Woodworking
with Your Kids

Woodworking with Your Kids

Richard Starr

The Taunton Press

Frontispiece: Eighth-grader Emily Kucer discusses the pedestal of her cherry music stand with teacher Richard Starr. The techniques Emily used to turn the piece are explained on pp. 197-201. The completed stand is shown on p. 142. Photo by Deborah Fillion.

Cover photo and all text photos by Richard Starr.

Library of Congress Cataloging-in-Publication Data

Starr, Richard.
    Woodworking with your kids / Richard Starr. — Rev. ed.
      p.   cm.
    ''A Fine woodworking book''—T.p. verso.
    Includes bibliographical references and index.
    ISBN 0-942391-61-6
    1. Woodwork (Manual training)   I. Title.
TT180.S714   1990
684'.08—dc20   90-39848
                               CIP

TAUNTON
BOOKS&VIDEOS

...by fellow enthusiasts

First printing: October 1990
Printed in the United States of America

A FINE WOODWORKING Book

FINE WOODWORKING ® is a trademark of The Taunton Press, Inc.,
registered in the U.S. Patent and Trademark Office.

The Taunton Press, Inc.
63 South Main Street
Box 5506
Newtown, Connecticut 06470-5506

As you can see from my photo, I'm sixteen now, but when I was six (see p. ix), I took a woodworking class after school with Richard Starr. It was not only my debut at working with wood, it was the first of any after-school activity.

I had always liked drawing, but something happened between the time I put the pencil to the paper and the time I viewed the finished product. Looking back, I know I couldn't create what I could visualize. When I started woodshop I had never made anything beautiful or incredibly useful, but Rich gave me the opportunity to make exactly what I wanted, and whatever it was it always turned out the way I wanted it. This made me feel more confident.

One of the greatest things was that Rich never said, "That's too hard." He only encouraged us to make things that we liked. Often, I'm sure he was surprised at the skill involved in some of the projects that we turned out, like beautiful drafting tables and ornate wine racks. When I was between projects, I often browsed among the projects in the store room. Many of my better project ideas I pirated from other woodworkers who didn't know they were sharing their ideas with me.

Woodworking made me feel grown up. Let's face it, when you're six years old there are very few ways to express yourself, and if drawing is not enjoyable, even fewer. When I worked with wood, I was using grown-up tools. I was making big, heavy things that were solid and looked great to me. I was very proud of what I made, and proud of my creativity as well. Looking back, I see Rich Starr not only as an instructor I had when I was younger, but also as a very special friend who happens to know a lot about wood.

Angus Chaney

This book was mostly written during a year's sabbatical leave from my teaching job. Few public schools offer such opportunities, so I am grateful to the Dresden School District of Hanover, New Hampshire, and Norwich, Vermont. I hope this book is a good argument for other districts to favor their faculties with the refreshing chance to do something different now and then, which can only increase their value in the classroom.

Some individuals who helped it happen: Dr. Hugh Watson, then superintendent of schools; Dr. Velma Saire, then principal; Patricia Davenport, then assistant principal; Ed Johnson and Roland Miller, the principal and assistant superintendent who took the chance to hire me; and Bruce Curtis-McLane, who taught my classes during my year away. Photographs of many children grace these pages, but several put in much time after school for certain sections: Angus Chaney; Crissy Chioffi, Wendy Fraser, David Hauri and Ken Varnum.

Most craftsmen learn their trades from an apprenticeship or by working alone. I think teachers acquire skill mostly from their students. This book is dedicated to the hundreds of kids who taught me to teach and who, through their enthusiasm, have kept me looking for better ways. And, of course, to my parents, who lit the fire to begin with. And to Susan, who helps to keep it going.

ids love
woodworking. They like the tools and
the ability to prevail over a tough
material, and they like making
something real. They get a thrill from
sitting on stools they made themselves,
storing junk in boxes of their own
design or playing with games that a few
weeks ago were only piles of boards.
But woodworking is not like finger
painting, which encourages children to
express themselves with abandon. The
material's strengths and limitations
require a discipline that most kids have
to learn.

In more than two decades of
teaching, I have found methods that
help kids develop discipline and harness
their innate enthusiasm and creativity to
make beautiful things of wood. These
methods will work for you and your
child, too.

Think of your child's woodworking
project as a cooperative venture. The
child provides the ideas; you offer the
know-how, support, materials and tools,
as well as a safe, secure environment in
which to work. With you as a partner,
the youngster will develop confidence in
the success of the project and will be
excited about doing more. As skills
develop, the child can become more
independent, but your supervision,

judgment and knowledge will still be
needed and valued.

When I was a kid I thought of wood
as a difficult and uncooperative material.
I thought that noisy, dusty, dangerous
and expensive machinery was required
to coerce it into shape. Then I met
a man who made beautiful things of
wood from the forest around him,
entirely by hand, in the 18th-century
fashion. That meeting was a gift
I'll always treasure. It initiated my
interest in hand woodworking and led
me to the realization that I could use
those skills in working with children.
You can too.

Who is this book written for?—If you
are a parent who wants to work wood
with your child, or even with a small
group of kids, this book is for you. I
assume only that you are excited about
making things of wood, not that you
know very much about the craft. I've
included all of the technical information
you'll need to make the project you and
your child select. If you are already an
experienced woodworker, you can use
the book as an idea bank of successful
methods for working with kids. If you
are a complete beginner or chiefly a
power-tool user, you can use this book
to learn hand-tool techniques.

How old must your child be before
you can begin? I think that children are
ready when they show an interest. Little
kids need close and constant
supervision, of course, but with your
helping hands on the tool, a three-year-
old will delight in drilling a hole through
a board. If you watch, listen and provide
opportunities, your child will tell you
when he or she is ready to make
wonderful wooden things.

How to use this book—The best way
to use this book is to browse through
the chapters with your child. Kids love
to look at pictures and will come away
with grand ideas. Before you begin,
however, you should carefully read the
rest of this section.

The book is divided into two parts.
The main portion is devoted to projects,
and each chapter describes a particular
type. The techniques box on p. xi
describes which pages you should read
before you and your child begin a
project. It refers you to the second part
of the book, Tools and Techniques. Here
you'll find detailed information on how
to use the tools or perform operations
described in the project chapters.
Among other things, you'll learn how to
sharpen tools, make wheels for a toy
car and design a workbench for kids.

The first four chapters of the book cover basic projects that work well with young kids (ages 5 to 10), although older children enjoy them too. Subsequent chapters are not sequenced according to skill level, so there is no reason to complete one project before another. You be the judge of where you want to begin.

There are no plans in this book. Instead, each chapter describes a method for making a particular type of project. These methods are only suggestions, and I leave the project's final dimensions, even the final shape in many cases, up to you and your child. At the end of each chapter are various other project ideas that you can make using the same techniques taught in the chapter. I hope these suggestions and the Gallery chapter (pp. 136-143) will stimulate your creativity and your child's too.

All the methods in this book have been developed with many children through the years. They are tried and true techniques, and they can be used on a wide range of projects. There are very few things a child will want to make in a woodworking shop that cannot be made with the techniques I've described in the book.

What to expect from your child—In your shop, a child's project isn't complete until you are satisfied with it. But when do you give the OK? What kinds of standards do you apply? After all, how much can you expect from a child?

As you browse through the photos in this book, you'll find that not every project is polished to perfection. You need to see the project through the child's eyes. Sometimes you'll have to ask, but more often the child will let you know exactly where the project stands.

"This is just the way I wanted it to be."

"I don't want it any smoother."

"I never thought I could make something like this."

On the other hand, sometimes children just want their projects to be finished because they're bored or frustrated.

All of these are good reasons for you to agree that the project is finished. It may be best to let the child work to his or her own standards, even if you think that the work could use a few more hours of sanding. In the next project, you can encourage your young craftsman to undertake something that is a little more challenging. You will need patience to let kids grow at their own speed.

Of course, a project is not finished if it isn't safe or doesn't work properly. A toy or a box that is likely to cause splinters needs more work; a stool with badly fitting joints will be dangerous to sit on. Kids need to learn that the maker has a responsibility to the user, and you may need to help them meet that responsibility with a lot of extra support at the end of a project.

"Something worth doing is worth doing well" is not a bad maxim, but I learned an important corollary from the superb woodworker who was my inspiration. He said that if a thing is really worth doing, it's even worth doing badly. Sometimes compromises motivate our best work. When you work with children, there must always be compromise. More important than demanding perfection from children is praising good effort and giving them time to grow.

(see the box at left)

A Safety Checklist

Before you can begin to teach safety, you must take a new look at your own habits and your shop environment. Remember that kids learn by example: "Do as I do" teaches more and more effectively than "Do as I say."

Ask yourself these questions:

● Is my shop well organized with everything in its place, or is it a jumble of things to trip over or objects that might fall from above?

● Are electric outlets available at safe and convenient places?

● Are there adequate trash cans and receptacles for scrap wood?

● Are my wood stacks secure or about to fall over?

● Is my bench or work table free of sharp edges and rough spots that could snag clothing or cause a splinter in someone's hand?

● Do I wear safety glasses whenever there's a possibility of flying debris?

● Is my workspace properly ventilated?

● Do I use ear muffs or plugs whenever there's a potential for loud noise?

● Have I checked and implemented the manufacturer's safety recommendations for my power tools? (Review owner's manuals.)

● Do I work in the shop when tired?

● Do I work when I've consumed alcohol or medications that affect my judgment? (Fatigue and even mild intoxication are probably responsible for more woodworking accidents than any other cause.)

Safety—Working safely must be the first thing on every woodworker's mind. When a child is in the shop, this prime concern is doubled. You are responsible not just for yourself, but also for the well-being of a youngster in a potentially hazardous setting. Be vigilant! Children are impulsive by nature, and that quality makes careful adult supervision the most important safety rule in a shop where a child is at work. No matter how many times you remind a youngster about safety and the correct way to do something, there will be moments when you will be glad you were there and watching.

The point is not simply to keep accidents to a minimum. You must also teach safe habits so the child will use them in every situation (see the box at left). You must teach that there are times and places where childish behavior is dangerous. Learning to behave safely may be one of the most important lessons the child will take from the shop experience.

At least a couple of thousand kids have passed through my school shop over the past two decades, and we've had very few accidents. It's because I'm never satisfied that I've got it right.

Take an active approach to safety—I don't think of safety only as a set of immutable rules. People are creative and often try to do things in new and better ways. While you let the creativity flow, back up your originality with a constant check for safety. Whenever I turn on a power tool, I go through my standard safety list, which includes checking guards, tightening adjustments and putting on appropriate eye and ear protection. I then ask myself, "Am I doing anything even slightly unusual?" If the answer is yes, I consider the possible safety consequences and adjust my procedures as necessary. I try to teach kids to ask themselves similar questions, and to consider the possible consequences of every action and behavior in the shop.

Accident prevention should be paramount in your shop. Eyes are easily the most vulnerable part of the body, and your accident-prevention efforts should begin there. Many industrial settings and schools require that eye protection be worn at all times. In your shop, the decision on when and where to wear safety glasses or a mask is yours to make. When in doubt, err on the side of caution.

Set an appropriate tone—Most children enjoy being silly, loud and outrageous. After all, kidding around is what makes them kids, and we love them for it. But for safety and productivity, children need to understand that a woodworking shop is a special place. Whether you have one child in your shop or ten, it's important that you set the tone by your own example and by clear rules of behavior. The tone of your shop goes beyond rules. It is a positive atmosphere that helps your child enjoy being safe and productive. A good tone is the product of your own infectious enthusiasm and clear rules of behavior.

In my school shop, kids know that running, pushing, loud behavior, fighting or even looking like you are fighting are all forbidden. They know they mustn't make believe a tool is a sword, for example. In fact, I make it clear that tools are never used for anything but their intended purposes. My students understand that rules are not up for discussion during class time. No means no, and immediately. In a home shop, you may not need to be so rigid, but it's essential that your child understand that he or she must stop doing anything the instant you say so. A shout from across the room may be the only way to stop an accident about to happen.

Rules of behavior in the shop must be taught from the very beginning. But there are hundreds of other rules associated with individual tools or processes that you'll need to teach as they come along. Don't overwhelm your kid with a litany of specific rules for each tool in the shop, for such lessons are quickly forgotten. Rather, teach safety with individual tools as you go along: for example, ''This is a brace and bit for drilling those holes you need. Remember to carry it through the shop with the sharp point down, and don't let the point hang over the edge of the table when you put it down;'' ''Let's make sure your work is clamped securely to the bench;'' and so forth.

Repeat these rules frequently as a reminder. Few people learn by hearing a lesson once. Check to see if the lesson is being absorbed by asking questions like, ''How do you carry a brace and bit?'' when you send the child for the tool. And always watch to see that those procedures are being followed. (Specific safety considerations are discussed throughout this book. Consider highlighting these passages for quick reference.)

Along with the rules, a good tone in the shop includes a warm and friendly feeling, a personal closeness and a sense of helpfulness. The tone in your shop reflects who you are and what you are willing to offer. It says, ''Come on in. This is a safe, friendly place. Let's work together. You're going to enjoy this.''

First aid — Most accidents with hand tools are minor cuts and bruises, the same kind that happen to children on a playground. You need to know when an injury is serious enough to require medical attention, and a good first-aid book will tell you what to look for. I've recommended one in the Bibliography on p. 203. Read up on injuries and first-aid measures in it or another such book. Make sure you have on hand the appropriate first-aid supplies, too. At the very least, have Band-Aids and antiseptic available, as well as a pair of tweezers for splinters.

Minor accidents in the shop often hurt a child's pride more than his or her flesh. Treat wounded pride as you would when a child falls off a bike.

Techniques Box

When your child wants to build:	Read pages:
A toy man (Chapter 1)	146-149, 151
An airplane (Chapter 2)	146-149, 151, 178-179
A car (Chapter 3)	152-154, 157-161, 177
Boxes (Chapter 4)	147, 157, 170, 180
A rabbeted box (Chapter 5)	162, 165-169, 180
A bookcase (Chapter 6)	146-149, 157, 165-169
A mitered box (Chapter 7)	150, 165-169, 180, 190
A board-on-frame box (Chapter 8)	146-149, 151, 152-154, 170
A table (Chapter 9)	146-149, 151, 190, 192
Signs and carvings (Chapter 10)	146-149, 180
Spoons and scoops (Chapter 11)	146-149, 178, 180, 188
Stools (Chapter 12)	152-156, 178, 188, 196
Games (Chapter 13)	146-150, 157, 170-173

Show concern, but try not to make a big deal of it. If kids know you expect a few cuts and scrapes, just as you would on a playground or athletic field, they are less likely to conceal a minor cut or to feel that a small accident reflects on their skill or on the quality of their work.

Let kids know that you expect to be told about every scrape that occurs in the shop. This helps you to take care of the accident properly and correct a child's bad habits. It also lets you discover a potentially dangerous situation that you may have overlooked.

Some accidents are a little more serious, and kids do get upset about them. Youngsters may need reassurance or hugs. When the injured child seems calm, I always discuss the accident to find out exactly what happened. It's important to help kids assume responsibility without making them feel they did something wrong.

We accept the risk of bicycles and baseball for children because they are richer for these experiences. Woodworking has risks too, but the blossoming of a child's skills and creativity makes these risks worth taking. With your close supervision, the risk is minimal.

Good luck, stay safe and have fun.

Richard Starr
October 1990

Toy Man

Chapter 1

Expect some
surprising answers when you ask a child
"What do you want to make?" Little kids
commonly ask for a horse, dog or man,
projects that make us think of sculpture
rather than woodworking. But don't
discourage a child who has these ideas,
because almost anything can be
expressed in wood once you know the
basic woodworking language.

Adult woodworkers usually begin a
project by planning it on paper. The
drawing is considered final, even
inviolable; then all that's needed is to
shape the pieces and join them together.
Young children, however, quickly
become frustrated with planning. So the
adult's task is to help the child connect a
drawing to the finished project without
extinguishing his or her precious
enthusiasm—it's important that kids get
busy with wood right away.

It's possible for even very young kids
to assemble pieces of wood into shapes
that suggest real objects. The key is to
use dowels to join the parts together.
This is easy to do and almost foolproof.
The dowel can be a hidden structural
member or an integral part of a form. By
using stick assemblies, a child's piece
can project realistically in three
dimensions rather than be just a flat
shape cut from a board.

Most young kids draw stick figures,
and these adapt readily to dowel
assembly. A child who's already seen an
example of dowel assembly may even
come up with a sketch that suggests this
kind of construction. This is cause to
celebrate, for the kid is picturing the
finished project while drawing it; one of
our goals is to develop this kind of
concrete thinking. But if the drawing
doesn't suggest doweled blocks, the
adult will have to translate the idea into
block shapes and draw them directly on
the wood. The finished figure needn't

look exactly like the child's drawing as
long as it has all the same basic
features; most young kids see things as
a conglomeration of parts rather than an
organized whole. When interpreting
parts, remember that arms, legs, necks,
noses, antennae and tails can all be
expressed using dowels. Let kids know
you're concerned with every detail.

Second-grader Angus Chaney decided
to make a toy man. Having seen several
in the workshop, his drawing reflected
the dowel-assembly technique closely
enough to be used as an actual pattern.

Angus began by placing carbon paper between his drawing and the wood and tracing around the body. Then he cut all the straight lines with a crosscut saw, leaning the saw against his left thumb to start it. Angus used a coping saw for the curves of the shoulders and for the head. Coping saws cut best on the pull stroke, so make sure the blade's teeth point toward the handle. Tell the child that the saw must be held at a right angle to the wood, then demonstrate: "Not up or down, like this or this. . . .or left or right, like this or this. . . ."

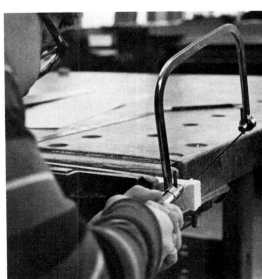

Angus chose to draw the head directly on the face of the wood rather than to use the pattern and carbon paper. He held the body in place on the wood so he could make the head exactly the right size. After cutting around three-quarters of the head, Angus found that the frame of the coping saw was hitting the vise. Moving the wood in the vise would have solved the problem temporarily, but a few more strokes and the frame would have been hitting the edge of the wood. The solution was to swing the frame out of the way (p. 149). Though Angus was able to do this himself, an adult will usually have to help.

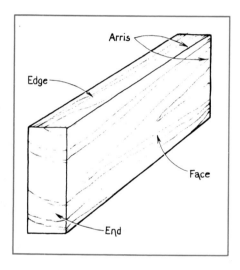

To position the toy man's head, Angus set it against the body and indicated on both pieces with his pencil where he wanted the neck to go. Then he marked across the edge of each piece of wood and marked the center of the line by eye. To keep the drill bit from sliding around, start the neck hole by dimpling the wood with a nail set or a nail. I helped Angus chuck a ¼-in. twist bit into an eggbeater drill and marked a distance of ¾ in. from the end of the bit with a little flag of masking tape. Angus bored into the head until the tape just touched the wood, then he bored a ¼-in. hole in the shoulders to the same depth.

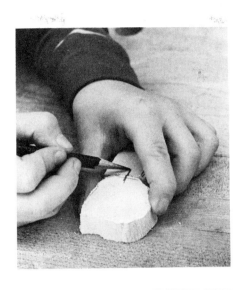

A short piece of ¼-in. dowel, cut with the coping saw, joins the head to the body. When Angus assembled his man, he found that the neck was too long, so he cut the dowel shorter and tried again.

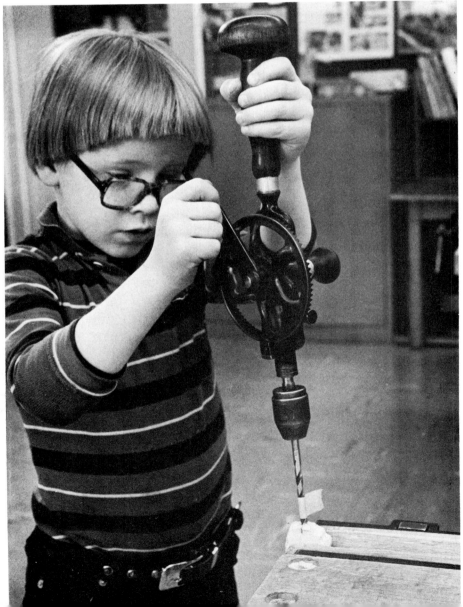

The legs of the toy man joined the body at an angle; Angus dimpled the wood with a nail set, holding it at about the same angle he would bore the holes. Angus felt he could guess the correct angle for boring the legs, but I helped him judge it by eye.

Then Angus drew one of the toy man's feet on a strip of wood, bored an angled ¼-in. hole in it and cut it out with the coping saw. He tried the foot on the man for size and it fit, so he traced the second foot from it, bored and cut it out. In an earlier attempt, Angus cut the foot out before boring the hole, but the little piece of wood was too delicate and the bit split it in two. If you bore the hole before sawing, and hold the wood between the jaws of the vise, it'll be less likely to split.

The man's arms were also at an angle, so Angus marked where they should go, fixed the body in the vise and bored the holes. Once the arms and feet were in place, Angus drew the details of the face. Bore holes for eyes and one for the dowel nose with a ¼-in. bit; the mouth is a series of adjacent ⅛-in. holes. Angus marked the length of the nose on the dowel and sawed off the excess with the coping saw.

Angus decided that his toy man was finished. He chose not to glue the dowels in their holes because the friction held them in just fine. Sometimes younger children wiggle the drill around and glue is needed to hold the dowels in the oversized holes.

The little horse below was made by a kindergarten child and painted with poster colors. Lisa Miles, right, also a kindergartener, took more time with her horse, even shaping the little dowel ears with a file. Later, Lisa made a tail of yarn, held in place with a short dowel plugged into a hole. She painted her horse with poster colors, too.

Jane Longnecker made this playground in fifth grade. The slide, glider and jungle gym are made of dowels and short pieces of wood. This Tinker-Toy approach to woodworking opens up endless possibilities.

Shelle Whitcomb, a sixth-grader, made this little doll. To make the elbow and knee joints, cut a slot in the end of one piece and a tongue on the end of the other. A ⅛-in. dowel pivot fits tightly in a hole bored through the slot and the tongue, which makes the joints stiff, so the limbs will hold a pose once they've been positioned.

Older children can do a great deal with simple stick figures. Susan Reeves, below, made her marionette when she was in seventh grade; its articulated joints move freely, as shown in the drawing. (Any resemblance between this puppet and Susan's woodworking teacher is purely intentional.)

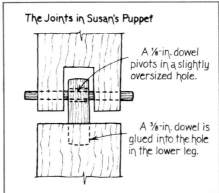

The Joints in Susan's Puppet

A ⅛-in. dowel pivots in a slightly oversized hole.

A ⅜-in. dowel is glued into the hole in the lower leg.

Susan's friend, Heidi Sternick, made a dragon. The legs, head and jaws pivot on joints similar to the ones on Susan's puppet. The tail flops like beads on a string, which is pretty much what it is. Even the leather wings of this monster are controlled by the puppeteer.

Airplane
Chapter 2

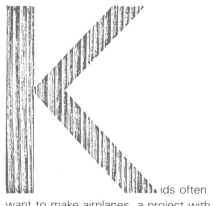ids often
want to make airplanes, a project with a
complex, three-dimensional shape.
Here's one way to make them, along
with suggestions for other methods.

First, ask the child to draw the airplane
the size he or she wants to make it, so
that the drawing can be used as a
pattern. The actual size of a project is
usually of little concern to young kids,
but it's important that the drawing have
practical dimensions: kids need to learn
about scale. When I noticed that the
fuselage of Angus's plane, which he
drew in profile, was going to be thinner
than the ¾-in. wood he was using for
the wings, I asked him to redraw it and
make it thicker.

Angus scissored the pattern out and traced around it on the wood. For young kids, this is more direct than transferring the pattern with carbon paper: the child can immediately relate the pattern to the wood. Because the tail of Angus's plane was perpendicular to the fuselage, I suggested he place the pattern at the end of the board to save two sawcuts.

To cut out the tail, Angus used a crosscut saw. Because it's easier for a child to saw straight down, chuck the wood in the vise on an angle whenever necessary. Use the coping saw to cut out the rest of the fuselage.

Angus wanted to smooth the sawn surfaces and round the edges of the fuselage. Of all the tools he tried (file, spokeshave, sandpaper, Surform), he found a combination rasp-file the most satisfying. This tool is about as heavy as you can get, but here is a case where "bigger is better" for small kids. The weight relieves a child of having to press down, and the coarseness of the file teeth gets the work done fast without tearing the wood. (The rasp teeth were too coarse for this job.) When the file clogs with sawdust, clean it with a file card, which is a short-bristled wire brush. For a really smooth surface, Angus could have sandpapered after filing, but he was satisfied with the surface left by the file.

With the finished fuselage in hand, Angus was able to decide just how the wings should look and then to make a pattern of exactly the right size. Place the fuselage, edge up, on a piece of paper and draw the parts in place full size; then mark on the fuselage where the wings will fit. This is an example of how a child can make critical judgments step-by-step as the work progresses.

Snip out the patterns, trace them on the wood, saw out the parts, and then spokeshave their edges smooth. A pleasant tool to use on edges that follow the grain, the spokeshave leaves a smoother surface than the file does. But the spokeshave requires more attention and skill to use, and it won't reach into tight places like the one between the tail and fuselage.

Now bore a ¼-in. hole through the fuselage for dowels to connect it to the wings. Keep the wood horizontal in the vise, and the drill vertical. An adult can help steer by placing a hand on top of the drill. Bore a hole in the end of each wing; use a tape flag ¾ in. above the end of the bit as a depth gauge. Hold the wing vertical in the vise and the drill straight up.

Here's how the plane goes together. Cut the ¼-in. dowels slightly shorter than the total length needed. Holes ¾ in. deep in each wing and through the fuselage add up to a total length of 2¼ in.: a 2-in.-long dowel will allow the pieces to fit together tightly. Make sure the child test-fits the assembly before starting to glue.

It's a good idea to cover the table with newspaper before gluing to protect it from drips and spills. Spread glue around one end of the dowel and push that end through the fuselage until an equal length of dowel sticks out each side. Now spread glue around both ends of the dowel. Put glue on the ends of the wings, but don't put any in the wing holes; glue on the dowel will be enough.

Push both wings onto the dowel at the same time, then look at the plane from all angles and adjust the wings while the glue is still wet. Even if the holes aren't quite accurate, there'll be enough leeway to straighten the wings. (Young kids usually need help with this step.)

Angus decided that his airplane needed motors in the wings. He made them out of ½-in. dowels and bored holes through the wings with a ½-in. auger bit chucked in a brace. (Eggbeater drills are awkward for holes with a diameter of more than ⅜ in.) The auger bit has a sharp screw tip, so there's no need to punch a dimple in the wood to start it. Angus could have stood on a low stool to bore the holes, but he preferred to climb up on the workbench.

Angus fixed a wing in the vise and bored the holes; working on the unsupported wing would have broken the joint. To prevent a ragged exit hole, stop boring when the point of the bit just protrudes from the wood. Then turn the plane over and counterbore each hole by starting the bit in the tiny hole where the point has come through.

For the motors, Angus cut dowel pieces long enough to stick out on both sides of the wing. He shaped the ends with a dowel pointer (a tool that fits in the brace and resembles a pencil sharpener). A spokeshave or file would also do the job. He tapped the motors into place (use glue if the fit isn't snug), supporting one end of the wing on the table, and the airplane was done.

Some kids have a peculiar vision of how things should look. A second-grader's unusual drawing developed into the airplane in the foreground. If the sketch had been looser, I might have tried to help the child come up with something more realistic, but the drawing clearly expressed the child's idea. The completed plane has a certain charm as it is, and the kid loved it. Its wings are nailed in place. Strips of wood were first nailed to the ends of the wings and then were glued and nailed to the fuselage. The more realistic plane in the background uses the same technique.

Sixth-grader Eric Wilson made a sophisticated airplane, more of a model than a toy. Instead of cutting a fuselage out of a board, he carved it out of 2x2 pine, using a drawknife and spokeshave. He shaped thin, realistic wings from ⅜-in. pine, smoothing and rounding them with a plane. This airplane required more planning and skill than the others described in this chapter—a job for an older child.

Car

Chapter 3

Kids love to make vehicles——cars, trucks, trains, wagons——anything, as long as it rolls. Simple vehicles can be made either by cutting the parts out of one board or by gluing up several blocks. More complicated vehicles can be made from box shapes and have moving parts such as hinged doors and hoods.

Angus began with a full-size pattern of a car resembling his mother's VW bug.

Because he was working with a piece of 2-in.-thick, rough-surfaced pine, the first step was to plane the faces smooth. The edges didn't have to be planed because they would be cut off later. Young kids like Angus are more comfortable with small planes (about 7 in. or 8 in. long). Larger ones, which are common in most shops, are a bit clumsy for small hands, but they'll do in a pinch. Make sure the child positions the wood in the vise high

enough so that the jaws of the vise don't get in the way of the plane.

I teach children to push a plane, but Angus discovered it was easier for him to pull it, the method preferred in Oriental cultures. Western planes are not designed to be pulled, so when Angus gets a little stronger, he will probably find it feels better to push. In the meantime, he should work in the way he feels the most comfortable.

When both faces are planed smooth, transfer the drawing to the board with carbon paper, holding the pattern in place with push pins. This method lets the child check his or her progress without spoiling the alignment. Angus had to lift the drawing several times to make sure he'd traced every line.

Boring out the wheel wells on the car is the next step: do this before cutting out the car shape. Put the board in the vise, drawing-side up, with a piece of scrap sandwiched between the vise jaw and the bottom of the car. Make sure the edge of the scrap is flush with the face of the board. Because the wheel wells are not complete circles, the scrap is needed to cut a complete hole; it keeps the edges from chipping and the bit from walking off center.

Set an expansion bit to the diameter of the wheel wells (p. 153). Then set a depth gauge on the bit so that the depth of the cut will equal the thickness of the wheel (young kids will need help with this). Estimate the centers of the wheel wells by eye and bore holes on one side.

After boring, project lines from the well centers across the bottom of the car and up the other side with a small square. By measuring from the center of a wheel well to the edge of the wood with dividers, a child can accurately transfer the center points. Poking the wood with the point of the dividers marks the spot.

This is what the wood looks like after boring the last two wheel wells.

The axle holes are bored using the point left by the expansion bit as a center. The hole must be sufficiently oversized to allow the ¼-in. axle to turn easily, so use a ⁵⁄₁₆-in. bit. To make sure the hole will be on center, bore in about halfway from one side, then complete the hole from the other side.

I cut out the body of the car on the bandsaw, leaving a little extra wood below the holes as a sort of axle housing. A child could cut out the body with a coping saw, but it takes practice to get clean results. When there is enough good-quality handwork in a project, I don't mind sometimes easing the way with a power tool.

Now make the wheels. (Several ways of making wheels are described on p. 177.) We used a piece of ¾-in. scrap wood, a little over twice the final thickness of the wheels. Sawing the wood in half later will make two identical wheels. To find the wheel diameter, Angus measured the distance between the edge of the axle hole and the edge of the wheel well with dividers. (The wheel will clear the well by half the thickness of the axle.) Then he scribed two circles on the scrap piece. Hold the dividers near the top and scribe by making a series of arcs. Leaning the dividers in the direction they are being turned will allow the scribing point to be dragged smoothly across the wood.

Bore a ¼-in. hole for an axle in each wheel. Use the dimple left by the dividers as a center and enlarge it with a punch so the bit won't slide around. Make sure the child bores carefully, because if these holes are off, the wheels will wobble as they turn.

I bandsawed Angus's wheels for him. First, I cut the piece a little wider than the wheels drawn on its face. Then I set this piece on edge and cut it in half through its thickness. By leaving the halves joined at one edge as you bandsaw around the scribed lines, the two halves will behave almost as one piece. Hold them together tightly; remember to keep your fingers to the side of the teeth when working close to a bandsaw blade. The wheel edges can be sanded smooth, but most kids are satisfied to use them right off the saw.

Axles are next. Here Angus marks the axle length by measuring directly from his car and wheels. Leave some space between the wheels and the body of the car so the wheels can move from side to side. The axles should be flush with the outside of the wheels, so leave them extra long and trim them later.

If the wheels fit tightly on the axle, hammer them on gently. If the wheels loosen later, they'll need to be glued on.

The car should roll easily on its wheels. If it doesn't, a wheel with a crooked hole may be wobbling against the well. Pull the wheels further out on the axle and try rolling the car again. (A very wobbly wheel should be replaced.) If a wheel isn't the problem, check that the axle holes are straight; because they were bored in from both sides, they may not meet accurately in the center. If they don't, run a round, rat-tail file through the hole.

Angus wanted to carve details into his car. He penciled them on and began to work with a No. 4 veiner, a small gouge with a *U*-shaped edge. Angus is right-handed and holds the handle of the gouge with that hand. He grasps the tool just behind its cutting edge with the fingers of his left, resting the heel of his hand on the wood. One hand works against the other to control the tool.

Tell kids always to keep both hands behind the edge of the tool, and never to work toward an arm or a hand. By always considering where the edge of a tool will go if it slips, kids can judge the difference between a safe and a risky move. Tools should be put down on the table when not in use. Also remind kids to carry gouges, chisels and drills with their edges down—not up, forward or sideways. Be strict about these rules and you'll keep accidents to a minimum. (For more on safety, see p. ix.)

Angus added headlights to his car, made from ¼-in. dowels. He also installed a radio antenna of ⅛-in. dowel. Angus thought the finished car looked fine, even without filing or sandpapering. You might want to encourage an older kid to file and sand to a smoother finish, but for a second-grader like Angus, good work is self-measured.

Here's an example of a more detailed car, made by fifth-grader Bobby Officer.

Angus shaped his car from a single piece of wood, but kids can also make vehicles by gluing or nailing small chunks of wood together. This approach works well with very young children because all the cuts are straight and can be made with a crosscut saw.

The train above was made by a nursery-school child. The engine is made from two boards nailed together, and the car is made from a third board. The axles are stubs of dowel glued into holes in the sides of the engine and car. The wheels run freely on these, retained by hubs made of string wrapped and glued around the dowel. This isn't as good as a moveable axle, but is simpler to make.

A Road Grader

Seventh-grader Joe Bourne made this road grader. The shaped grader blade can be rotated by lifting it and lowering the crossbar pins into holes in the indexing disc. The front axle assembly and the pairs of rear wheels pivot on central pins.

The axle carrier rotates on a ½-in. dowel fixed in the frame.

The ¼-in. dowel axles ride in ½-in. holes in the axle carrier.

¼-in. dowel kingpin

The axle carrier pivots on a ¼-in. dowel fixed to the grader.

Axle carrier

Fix a ⅛-in. dowel in the knuckle.

⅛-in. dowel

Axle carrier

Tie bar

The wheel runs free on the ¼-in. axle and is retained by a pin.

Make an oversized hole for the kingpin.

Steering knuckle

Bore an oversized hole in the tie bar.

Here's a truck constructed by a first-grader and made from chunks of 2x4, with a dumpster made of scrap boards. The dumpster pivots on the rear axle.

Box vehicles are hollow, so more details and moving parts are possible than with block vehicles. Also, a child can make larger toys without having to use a lot of extra wood. The methods described in Chapter 4 work well for box vehicles, but curves require some pattern work.

The van below was made by a first-grader and modeled after the child's school bus. It has seats, a steering wheel and front and rear doors that open and close. Before nailing the sides to the bottom, bore out the windows and cut off the front door. Round the door edges with a file so the doors won't hit the frame when they close. For axle hangers, bore holes through 1-in. by 1-in. strips of wood, oversized so the axles can turn freely, and glue the strips to the bottom of the van. Boring end grain is tricky with a standard auger bit; many children will need help to aim accurately and push the bit through. This van is painted with poster paint—blue, if my memory serves.

Box-built vehicles can get quite complex. The jeep above was built by a third-grader and has a fold-down, Plexiglas windshield and a raise-up hood.

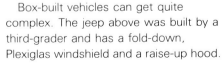

Box Without Measuring

Chapter 4

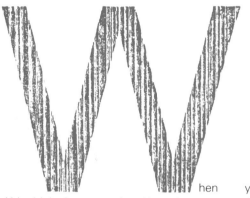

When kids think about woodworking, they often imagine boxes or boxlike objects, such as birdhouses, benches and cabinets. Here's an easy way for young children to make boxes using only a square, pencil, saw and hammer. The trick is to build the box from the bottom up. The bottom determines the size of the first side, the bottom and first side determine the size of the second side, and so on; this method is forgiving of the inaccuracies likely to occur when young kids use a saw. It's also a good way to help children understand right angles and rectangles, without having to resort to geometry.

Although young kids are concerned with shape and function, they are apt to be somewhat arbitrary about size. If the box is intended to hold something specific (you should always ask about this), size becomes a practical concern; even if it is not, go through the decision-making process to emphasize its importance: how high, how wide, how deep? Though older kids should be able to specify measurements in advance, young kids can decide on each dimension as they're making the box. They can be working with wood while learning to think in three dimensions.

"How big do you want the bottom of your box?" Working at one corner, have the child move his or her fingers around the surface to describe the size of the bottom. Let the child know the box can be just the way he or she imagines it.

When the size looked right to Angus, he marked the final position of his fingers on the edge and end of the board and drew a rectangle by placing a trysquare along the marks. Make sure the child pushes the square tight against the edge of the board.

After sawing the bottom out, make the ends of the box. Hold the bottom against a corner of the board and mark its width, then decide how deep the box will be. Label the joint so it will be nailed together the right way. Lay out the rectangle with the square and saw out the first end.

Next glue and nail the end to the bottom. Hold the bottom of the box in the vise, spread a bead of white glue on the end and nail it on with three or four nails. Angus was able to hold the piece in place while he drove in the first nail; many kids will need help until two of the nails have been driven in.

Angus marked the width of the other end of the box as before. He marked the height of the second end using the first end as a template. Then he labeled the joint, squared up the rectangle, cut out the end and nailed it on.

Here Angus marks out the first side. He placed one end of the box against the end of the board and lined up the tops of the ends with the adjacent edge. Angus didn't hold the saw perpendicular to the board when he cut out the bottom, so one of the ends of his box tilted outward. He placed the end that didn't tilt flush with the end of the board and traced around the box. If neither end of the box is perpendicular to the bottom, just make sure the tops of the box ends are flush with one edge of the board and trace the other three sides. Label this piece so it's sure to go on the correct side of the box. After tracing, saw out the side.

Glue and nail the side to all three edges of the box. The box can be set on its side while being nailed, but if it bounces, hold it in a vise. If, because of inaccurate sawing, the side of the box doesn't fit snugly against all three surfaces, the child (or adult) can remove high spots by filing, planing or sawing. With young children, I've found it's best to emphasize accomplishment rather than perfection; kids are usually happy to nail the side on and ignore the spaces.

Now trace the other side of the box, saw it out and nail it on. Angus insisted that even a basic box needs a lid, so he traced one and sawed it out. He made hinges from strips of leather, and with the lid held in place against the box with a vise, nailed them on with ½-in. wire nails. Each hinge is nailed close to the joint between the lid and the box and all around the perimeter of the hinge.

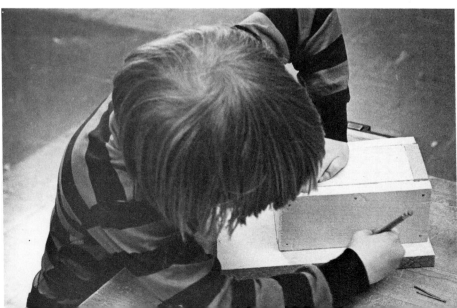

Here are some variations on the basic box without measuring:

The ends and sides of a box don't have to be the same height. Birdhouses, toolboxes and stools, for example, are objects whose ends project above their sides. These projecting parts make the birdhouse gables, hold the handle of the toolbox and form the legs of the stool. For these projects, the grain of the ends should run vertically. Make a pattern for the ends of the stool and toolbox and saw them to shape before nailing them to the bottom and adding the sides.

When making a birdhouse, however, fit the sides to the bottom first, then fit the ends. This makes it easier to fit the roof pieces because the sides won't form a ledge, which is difficult to roof over. One roof piece should overlap the other at the peak. Nailing one roof piece onto the birdhouse and hinging the other to it at the peak makes it easy to open the house for cleaning.

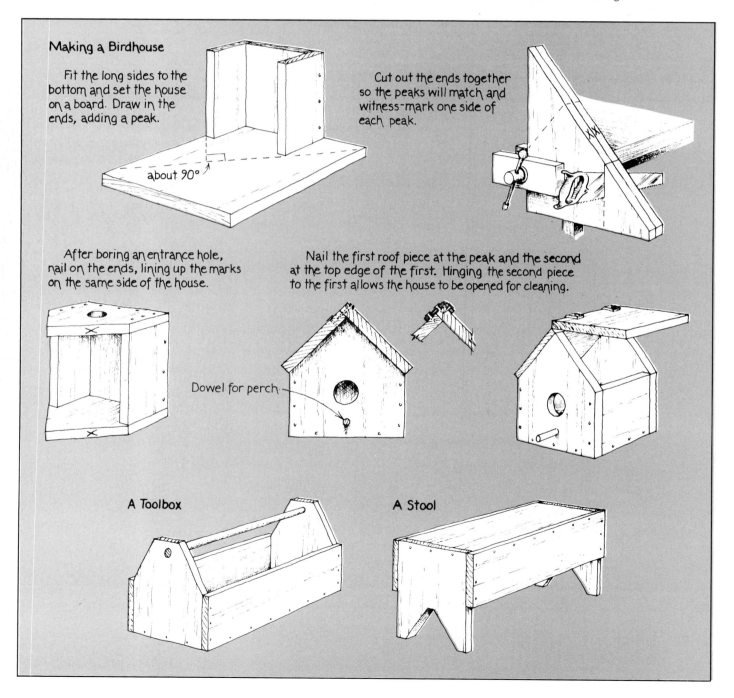

Making a Birdhouse

Fit the long sides to the bottom and set the house on a board. Draw in the ends, adding a peak.

about 90°

Cut out the ends together so the peaks will match and witness-mark one side of each peak.

After boring an entrance hole, nail on the ends, lining up the marks on the same side of the house.

Nail the first roof piece at the peak and the second at the top edge of the first. Hinging the second piece to the first allows the house to be opened for cleaning.

Dowel for perch

A Toolbox

A Stool

This toy house, built by Rebecca Schlosser, a kindergartener, has a door that pivots on ¼-in. dowels protruding from its top and bottom. To support the door, Rebecca had to construct the house so its ends rested on the bottom and fit between the sides. Then she planed the tops of the sides at an angle to accommodate the roof. She held the house in a vise, using the gable ends as a guide for the plane.

Rebecca wanted square windows in her house, so she used a chisel to square the holes she bored. The wood is clamped to a piece of scrap, so the exit side of the hole won't chip. The paper in between tells Rebecca when she has chiseled deep enough. This house is pretty high-level work for a five-year-old, but many kids that age can do it.

Rabbeted Box

Chapter 5

There are always boxes being made in my shop at school: jewelry boxes, toy boxes, bread boxes and "anything boxes." There are also plenty of boxlike projects, such as bookshelves, stereo cabinets and doghouses. The way we choose to make a box depends mainly on what the box is intended to do: will it be a tiny ring box of exotic wood, a locker to store athletic equipment or a nightstand equipped with a drawer? Older kids rarely use the box method described in the previous chapter; kids with more experience want to produce more grown-up results and develop new skills, such as rabbeting and mitering. Though dovetailing is too difficult for most kids, I keep a sample dovetail joint in the shop to show to skilled kids who want to try more advanced joinery.

Like young kids, some older children have trouble determining the size of the boxes they want to make. I ask my students to dimension their drawings, so they have to think carefully about size. Incorrect or omitted dimensions indicate that the child is having trouble translating size into numbers. You know a child isn't clear if a drawing of an oblong box has measurements for a square one. Or perhaps the child has offered two reasonable dimensions but has left out a

third. Some children will understand that a dimension is missing if you simply remind them that more information is needed. Others get the point if you ask them to draw a front or top view. But if you suspect that a child is pulling numbers from thin air, try exaggerating the missing or awkward dimension—children always understand absurdity.

"Let's see, you want a box 14 inches long, 10 inches wide and, um . . . 3 feet deep?" (Gesturing with the hands.)

"No." (Giggling.)

"Oh, then maybe an inch and a half deep?" (Gesturing again.)

"No, that's silly."

"Well then, how deep do you want it? Show me with your hands."

Measure the size the child indicates and go from there. You can also have the child measure several boxes that are close in size to the one he or she wants to make. Eventually, most kids will make the connection between actual sizes and the dimensions on a drawing.

This chapter and several others in the book describe different ways to make simple boxes. The rabbeted box is one of the simplest of all. A rabbet is nothing more than a rectangular recess along the edge of a board. The only corner joint simpler than a rabbet is a butt joint, used to make the box without measuring

(Chapter 4). In a butt joint, the end of one side butts against the face of another, and the two are nailed or doweled together. A rabbet joint is stronger than a butt joint because it has more gluing surface and can be nailed from two directions for extra strength, and the ledge of the rabbeted board helps hold the joint square. A rabbeted corner looks neater than a butt joint, and it displays the skill and care of the kid who made it. Older kids are seldom allowed to use butt joints in my shop.

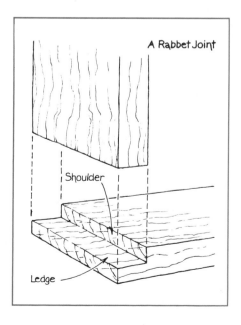

A Rabbet Joint

Shoulder

Ledge

Once I'm satisfied with a kid's drawing of a box, I provide the wood, cut to size. The long sides of the box are cut to full length because they're usually the pieces that are rabbeted. The short sides fit into the rabbets and are shorter than the outside dimensions of the box by twice the depth of the rabbet. For example, if the sides of the box are ¾ in. thick and the rabbets are cut halfway through, cut the short sides of the box ¾ in. less than the outside dimension. Avoid boards with knots on the edges or ends that have to be rabbeted: knots are hard to plane through and may fall out. When kids wonder why I've only given them the four pieces of wood they're going to need for the sides, I assure them they'll be making the bottom later on.

A rabbet plane, shown below, is used to cut rabbets, as described on p. 165. I mark the boards before planing as a reminder of where to cut: the two ends of each long side are rabbeted to make the corner joints, and the bottom edges of all four sides are rabbeted to accept the bottom of the box.

Eighth-grader Chrissy Chioffi's board was flat, so she was able to hold it in the vise while she planed the rabbets. But most boards aren't flat across the grain: this is called cupping and is shown in the drawing below. You can see cupping by sighting across the end of the board with one eye. On cupped boards, rabbets should be laid out on the hollow side of the cup. (See p. 166 for how to clamp the board to the bench to flatten the cup while rabbeting.)

Sight along the end of the board to see cupping.

Here's how Chrissy's box went together. She put a short side in the vise, spread glue on its end and positioned a long side on it. The ledges of the rabbets for the bottom must line up; Chrissy checked this alignment with her forefinger. The bottom will be glued to these ledges, and there'll be a gap between the sides and the bottom if they're not aligned.

Nail the sides together with four or five 4-penny (1½-in.) finishing nails. Don't nail through the rabbets for the bottom: there isn't enough wood there to hold the nail. Lean on the side of the box to push the rabbet tight during nailing.

The sides of Chrissy's box didn't line up perfectly at the last joint, so she forced them into place and clamped them together before nailing. Before the glue set (about half an hour for white glue), she clamped tight any spaces in the joints. Using a nail set, she drove all the nailheads slightly below the surface.

Checking to see if the box is square is the next step. Use a large trysquare or measure the diagonals, which should be equal. If it isn't square, pull across opposite corners of the longer diagonal with a bar clamp. Swab up squeezed-out glue with a wet paper towel.

The bottom of the box fits inside the rabbets on the edges. Measure from the wall of one rabbet to the wall of its opposite. Inside measurements can throw kids, so they may need help. The bottom should be slightly smaller than the opening—an easy fit. The bottom will shrink and expand across the grain with variations in humidity; if the fit is too tight, the bottom could push the box apart when it expands in wet weather.

Spread glue on the shoulders of the rabbets, put in the bottom and nail it in place. Nail at a slight angle so that the nail goes through a thick portion of the bottom and well into the side of the box. Too small an angle and the nail may come out inside the box; too large and it may stick out of the side. Never nail into the bottom from the side; you might split the bottom rabbet right off the sides.

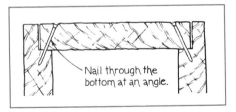

Nail through the bottom at an angle.

Chrissy wanted a flanged, overhanging lid for her box. The flange fits inside the box and keeps the lid in position. The overhang makes the lid easy to lift, and conceals the line between lid and box. An overhang also gives the box a pleasant shape, breaking the stark rectangle, and the thin edge of a rabbeted lid is more attractive than an edge of full thickness. Chrissy decided on an overhang of ½ in. on all four sides. She rabbeted the lid, setting the plane to cut slightly wider than 1¼ in.—the overhang plus the thickness of the box side plus a little extra for a loose fit. Note that Chrissy rests her left hand beside the blade; she risks a cut finger.

With the rabbets cut, check the fit of the lid. If it fits too tightly, widen the rabbet slightly with a shoulder plane or the rabbet plane with its fence and depth gauge removed.

Level the rim of the box with a bench plane. A fore plane (18 in.) works well cutting at an angle to the side, its tail supported by an adjacent side of the box. Planing at an angle across the box corners helps prevent chipped edges.

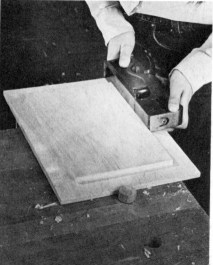

If you cut the side rabbets slightly oversized, you'll need to plane the projecting ends of the box sides. A block plane or a small bench plane will do. Hold the plane flat on the end-grain surface and slightly skewed, its nose pointing toward, not away from, the center of the board. Plane toward the center from each end; planing off the end will pull a chip from the wood.

When the box is assembled, check that all the nailheads are set below the surface and sand with 100-grit paper, finishing with 220 grit. Wrap the sandpaper around a rubber block and hold the block in both hands for even pressure as you sand. Chrissy finished her box with oil.

Lisa McCleery made this cherry jewelry box when she was in eighth grade. She rabbeted a lip around the box to accept the lid, and made an upper compartment by setting a piece of wood in grooves cut in the sides of the box. To make the drawer front, Lisa cut a strip from the bottom of the box front and widened the rabbets to accept drawer sides. (See p. 174 for details on how to make a drawer.)

Here's a cradle made by D'arcy Hyde, a seventh-grader. The bottom piece fits into the rabbets in the sides and ends. The end pieces are nailed and glued to rabbets in the sides. The rockers are screwed onto the bottom.

A Pirate's Chest with a Rounded Lid

Laura di Bonaventure made this pirate's chest in eighth grade. The rounded top isn't as tricky to make as it looks.

Make a pattern for the end pieces by folding a large piece of paper into quarters. Mark half the width of the box from the vertical fold. The first ¾-in. by 1¾-in. strip on each side is perpendicular to the bottom of the lid; mark their positions up from the baseline fold.

Make a large compass from two 1x2s, a bolt and wingnut, a nail, pencil and rubber band. Strike an arc as shown at right. Position the compass point on the centerline by trial and error to get the curve you want.

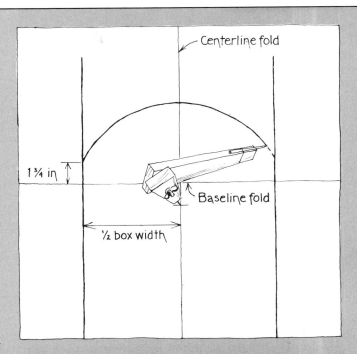

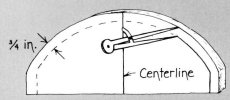

Cut out the pattern and trace it on four pieces of ¾-in. pine. Mark the centerline on each piece. Saw out the pieces. On two of the pieces, mark a line ¾ in. from the outside edge with dividers, as shown. Saw on this line and nail the small ends to the large ends, lining up their bottom edges and centerlines.

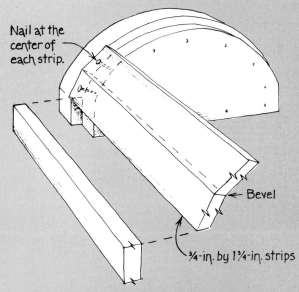

Nail at the center of each strip.

Bevel

¾-in. by 1¾-in. strips

Nail and glue the strips to the ledges. The strips should bear on the curve at their centers. Bevel one edge of each strip to mate it to its neighbor. Glue tapered fillets in any gaps. Plane and sand the lid smooth.

Bookcase

Chapter 6

et a box on its side, put in a shelf or two, and you have a cabinet. Most cabinets made in my shop have rabbeted corners, so if a kid knows how to use a rabbet plane, he or she is halfway there. We install shelves in a cross-grain groove called a dado; like a rabbet, a dado is an improvement over a nailed butt joint because there's more contact between the surfaces of the parts. A snug dado will hold a shelf flat and help keep the cabinet sides from bulging. Dadoes aren't hard to cut by hand, but they do take some time. Young children may find them tedious and prefer a butt joint, or a butt joint reinforced by a strip of wood nailed or glued beneath it.

Backs aren't really needed in many of the shelf units made in my shop. A cabinet back has three purposes: it keeps dust from coming in, things from falling out, and it holds the cabinet square and stiff. (If you want a back, recess ¼-in. plywood in a rabbet cut along the back edges of the sides. It's strong and neat.) To stiffen a cabinet without a back, we nail a brace to the

shelf and cabinet sides. When placed beneath a long shelf, the brace prevents the shelf from sagging under the weight of heavy loads; set it above the shelf as a backstop for books and bric-a-brac. We house the ends of the braces in the cabinet sides; cutting these housings is good practice in careful layout and teaches the child to work accurately with a chisel.

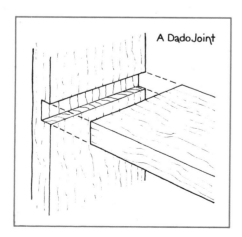

A Dado Joint

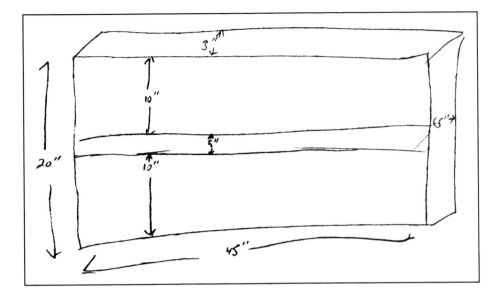

Eighth-grader Ken Varnum made a loose sketch of his bookcase and specified its dimensions, but he didn't indicate the thicknesses of the pieces. I pointed out that they would be ¾ in. thick—would there still be room for his books? He assured me he had thought about this and most of his paperbacks measured less than 10 in. high. In his drawing, he meant only to indicate the placement of the pieces and he wanted to show that the shelf was centered on the sides of the case.

I usually supply a board for each of the four sides of a cabinet, but because Ken's bookcase was only 5 in. deep, we were able to take a shortcut. I gave him two boards, 10 in. wide, so he could cut two rabbets instead of four and one dado instead of two. Then I ripped each board in half to make two identical sides. This shortcut is also useful when making rabbeted boxes.

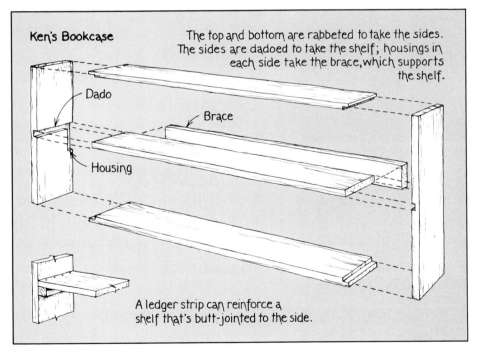

Ken's Bookcase

The top and bottom are rabbeted to take the sides. The sides are dadoed to take the shelf; housings in each side take the brace, which supports the shelf.

Dado

Brace

Housing

A ledger strip can reinforce a shelf that's butt-jointed to the side.

Ken began his bookcase as if he were making a box, rabbeting both ends of the wide board that would become the top and bottom. If the board (or boards, if you're not using the shortcut) is cupped, place the hollow side of the cup on the inside of the cabinet and clamp the board flat to the bench when cutting the joints. During assembly, you'll flatten out the cup.

Ken wanted his shelf in the middle of the cabinet, so to place the dado, he first marked the center of the cabinet side. Then he measured half the shelf's thickness from either side of the mark. With a square, he projected the shelf measurements across the inside face of the board. If you have two side boards, align their edges and ends and transfer the marks on the inside face of one side to the inside face of the other, as shown in the drawing at right. Try not to run shelves through a knot, as this makes cutting the dado more difficult. You may be able to avoid a knot by turning the board, end for end.

Extend the dado lines down both edges of the board with a combination square, as in the photo at right. Mark the depth of the dado on each edge with a marking gauge, set to one-half the board's thickness. (Or mark along the end of the blade of a combination square, set to the depth of the dado.)

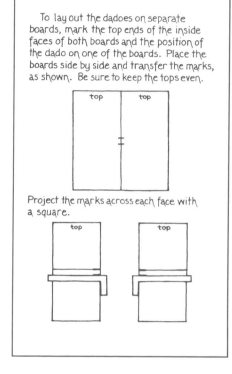

To lay out the dadoes on separate boards, mark the top ends of the inside faces of both boards and the position of the dado on one of the boards. Place the boards side by side and transfer the marks, as shown. Be sure to keep the tops even.

Project the marks across each face with a square.

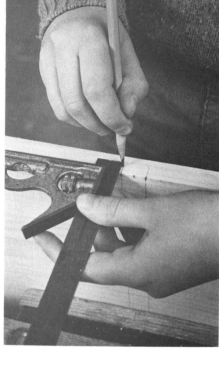

The dado is cut by sawing to depth along the layout lines, chiseling out the wood between the kerfs and smoothing the bottom with a small hand router. The saw is guided with a straight piece of wood, called a batten, clamped to the outside of the layout line. This way, the saw kerf will fall within the dado.

Ken used an 8-point crosscut saw; a finer saw, like a 12-point backsaw, will clog too quickly with sawdust. Push the saw gently, but firmly, against the batten with your fingers, and keep it vertical. Work carefully; try to keep from rocking end for end so the cut will be the same depth all the way across.

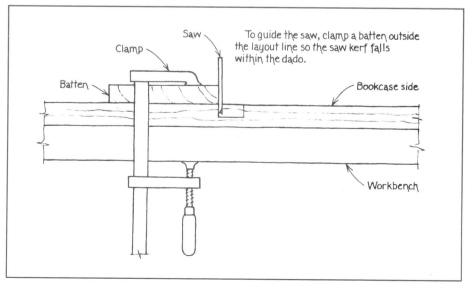

To guide the saw, clamp a batten outside the layout line so the saw kerf falls within the dado.

Saw

Clamp

Batten

Bookcase side

Workbench

Keep track of progress by checking against the depth marks on both edges. If the cut seems deeper at one edge, raise or lower the saw handle slightly to compensate. Stop when the sawteeth reach the depth mark, as in the photo at right. The saw should touch both marks at once; if it doesn't, the kerf is high in the middle. Try to level the kerf by rocking the saw until it's the same distance above both marks. Then gently saw straight across until you reach the mark on both edges.

Now set the batten on the other layout line. Remember not to cover the dado with it. If you do, the sawcut will come out on the wrong side of the line, and the dado will be much too wide.

Ken cleaned out his ¾-in. dado with a ⅝-in. chisel (a chisel the same width as the dado is likely to chip the edges). Lightly score the depth marks on each edge to prevent chipping below them. Use the chisel with its bevel down (toward the wood) and drive it with the palm of your hand, as shown below.

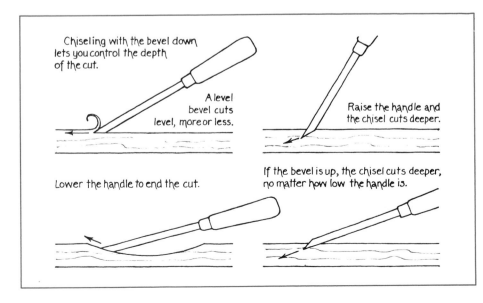

Chiseling with the bevel down lets you control the depth of the cut.

A level bevel cuts level, more or less.

Lower the handle to end the cut.

Raise the handle and the chisel cuts deeper.

If the bevel is up, the chisel cuts deeper, no matter how low the handle is.

Working with the bevel down allows you to control the depth of cut: raise the handle to go deeper, lower it to cut parallel to the surface, lower it further to cut up out of the wood. Kids who use the chisel with the bevel up will find it impossible to control depth and will get a very rough cut.

Working across the grain and with the bevel down, you can remove large chunks of wood with no fear of going too far. Chisel in from each end of the dado to avoid chipping out the edges of the board. I tell kids not to go all the way to the bottom of the kerf and not to worry about leaving a rough surface as the hand router will take care of that.

The little router (Stanley 271) smooths the dado bottom and ensures a uniform depth. If there's more than one dado, the router can cut them all to the same depth, so that the shelves can be of equal length. To set the router, place it astride the dado over what seems to be the shallowest point. Loosen the set screw and lower the blade to touch the bottom, then push it a little further so it will cut, and tighten the screw. The router should take a plane-shaving thickness off the bottom of the groove.

Hold the router with two hands, pushing it down firmly as you move it forward. If set correctly, it will move easily and smoothly. If it's hard to push and takes a rough cut, it's set too deep. Push the tool all over the dado until it removes no more wood anywhere. Work all the other dadoes at the same setting.

Now lower the blade slightly. (I loosen the screw just a little, tap the top of the blade shaft with the handle of the screwdriver, then tighten the screw.) Continue lowering the blade and cutting the dadoes until they are all smooth-bottomed. This may take as many as ten adjustments. If a dado passes through a knot, you will have to increase the depth in tiny increments; it's too hard to push the router through a knot when it's set to take a deep shaving.

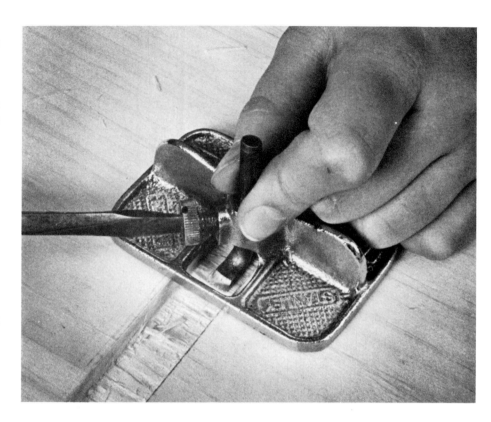

When the dadoes are cut to full depth, check each for fit with a board of shelf thickness. If a dado is too narrow, widen it with a side rabbet plane (Stanley 79). This plane has a bottom so thin it can fit into a groove less than $\frac{5}{16}$ in. wide and take shavings off its wall. It has two blades, so you can cut in either direction. Work toward the center of the board to avoid splitting the edges. Set the depth gauge so the points of the blade just reach the bottom of the dado, and hold the plane vertically against the dado wall as you push it along.

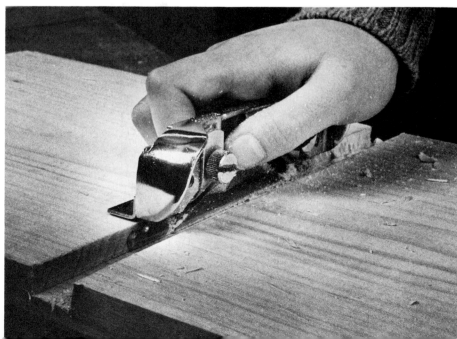

Keep checking the fit until the board goes in snugly, but without being forced. If a dado is too wide, not much can be done—the shelf fits loosely and the child tries to do more accurate work on the next project.

Once the dadoes are finished, the brace housings are chiseled out next to them. Ken decided to put his brace below the shelf, where it would be almost hidden from view. He marked the locations of the housings with little *x*'s to make sure they would be in the same position on each side: on the back edge below the dado, as shown in the drawing. Do this carefully or there'll be trouble later on. As with the dadoes, Ken avoided placing a housing over a knot. In knotty wood, it's a good idea to lay out dadoes and braces at the same time.

Use the small combination square to mark out the width and depth of the housings. Hold a pencil against the end of the blade and pull the square along the edge, as shown in the photo at right.

Ken used a sharp chisel of about the same width as the housing (here, ¾ in.) to rough it out. He gently scored just inside all four lines to prevent cuts from chipping beyond them. Caution kids that too deep a score along the grain of the wood could split the piece. Chisel out most of the wood, working with the bevel down. Start near the dado, and chiseling toward it, work back to the other end of the housing. The chips will come out easily as the wood fibers have been severed on one end by the dado.

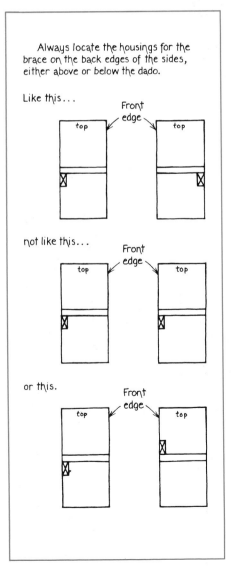

Always locate the housings for the brace on the back edges of the sides, either above or below the dado.

Like this . . .

Front edge

or this.

Front edge

not like this . . .

Front edge

When you get close to the lines, turn the chisel over and pare the rest of the wood away. Power the tool by hand, not by mallet. Take fine shavings, keeping the handle almost parallel to the face of the board for the bottom and vertical for the walls. Alternately trim the bottom and the walls, working slowly down to the lines.

When the rabbets, dadoes and housings are cut, the cabinet is ready to be assembled. If you've been working with wide boards, now is the time to cut them down the middle to make the four sides. Ken decided that his bookshelf would look better if the nails went through the sides rather than through the top and bottom, so he put the top in the vise, glued both surfaces of the rabbet, and nailed the side to it. It helps if a second person holds the horizontal pieces during nailing. When nailing a rabbet from the side, be sure to put the nails in at an angle, as shown at right.

You must assemble the top and bottom to the correct ends of the sides, or the dadoes and housings won't line up across the cabinet. You may discover that the child's cabinet has two right sides, that is, the housings on one side are in back, the others are in front. Or the housings might be above the shelves on one side, below them on the other. These are the results of layout errors. I check everything before giving the okay to start cutting, but mistakes creep in anyway. One solution that doesn't require making a whole side over is to rip the housings off the edge of one of the side boards while trimming the other three to the same width. Recut one set of housings and assemble the cabinet.

When Ken's frame was assembled, he measured shelf length, bottom of dado to bottom of dado. I checked the measurement—it's best to err on the long side. If the piece is too long, it can be trimmed for a perfect fit; if it's too short, it's scrap. Sliding the shelf into place, Ken tapped it home with a mallet, protecting the shelf edge with a piece of scrap, as in the photo at left. Keep the shelf straight by tapping on one side, then on the other. Remove the shelf, if necessary, in the same way. Ken didn't feel glue was needed, but he did nail through the sides into the shelf.

The length of the brace is the same as the shelf's, and its width is equal to the length of the housing. Cut the brace slightly wider than it needs to be and plane it to fit; once the brace has been installed, it will be difficult to plane a rough, exposed edge. After checking the fit, glue along the edge of the brace and all surfaces of the housing. Nail through the back of the brace into the housing, and through the side into the brace. Then nail through the shelf. A brace this long can bounce in the middle, so it's a good idea to hang it on a bench corner while nailing.

After planing the joints and sanding, Ken put a finish on his bookshelf.

Wildflower Stockbridge, a seventh-grader, made this "rabbet shelf," its shaped sides topped with animal heads. I bandsawed out the sides and Wildflower smoothed them with a spokeshave and file. Her cabinet is small enough not to need braces for stiffness, but cabinets over 18 in. in any dimension will need braces or backs.

Heather Johnston made this little cabinet when she was in seventh grade. It has a plywood back and two side-hung drawers (p. 175). Little blocks glued to the drawer fronts serve as pulls.

Paul Domingue's project, made in the seventh grade, is a good illustration of how to embellish a simple rabbeted cabinet. It has a plywood back, a mitered base with ornamental cutouts, doors and a drawer. The doors are single boards fitted between the cabinet sides and flush with the front edges. A catch mounted on a block below the shelf works as a doorstop. The attractive hinges are surface-mounted and simple to install because they require no fitting.

Eighth-grader Keith Thompson made this corner cabinet. He laid out the triangular top, bottom and shelf with a framing square, and I cut them out on the bandsaw. Keith rabbeted the top and bottom on two sides, dadoed the side boards to accept the shelf, and rabbeted the edge of one side board to join to the other. The sides were nailed together, then the top and bottom were added. Next, Keith used a fore plane (18 in.) to shave the front edges of the sides to match the angle of the top and bottom. The shelf was slid in, nailed, then planed to match the sides.

Mitered Box

Chapter 7

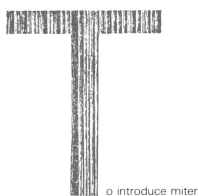

To introduce miter joints to a child, I say, "You know, like on a picture frame," and point to an old oak frame hung conspicuously for just this purpose. Most kids understand immediately, so accustomed are they to seeing these corners.

In my shop, we use miter joints in picture frames and in pretty little four, six or eight-sided boxes used for jewelry, knickknacks or odd treasures. There's a quiet grace to the simple diagonal line of a miter—no change of direction in the joint, no end-grain surfaces of different color and texture to distract the eye.

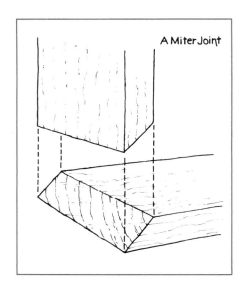

A Miter Joint

You can think of a mitered box as a single strip of wood folded in three places (with the little pieces of waste on the folds removed). Working with this single strip simplifies box making, but you can also cut the parts from separate boards. Use a miter box to make mitered boxes, but don't confuse the tool with its product; the miter box simply guides a saw at a precise angle. Unfortunately, most miter boxes won't accept boards of much more than 4 in. or 5 in. in width, which limits us as to how deep we are able to make our mitered boxes. Metal miter boxes are accurate, but they're also expensive. (How you can make a simple wooden one is described on p. 150.)

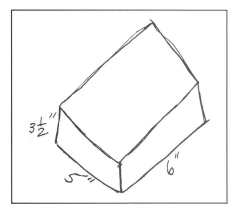

In eighth-grader Wendy Fraser's rough, isometric drawing, the upper right end should have been parallel to the opposite end. But no matter, all the information was there. I added up the lengths of the sides, plus a bit extra for waste, and cut a strip of ¾-in. pine about 2 ft. long. Then I ripsawed it as wide as the depth of the box.

Wendy rabbeted one edge of the strip to take the bottom of the box. The rabbet was ¾ in. wide (the thickness of the bottom) and ⅜ in. deep (half the thickness of the sides). Because the strip was narrow, she secured a bar clamp in the vise, then fixed the strip in the clamp. Make sure the clamp jaws are below the wood surface and clear of the rabbet, and that the middle of the strip rests on the vise jaws.

After making the rabbets, Wendy was ready to cut the miters. Which way does the cut go? Kids get this straight only by looking at a mitered object. So I point again to the oak frame and tell them that "mitered surfaces always point like arrows away from the center of the box." Back at the miter box, I draw the other three sides of the box in the air with my hands to show how the piece to be cut will relate to the box center.

If the children still don't get it, I ask them once again to imagine the box as a folded strip and to sketch the miters on the wood. Accurate measurements are made as each piece is cut, but the lines help keep the miters straight. You may need to use separate pieces for large boxes; if so, mark each piece so its position in the box and the direction of the miters are clear.

Wendy fixed the miter box in the bench vise so it wouldn't move or fall to the floor. If the child will be working on a tabletop, make sure to clamp the box down. Put the wood in the miter box so its rabbeted side (the inside of the box) faces the saw handle. The saw will chip the other side slightly as it exits the cut, but it's easier to clean up the outside of an assembled box than the inside.

Wendy chose not to mark her miters. For the first cut, she positioned the saw just slightly in from the end so there was wood on each side of the sawblade; this keeps the saw cutting straight down.

Make sure the strip is flat against the bottom of the miter box and clamp it in place. Tell kids to saw in a relaxed way and to use most of the length of the saw. Let the saw descend by its own weight, without using extra downward pressure. If the saw sticks now and then, aim it up or down and it will take less of a bite.

After cutting the first miter, Wendy measured along the outside of the strip to mark the second; measuring from an already-cut miter reduces error. The miters on each end of a side run in opposite directions, so Wendy swung the saw around to the miter box's other 45° setting. To position the saw, lower it so it barely touches the line. Then move the wood so that one sawtooth, bent toward the piece you want to keep, splits the line just where it crosses the board's edge and cut the second miter.

After swinging the saw back again, Wendy positioned the end of the strip to cut the first miter for the next piece, which should be a side adjacent to the one just cut.

The remaining two sides should be marked out using the first two as templates, so the opposite sides of the box will be exactly the same size. It's easier and more accurate to mark length in this way than to measure with a ruler.

Holding the pieces together, outside surface to outside surface, Wendy evened up the two cut ends and marked the end to be mitered. Then she drew an arrow on the piece to indicate the direction of the cut.

When all the sides were cut, Wendy was ready to glue the box together. She covered the benchtop with paper to protect it from glue and laid out the parts as they would go together. She spread glue on the miters and pulled the box together with a band clamp, a strip of webbing tightened by a tensioning mechanism. The heavy-duty model Wendy used is expensive and more powerful than necessary for a box this size. But it's easier to use than smaller, cheaper band clamps, though the cheaper ones will still do the job.

To use this type of band clamp, first unscrew the crank until the two castings are close together. Fit the band loosely around the box, adjust the boards so the ledges of the rabbets match, then crank the clamp tight. When glue squeezes out of all four joints, the band is tight enough. Use a wet paper towel to clean up squeeze-out. While the glue dries, cut and fit the bottom (p. 33).

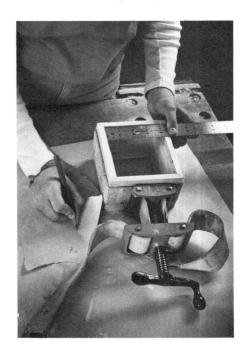

Glue is strongest when joining long grain to long grain, weakest when joining end grain. Miter joints run diagonally across the grain, halfway between end grain and long grain, so glued miters aren't very strong. For small boxes, glued miters are adequate, and the bottom will help to hold them together. If you want more strength, nail or dowel the corners from one or both sides, or saw the corners and add fillets.

After the glue dried, Wendy reinforced each corner by nailing from both sides. She set the nailheads beneath the surface so she wouldn't nick the blade when planing the sides. After planing, Wendy sanded the sides smooth. A gap appeared at the point of one miter, so she lightly bruised the sharp edge with a hammer to fold the wood fibers into the gap. Here's Wendy and her rough-and-ready mitered box.

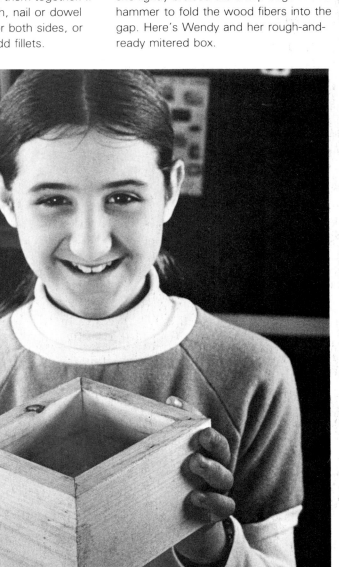

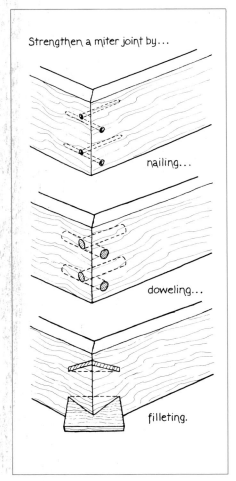

Strengthen a miter joint by...

nailing...

doweling...

filleting.

Another Mitered Box

Wendy decided to make a delicate, thin-walled mitered box after she had completed her rough-and-ready one. We make all four sides of this sort of box from one thick piece of wood whose faces have been planed flat and parallel to one another. By bandsawing the piece down the middle and opening it up like a book, we can lay out two box sides on each half. The planed-smooth sides of the board become the inside of the box. After assembly, the rough outsides are planed, too. The grain patterns on the two halves of the board will almost be mirror images, so the assembled box can have matching grain at each corner.

For making delicate boxes, I choose wood with distinctive grain patterns and annual rings that are almost vertical to the surface (wood cut this way is called quartersawn). The grain pattern in the middle of a quartersawn board looks much the same as that on its face, so a look at the outside surface of the 1-in.-thick butternut board Wendy and I selected gave us an idea of what it would look like inside.

I cut the board as wide as the box would be deep (in this case, 3 in.) and long enough to make both a long and a short side, plus extra for waste. Then Wendy planed the faces of the board flat and planed the edges square to the faces (p. 191). After studying the figure of the wood and deciding which edge would go at the top of the box, she cut two rabbets along the other edge to take the box's bottom. The rabbets were about ¼ in. deep and one-quarter as wide as the board was thick.

Then I bandsawed the board in half. Here's a trick to mark the center of an edge. Set a marking gauge to the estimated center of the board, then scribe down the edge twice, once with the gauge bearing on one face, once bearing on the other. A good guess results in a single line, a guess that's slightly off will yield two lines: saw down the center of the two and get a perfectly centered cut. Rather than take time to set up a fence, I bandsaw the line by eye, keeping the wood vertical against a 6-in. combination square. When pushing wood into a bandsaw, keep the heels of your hands low to act as a stop against the table's edge; when the end of the wood gets close to the blade, pull it through from the other side.

Wendy placed the two boards sawn-side up and laid out the position of the box sides. This step is critical: put an arrow on side one pointing toward side two and be sure to assemble the box in that order so the grain will match on all corners. Allow a little extra length on each board for waste.

Now Wendy made a mitered box in almost the same way as she had done before. As was the case with her other mitered box, the opposing sides had to be equal. After cutting two adjacent sides to length, Wendy used them to gauge the size of their opposites. Because the outside faces of the board were rough, she put the inside faces together and marked from the inside edges of the miter. Placing the smooth inside faces against the miter-box fence ensured accurate cuts, but left a fuzzy inside corner that had to be cleaned up with fine sandpaper before assembling the box.

Wendy made sure the ledges of the rabbet were even and the inner corners of the box were lined up as she tightened a small band clamp to assemble the box. Inaccurate resawing will sometimes cause one side to have a thick end, and with the band applying pressure from the outside, the thicker end may push the corners out of line. Insert a wooden shim under the band to compensate, as shown in the drawing.

The band pushes against the thicker end, forcing the inside corner out of line.

Shim the thin end to align the inside corner.

For small boxes or boxes of odd shape, I ask kids to make a pattern out of stiff paper to test the fit of the bottom before cutting it out of wood. Wendy cut out and trimmed the pattern to fit by trial and error, then witness-marked it and the box from the inside of the box. We make the bottoms for delicate boxes out of thick wood (Wendy's was 1⅛ in. thick), bandsawing and planing it to finished thickness after gluing it in the box. She planed flat the face that was to go inside and traced the pattern on it. I checked that she had transferred the witness marks, then bandsawed out the bottom. Wendy trimmed the bottom to fit the rabbet, glued and clamped it in place. Use a minimum amount of glue because it's impossible to clean up squeeze-out on the inside of the box while the clamp is on.

When the glue had dried, I bandsawed the bulk of the waste off the bottom of the box, and Wendy planed off the rest. Tenderly chuck the box in a vise, placing one end between the jaws to avoid squeezing in the sides. Support the top of the box on a board laid on the vise bars to raise the box sides above the vise jaws. Take coarse shavings at first, and finish with a thin cut when almost down to the box sides. Push the plane sideways at about 45° to avoid hitting a side of the box with the whole plane blade at once.

Now plane the sides to uniform thickness, gauging how much wood to take off by comparing the edges as you go along. Wendy worked in from the mitered corners toward the center of a side as the grain would allow. When she had to plane in the other direction to avoid tearing some difficult grain, she first chamfered the corners, as shown in the photo at right. This prevents the plane from catching on the end grain of the adjacent side and chipping a piece out of its face.

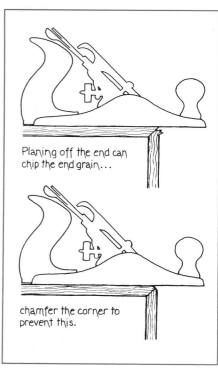

Planing off the end can chip the end grain...

chamfer the corner to prevent this.

To finish and flatten the top edges of small boxes, I made a special plane by mounting the iron frame from an old iron and wood hand plane in a board 30 in. long and 6 in. wide. The blade is off to one side to allow maximum use of the extra width. Fix the sole of the upside-down plane in a vise so it comes just above the jaws and push the top edges of the box over it at a 45° angle to the blade. When the plane had shaved everywhere along the edges, Wendy knew the top was flat.

You can also do the job by clamping a long, metal jointer plane upside down in a vise, but make sure the sole projects just above the jaws of the vise or you'll crush its sides. Be sure the cutting edge of the plane is sharp, straight and set very fine. Remind kids that if they don't keep their fingers above the blade of the plane, they risk a nasty cut. Wear work gloves when planing small pieces.

Wendy took time to sand the box carefully before applying an oil finish. Then she added the lid, which is flanged to hold it in place.

Darby Garrity made this cherry box as his final eighth-grade project. It has a mirror inlaid in the hinged lid and a drawer. Darby mitered the front side before he cut the drawer from it.

The butternut mitered box at right has compartment dividers that are housed in dadoes cut into the sides. The dadoes and miters were cut in a wide board, then the board was ripped down the middle to make two identical sides. The grain in the dividers runs vertically, but it shouldn't; in humid weather, the dividers are likely to expand slightly and push the box apart. If the grain ran horizontally, the dividers would slide up and down harmlessly in the dadoes with humidity changes. Butternut is a forgiving wood: this box was still intact several years after it was made. The lid is glued to a mitered frame, which engages the rabbet around the top edge of the box.

Pilar Ochoa made this picture frame in sixth grade. She made the ornamental beading around the edges with a Stanley 66 scratch stock, also called a beading scraper (p. 187). To make a picture frame, we rabbet the strips of wood to accept the picture, backing and glass; then we miter and glue the strips, pulling them together with a band clamp. A couple of nails put through each corner after the glue dries reinforce the joint.

Sixth-grader Nathan Faulkner's tray is really just a shallow mitered box. Its wide bottom fits loosely in a groove so it can move with changes in humidity. The carved handles are thin for butternut; in cherry or maple they would be fine.

Tara Hargraves made the little hexagonal box of rosewood at right in eighth grade. The lid is located by three strips of wood glued to its bottom face. To make a hexagonal box, set the saw guide on the miter box to 60°.

Victor Milo made this octagonal bookshelf in seventh grade. For octagonal boxes, set the saw guide to cut an angle of 67½°.

Board-on-Frame Box

Chapter 8

Large boxes, from stereo cabinets to doghouses, are difficult to make by rabbeting or mitering. Boards over 12 in. wide are hard to find, and gluing narrower boards edge to edge is demanding and time-consuming. An easier, faster way is to nail a lot of separate boards to a pair of frames. Cutting matched, overlapping rabbets (called shiplaps) or tongues and grooves in the edges of the boards is stronger and neater than simply butting the boards against each other. Tongue-and-grooving makes a nice, tight box, and in my shop the kids usually build boxes over 12 in. deep this way.

The tongue-and-groove joint is strong, even without glue, because the boards share a load as though they were a single board. But unlike a glued-up side, which expands and contracts as a single board, each tongue-and-grooved board can move independently with changes in humidity. As each board shrinks, its tongue slides further out of the neighboring groove; if the tongues are cut long enough, no space will be visible between the boards, even in the driest weather. Another advantage of the tongue-and-groove method of making boxes is that kids can use boards rejected from other projects; a tongue and groove can hold a twisted piece flat between two straight pieces.

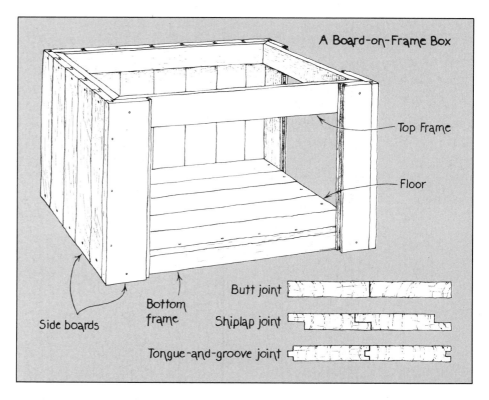

A Board-on-Frame Box

Top Frame

Floor

Side boards

Bottom frame

Butt joint

Shiplap joint

Tongue-and-groove joint

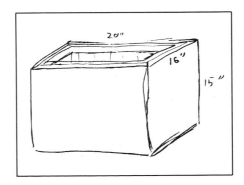

A board-on-frame box begins with the frames. Seventh-grader David Hauri calculated his box's frame dimensions from his drawing by subtracting twice the thickness of the sides from the outside measurements. The bottom frame is reinforced by nailing the floor of the box to it, so it can be made from narrow strips: David used ¾-in. by 1½-in. pine. The top frame has no reinforcement and the pieces must be sound (no knots or cracks) and more substantial: David's were 2½ in. wide. Using thicker stock would increase the strength considerably.

David chose to miter the frames, though he could have rabbeted them. Mitered frames are strong enough for this box, and miters are easier to cut than rabbets. Hold miters together with corner clamps while gluing and nailing. (The Stanley 83-404 clamps shown here are inexpensive, but they pull themselves apart when tightened; have the washer brazed to the end of the screw to prevent this.) Align the joint, slip the clamp into place and pull it against the inside corner of the joint, squeezing the clamp between fingers and thumb. Tighten both screws. (For wide boards, use a second clamp at the other edge of the joint.) Then loosen the top screw and slide the board out far enough to put glue on the miter. Slide the board back; the clamp will help to realign the miter perfectly. This is how I teach it, but after kids get comfortable with the procedure, they usually glue and clamp in one step.

Now nail through the joint from both sides. Put the board to be nailed into the vise and angle the nails slightly toward its middle. Glue and nail the other miters the same way. Some kids nail up two L-shaped pieces, then join the halves, but I find this awkward and encourage them to work in sequence around the frame.

Next, David filled in the sides, using boards of random width. The width of the last board placed on each side will vary according to the space remaining, so working with boards of random width will help keep the sides visually consistent. Using a spot of glue and one nail in the center of each end, place all boards referenced-face out.

David planed a tongue on the last board, laid the board flat on the unfinished side and marked the width needed to fill the space. He marked both ends (in case the space was tapered), joined the marks with a straightedge, sawed and planed to the line. Then he plowed the groove. If the board doesn't slide in easily, mark and plane off the excess and recut the groove.

Corner joints are the weak links in this type of box. After the sides are assembled, you could reinforce the corners by gluing and nailing battens to the top of the box. Battens also cover the end grain of the tongue-and-grooved boards and make the box look neater.

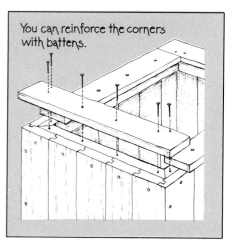

You can reinforce the corners with battens.

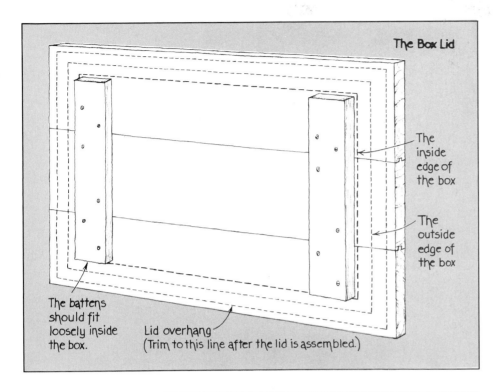

The Box Lid

The inside edge of the box

The outside edge of the box

The battens should fit loosely inside the box.

Lid overhang (Trim to this line after the lid is assembled.)

David chose to make a lid for his box from tongue-and-grooved boards screwed to battens. The battens hold the boards together and form a stop to hold the lid in place. After tongue-and-grooving the boards for the lid, David measured the inside of the frame. He cut two ¾-in. by 3½-in. battens slightly shorter than the box width, then placed them on the lid so their outer edges fit between the box ends. After marking their position, he marked the placement for two screws on each board.

The boards must be free to expand and contract with changes in humidity, even while they're screwed to the battens. Holes in the battens, made larger than the screw shanks, will allow enough movement. David flared each clearance hole with a countersink mounted in a brace so that the head of the screw would be out of the way, just below the surface of the wood.

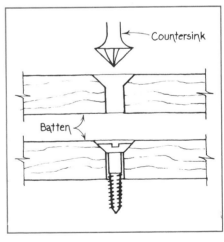

Countersink

Batten

Then David clamped the battens to the boards and screwed them down. Because the boards were soft, he didn't need to bore pilot holes. When both battens were screwed in place, I trimmed the lid to size on the bandsaw. David planed and chamfered the edges and then sanded the whole box.

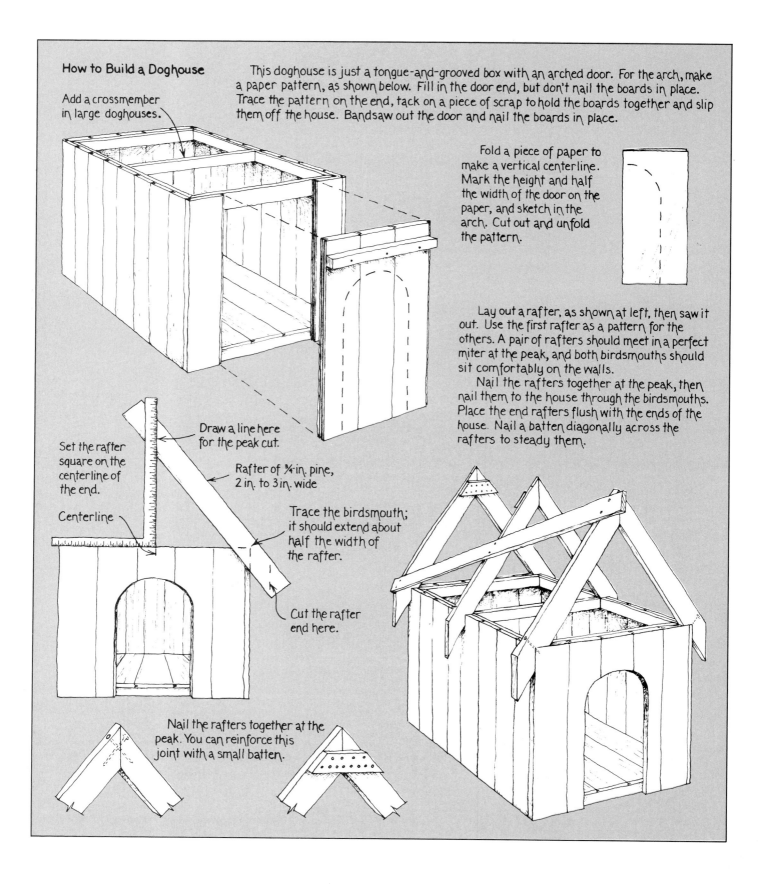

How to Build a Doghouse

Add a crossmember in large doghouses.

This doghouse is just a tongue-and-grooved box with an arched door. For the arch, make a paper pattern, as shown below. Fill in the door end, but don't nail the boards in place. Trace the pattern on the end, tack on a piece of scrap to hold the boards together and slip them off the house. Bandsaw out the door and nail the boards in place.

Fold a piece of paper to make a vertical centerline. Mark the height and half the width of the door on the paper, and sketch in the arch. Cut out and unfold the pattern.

Lay out a rafter, as shown at left, then saw it out. Use the first rafter as a pattern for the others. A pair of rafters should meet in a perfect miter at the peak, and both birdsmouths should sit comfortably on the walls.

Nail the rafters together at the peak, then nail them to the house through the birdsmouths. Place the end rafters flush with the ends of the house. Nail a batten diagonally across the rafters to steady them.

Draw a line here for the peak cut.

Set the rafter square on the centerline of the end.

Centerline

Rafter of ¾-in. pine, 2 in. to 3 in. wide

Trace the birdsmouth; it should extend about half the width of the rafter.

Cut the rafter end here.

Nail the rafters together at the peak. You can reinforce this joint with a small batten.

Tongue-and-grooved gable walls help secure the roof to the house. The bottom of the gable wall should overlap the end of the house by about 1½ in. Trace the rafter outline on the assembled boards, then cut out the shape.

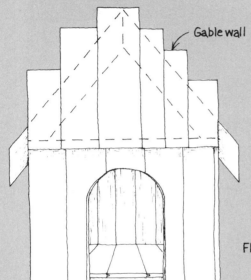

Gable wall

Tip the house on end on a flat surface, then nail through the end rafters into the gable wall. Position a shim to level the house while nailing.

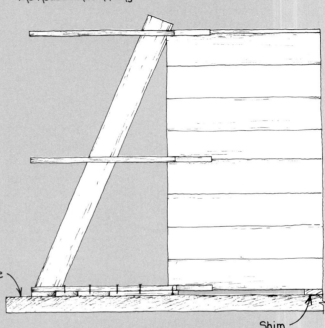

Flat surface

Shim

Nail through the center of the roof boards into the rafters.

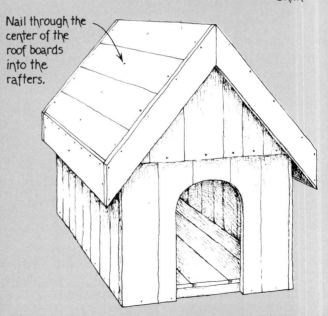

Nail on tongue-and-grooved roof boards. They should overhang the ends of the house by 1-2 in., as on Liz Brinkerhoff's house, at left. Then nail on trim boards, as shown in the drawing. If the ends of the rafters are vertical, you can carry the trim around the sides. Finish the roof with shingles or roofing paper.

Table

Chapter 9

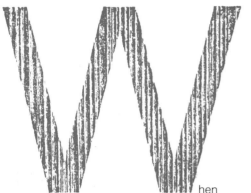

When a child in my shop wants to make a table, the first question I ask is whether the table is to have square legs or round ones. A square-leg design is formal and angular; a round-leg design has fewer right angles and a more relaxed feel. The methods for making each are also quite different. Square-legged tables call for cabinetmaker's methods: they require sawn boards, doweling, mitering and lots of planing (this is the type of table I'll show how to make here). We make round-legged tables using the skills of the country craftsman: the legs are split from a log and shaved round and have round mortise-and-tenon joints (as explained in Chapter 12); only the tabletop is sawn from a board. Both methods can express a kid's ideas.

In table making, more than in most projects, the cause-and-effect relationship between carelessness and frustration is evident to a child. Planning and careful work are required at several points or the table won't go together. Yet every mistake is correctable; if a child perseveres (and gets enough adult help), he or she will eventually succeed. When the project finally works out, the child will understand how important it is to follow instructions and that persistence pays off. It's a good experience.

I was pleased with seventh-grader Amy Lord's drawing. It was quick and rough, but it showed me that she understood the structure of the table. To make sure I understood, she and I went over the drawing together: I asked her, "You want a square-legged table with a top 24 inches by 36 inches, right? The height is 31 inches? The apron is 3 inches wide? You haven't given me the overhang of the top; we'll need to know that before I can give you any wood."

Checking like this confirms the child's power to communicate ideas—a valuable pat on the back for any kid. Sometimes you'll find you've completely misinterpreted the drawing. Let the child know adults make mistakes too: "Oh, you're right. I misunderstood. Sorry." Kids need to hear that once in a while.

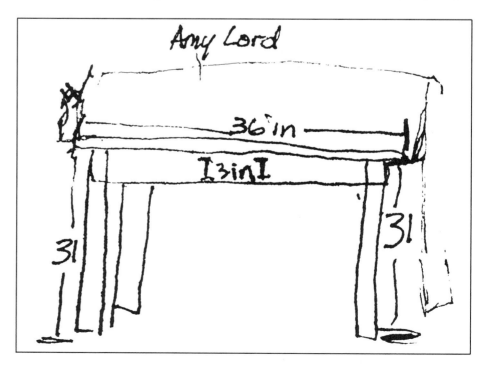

Table | **69**

Amy chose to overhang her tabletop 3 in. on the ends and 2 in. on the sides. Knowing this and the approximate thickness of the legs (1½ in.), she was able to work out the length of the aprons. I ripped the legs from rough pine cut to a length of 30¼ in. This is ¾ in. less than the height of the table because the top will make up the difference.

The legs must be planed smooth on four sides; keep each leg square in section and uniform in thickness. This is easier if the child goes the full length of the leg with each stroke and doesn't tip the plane. A leg that has a little taper or is slightly off square is okay, but kids new to planing may get carried away. Replace any leg that's badly out of shape.

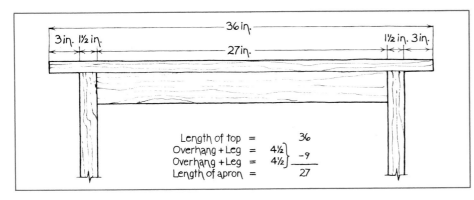

Length of top =	36	
Overhang + Leg =	4½	
Overhang + Leg =	4½	−9
Length of apron =	27	

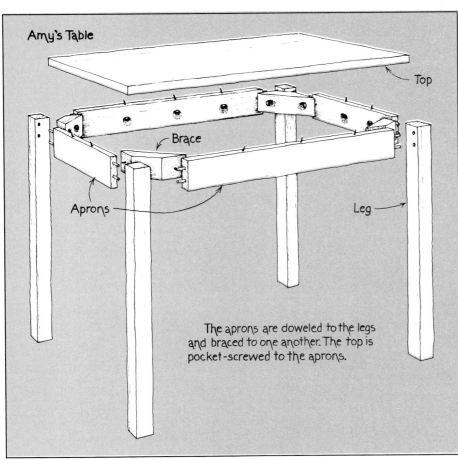

Amy's Table

Top

Brace

Aprons

Leg

The aprons are doweled to the legs and braced to one another. The top is pocket-screwed to the aprons.

For a table to be sturdy, the legs must be locked rigidly to the top. Just nailing them to the top won't do because the legs will wobble on the nail. We add the apron rails between the legs just below the top to stiffen the structure. The wider the apron the stiffer the leg, but if the apron is too wide, the table will look top-heavy. Kids can judge the best width by looking at aprons on a finished table or by doing a scale drawing.

The apron is joined to the leg with hidden dowels, but the dowel joint alone isn't very strong. We reinforce it with a brace, mitered into the corner and glued between aprons. Aprons, legs and bracing make a sturdy frame, but it's even stiffer when fixed to the tabletop. The tabletop, like the back of a cabinet, holds the frame square, preventing any sideways racking motion from loosening the corner joints.

Amy made her aprons from pre-planed, ¾-in. pine. She decided to place them flush with the outside faces of the legs, though she could have recessed them. Set the legs and aprons upside down on the benchtop and align them. Carefully label each joint with small letters written closely together, so that later on there will be no mistaking where the apron goes on the leg. Check a child's work at this point because this is where many tables start to go astray. Kids often use huge letters across the whole face of a leg, then later can't position the apron.

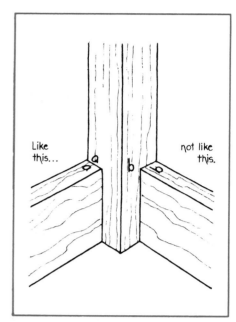

Like this...

not like this.

Next, Amy bored ¼-in. holes about 1 in. deep into the apron ends to take the dowels. She placed them about ¾ in. from the edges, centered between the faces of the apron. The straighter the hole the better, though ¼-in. dowels are flexible enough to forgive small errors.

After boring, Amy put an apron, end up, in the vise and inserted a dowel center in each hole. (Dowel centers allow you to mate holes accurately in two pieces of wood.)

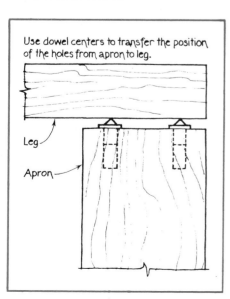

Use dowel centers to transfer the position of the holes from apron to leg.

Leg

Apron

Table | **71**

Amy then held the face of the corresponding leg in position so that the labels were close together. Squinting down at the leg and apron from above, she made sure the top edge of the apron was lined up with the top end of the leg, and that the face of the apron was aligned with the face of the leg. Don't let the leg touch the dowel-center points until the position looks and feels just right; when it does, push down hard on the leg so the dowel centers make a good, clear mark.

Amy bored ¼-in. holes, about 1 in. deep, in the legs on these marks. Be sure that the leg is horizontal in the vise and the drill is held vertically. Kids should test each joint before marking and boring the next, so that errors will be caught and corrected, not repeated. Each dowel should be 1¾ in. long; though the length of the holes is 2 in., shorter dowels ensure that the joint will close.

Most of the errors on a table will show up at this point. If the holes on mating pieces don't match, the pieces won't go together, but you can usually save an imperfect piece. If a hole is just slightly off or angled, try whittling a point on one or both dowels to guide them into place, or shave the dowel.

Check the alignment before deciding which dowel to trim. If both holes are off, bore new ones, leaving at least ¼ in. between new and old, then re-mark the leg with dowel centers. If only one new hole is needed, align the good hole with a dowel while marking the new one with a dowel center. If all else fails, give the child a new leg and apron. Don't worry if the apron is twisted or its top edge doesn't match the leg top; small errors can be planed away after the frame is glued up.

You can avoid planing and aligning the faces of apron and leg if you recess the apron, as in the drawing at right. Decide how far in from the front face of the leg you want the apron and scribe a line to mark it. Align the apron and the line and label the joint. When you bore the holes, make sure the dowels won't intersect in the legs—the hole centers should be at least ⅜ in. apart, and no hole closer than ½ in. to an edge. Hold the leg in the vise and bring the apron down to meet it to mark the position of the holes on the leg. This way you can line up the edge of the apron with the scribed line. If the dowel centers drop out of the holes, wrap masking tape around their shanks to fill them out.

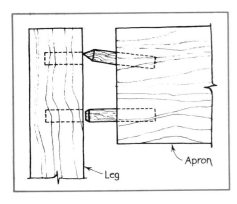

Apron

Leg

Recess the apron to avoid alignment and planing problems.

Before gluing, assemble the frame dry to make sure that all the joints fit. Gluing is tricky business and requires an adult's help. Glue and clamp two opposite sides together first, then add the other aprons to complete the frame. (Some kids will try to assemble the joints in sequence around the table, but this is awkward.) Roll one end of each dowel in a puddle of glue and tap it into a leg hole with a hammer as far as it will go. (If you've shaved any dowels to improve fit, be sure to glue these in the correct position.) Then spread glue on the rest of the dowel and the ends of the apron. Push the joint together with bar clamps, pipe clamps or quick-set clamps. The clamps must be centered on the width and thickness of the apron as they press against the leg, as in the drawing. If they're not, the joint won't close square or the legs won't be parallel. Place wooden pads under each of the clamp's ends to keep from denting the wood.

Complete the assembly with the other two aprons. The end clamps prevented Amy from centering single clamps on the last two sides, so she used two clamps on each side, above and below the end clamps. (You could wait until the glue on the first two ends has dried, remove the clamps and glue the whole assembly.) View the frame from above; if it isn't close to square, clamp it across the long diagonal. Clean up any squeezed-out glue with wet paper towels.

Position the clamps to press here... not here.

Table | **73**

The glued-up legs and aprons will be fragile until the braces are installed, so handle them gently. Amy's braces were thick and about ½ in. narrower than the apron. She planed the stock smooth and mitered both ends so that the brace just cleared the corner of the leg. To ensure an accurate fit, I made sure that she sawed both ends of each brace with the same surface against the back of the miter box.

Amy spread glue on the ends of the braces and clamped them in place. Wooden pads on the arrises of the legs provide a bearing surface for the clamps. (Bandsaw them from scrap.) For Amy's small pine table, glue was enough to hold the braces; on larger tables and hardwood tables, reinforce the braces by pocket-screwing them to the aprons. Cut and fit the brace as usual but, before gluing, cut pocketscrew seats, as shown in the drawing.

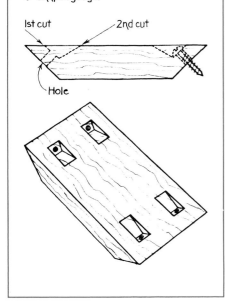

To make pocketscrew seats, first bore a hole perpendicular to the mitered surface, larger than the screw shank, but smaller than the screw head. Then carve a channel for the screw head with a chisel or U-shaped gouge.

1st cut   2nd cut

Hole

There wasn't a single board wide enough for Amy's tabletop, so she had to edge-joint and glue narrow boards together (p. 192). Jointing requires a good deal of aptitude—not every kid can do it and even some adults have difficulty learning the skill. You could butt joint, shiplap or tongue-and-groove the edges of narrow boards and screw or nail them to the aprons, as when making the side of the board-on-frame box in Chapter 8. There'll be little gaps between the boards and spaces will show on the ends, but these tops are easier for young kids and for kids who want to make a table quickly.

After the glue dried, Amy planed both faces of the top, taking a fairly thick shaving with a smoothing plane. She continued with a longer plane set to take a fine shaving. Then she planed the edges and chamfered the corners.

To pocket-screw the apron for mounting the top, Amy used a drill bit that was larger than the screw shank but smaller than the head. Start the bit on top of the apron, just outside the center of the edge, and bore straight down for about ⅛ in. to seat the drill. Then angle the drill so the hole bursts out 1½ in. to 2 in. below the apron edge on the inside face of the frame. Bore two or three holes on each apron, then carve a channel for the screw head with a *U*-shaped gouge or a chisel. Cut this seat deep enough so the screw sticks out of the top of the apron slightly less than half the thickness of the tabletop.

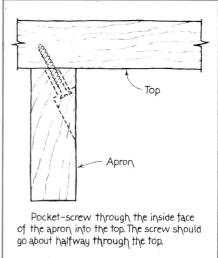

Pocket-screw through the inside face of the apron into the top. The screw should go about halfway through the top.

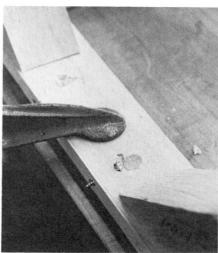

Table | 75

Center the frame on the tabletop, checking the overhang on every side with a ruler. Amy clamped the assembly to the top of the bench and traced around the aprons so she would be sure later on to position the pieces properly. She started each screw by tapping the screwdriver with a hammer, then she snugged the screws down. Don't overtighten them because that could strip the holes.

When the table is assembled, measure each of the legs to see if they are all the same length. If not, trim them to the length of the shortest. If the top and frame are close to true, the table won't rock.

Amy completed her table by sanding everything with 100-grit and 220-grit paper wrapped around a sanding block. She then applied a clear oil finish.

Jane Longnecker made the fine butternut table at right in seventh grade. The aprons are recessed and each leg is tapered on the two inside surfaces. Tapered legs add grace and visual lightness to a table without reducing strength. Tapering isn't hard to do but it takes extra time. I suggest it to kids who have the patience to add a refinement.

There is no need to taper all four faces of a leg. Tapering only the inner faces gives the effect of slightly splayed legs, which are pleasing to look at. Jane planed the legs smooth and square, then marked the taper on the two inside surfaces of the leg.

A taper of ⅜ in. to ½ in. on a 1½-in.-thick leg is plenty; measure and mark the bottom of the leg on the inside faces. The taper should start about ½ in. below the apron. Project a line around the leg at this point with a square and mark out the taper by joining these lines to those on the bottom of the leg. Hold the leg in a vise so the taper line is horizontal. Use a fore plane or jointer plane (18 in. or 22 in. long) to ensure a flat surface, and start planing near the bottom of the leg. Move toward the top lines as you remove more wood, increasing the length of the stroke. Go slowly as you approach the top lines and work right up to them, but don't go beyond them. Now taper the adjacent face. You will have to redraw the taper line on the face you have just planed.

This table was made by seventh-grader Debbie Miles. She added stretchers for extra strength, and because she liked the way they looked.

Table | 77

Rebecca Roebuck, near right, also a seventh-grader, made her table of oak and set a shelf on the stretchers.

Seventh-grader Jordy Green, far right, added a drawer to his little table. This isn't too difficult to do, but it must be planned from the beginning (p. 174).

Tom Boswell made his cherry drop-leaf table with tapered legs in eighth grade. He did a careful job with this difficult table. He had the special rule joints on the edges of the leafs and tabletop milled by a local cabinet shop because we didn't have the molding planes required to do the job by hand.

Signs and Carving
Chapter 10

There's a good chance that when a kid is between major projects in my shop, he or she will carve a sign. Signs become especially popular around the holidays, for they make nice gifts. If you enjoy carving, kids will catch your enthusiasm, and it will become an important shop activity. Some kids really become excited about signs and, like sixth-grader Dan Adams, take pride in giving them decorative, personal details.

There's nothing automatic about carving a sign—almost every cut counts. I teach a simple method that allows all but the youngest or most impatient child to succeed; all that's needed is a chunk of wood and a *U*-shaped gouge called a veiner. A veiner can cut deeper than a shallow gouge of the same width, with less risk of the tool's corner catching in the wood. I usually keep 3mm, 5mm and 7mm veiners on hand, but choose a tool closest in size to the detail in the child's drawing. The whole job can be done with just one veiner, but kids may use several to produce a variety of textures.

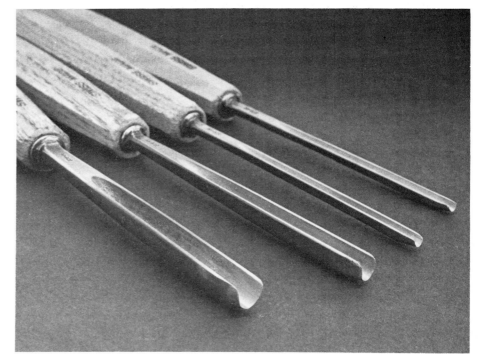

Softwoods are easiest to carve, so I usually offer my students white pine or basswood. Poplar, walnut and butternut are good, too. Occasionally a child will insist on cherry because of its color; though it's hard, it carves well. Avoid coarse-textured woods such as the ashes, oaks and southern yellow pine. Try to choose a board that is knot free and straight grained (with fibers running parallel to its faces and edges). The way a board looks is usually a good indication of the orientation of its grain. If the board is straight grained, the veiner will cut smoothly in any direction; if it's not, carving with the grain may cause the wood to split ahead of the tool.

To begin, ask the child to do a full-size drawing of the sign. Some kids are comfortable drawing directly on the wood, but unless a kid is adept, I prefer the drawing be done on paper first, so that the layout of the letters can be easily adjusted. The letters must have thickness; simple lines will not do. Any style of lettering can be used, and I like to keep typography and calligraphy books around for inspiration. Kids who have a hard time arranging their letters in the available space should cut them out and push them around the board until the spacing looks right. This is helpful even for kids with good design sense.

During the design process, decide whether the letters will be carved into the wood (incised) or the background will be carved away, leaving the letters raised. At first, most kids will want the letters incised, but many will change their minds when they see samples of the alternative. If any part of the design is superimposed over another, as in balloon lettering, there's no choice: the background must be carved away.

Have the child transfer the drawing to the wood using carbon paper (or by tracing around the cutout letters). Then secure the board to the bench with a clamp or bench stop, or put the board in a vise. Never allow a child to carve with one hand while holding the board down with the other.

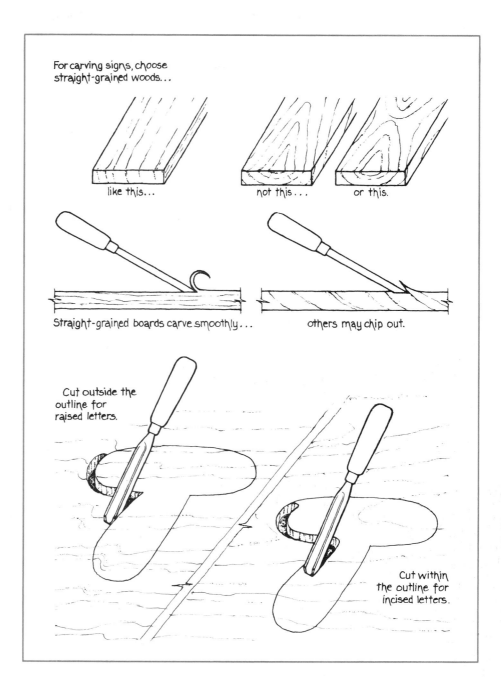

For carving signs, choose straight-grained woods...

like this...   not this...   or this.

Straight-grained boards carve smoothly...   others may chip out.

Cut outside the outline for raised letters.

Cut within the outline for incised letters.

Carving is the next step, but before giving a child a tool, remind him or her of the basic safety precautions: Carry the tool with its edge down, work with both hands behind the edge, and never leave the tool extending over a table edge. A child hasn't absorbed the rules if he or she takes wild cuts, carves without the hand that holds the blade resting against the wood, or without securing the wood to the bench. Let kids know they may not use the tool unless it's used properly.

Begin to carve by outlining the design with the veiner. If the letters are to be raised, the child should cut outside the pencil lines; for incised letters, inside them. Always try to remove wood to just beyond the line so you won't need to clean it up later. Kids should practice on scrap before trying this on their signs.

I don't suggest using a mallet to drive the veiner except in very hard woods; hand power is all that's needed. Good control comes from using both hands on the tool. I tell kids that the right hand, like the motor of a car, provides the power, and the left hand is like the brake. The power hand holds the handle of the tool while the brake hand presses on the blade just behind the edge. The brake hand must always rest on the wood or on the table near the wood, as demonstrated in the photos. For extra accuracy, hold the tool by the blade in the left hand and tap the end of the handle with the heel of the right hand. This advances the tool in tiny steps, allowing the child to stop on a dime. It's particularly important to have this control when approaching an intersecting line.

After outlining, go to work on the background. The surface need not be cut deeply: just introduce a texture within or around the letters. Start the tool on one outline and stop at the other; near the outlines, try driving the tool with the heel of one hand for extra control. A large veiner will cut deeply and quickly; a fine one will allow a more delicate texture. Some kids vary the direction of their cuts or go in for cross-hatching. Cutting across the grain will give the cleanest results in some woods.

A child may consider the sign finished once the background is carved. For deeper relief, outline the letters again and take out more wood. For a smooth background, finish up with a shallow fishtail gouge and sand lightly. The completed sign may be oiled, stained or painted, which will increase the contrast between textured and smooth surfaces and make the sign striking to look at.

The method I have just described is also ideal for cutting blocks for printing, though we seldom do this in my shop. To lay out the image you want to print, remember to reverse it from left to right. The easiest way to do this is to draw the image the way you want it to appear when printed, working with a piece of carbon paper, carbon-side up, under your paper; the drawing will appear reversed on the back of the paper. Now turn the paper over and trace the reversed pattern through the carbon paper onto the wood. Water or oil-based printing inks are available at most art supply houses.

Here are some examples of carved work. "Nicky!" was neatly carved with a 5mm veiner; the background cuts go across the grain.

Seventh-grader John DeGange, near right, incised his letters.

Eighth-grader Heidi Conrad, far right, did an attractive job texturing the background of her backgammon board.

Sixth-grader Marci Hawthorne made her box using the techniques described in Chapter 7, then she carved a name in its side.

Eighth-grader Katie Crow made this unusual pendant by gluing a layer of butternut to a piece of rosewood, then planing the butternut very thin. By carving through the butternut, she created a design with sharply contrasting colors.

Chrissy Chioffi made her cherry cutting board in seventh grade. She used a mallet to drive the large veiner when removing wood between the outlines of her design.

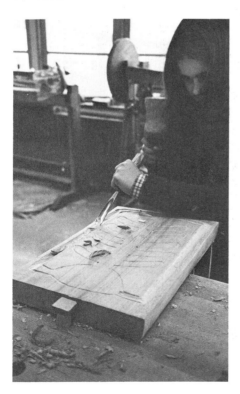

Sometimes a sign turns into a major project. Eighth-grader Tom Porter carved this beauty in walnut for his father's business. To incise the letters, he used a straight chisel to make a plunge cut on the centerline, then he carved to the central cut from the outlines. The rest of the sign was carved using methods similar to those I've described, though the relief is fairly deep and the background has been smoothed. Tom gave the hammer and saw handles some three-dimensional shape by rounding their raised surfaces.

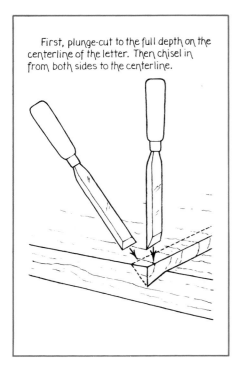

First, plunge-cut to the full depth on the centerline of the letter. Then chisel in from both sides to the centerline.

Carving can also be done on projects other than signs. Sixth-grader Jay Sailor drew his horse carefully on paper, then transferred the top and side views to the face and edge of a piece of pine; I cut it out for him on the bandsaw. But before Jay got his horse to look this good, there was still an enormous amount of handwork for him to do using gouges, files, rasps and sandpaper.

Spoons and Scoops

Chapter 11

Kitchenware has always been popular in my shop. Kids frequently choose a wooden spoon as a first project because it's small and looks simple, and they know that it will be welcome at home. I encourage this sort of project by displaying sample spoons and scoops conspicuously; children can either copy these designs or create their own. Either way, making spoons and scoops is a fine introductory sculptural experience, involving the use of carving tools to produce gracefully curved shapes. But it's also practical sculpture, for the piece must work well and be comfortable to use.

Cherry and butternut have beautiful color and grain and are favorite woods for spoons. Kids less often select maple, birch and beech because their colors aren't as exciting, but I've heard it said that light-colored woods are kinder to the flavor of foods. On the other hand, one professional spoon maker I know uses almost any kind of native wood, from apple and dogwood to locust. Seventh-grader Becca Brackett chose to make her salad set from butternut.

Green wood is good for spoon making for the same reason it's good for stool making: it's easy to carve but dries hard. If you can get freshly felled logs, use the techniques described in Chapter 12 to split out the material. Store the spoon in a closed plastic bag to keep it wet until it's completed.

If you can't get green wood, don't worry. Many woods carve easily when dry: butternut, pine, beech and bass, for example. Cherry, walnut and birch are harder, but not too difficult to work when seasoned. Maple and oak are very hard and should be carved green. Red oak has large pores that allow liquid to pass through, so don't use it for spoons or bowls that will hold fluids. White oak is relatively impervious to liquids. But all oak is high in tannic acid and may affect the flavor of foods.

This drawing shows a progression of spoon designs—from flat spoon to curved dipper. All spoons require careful shaping below the bowl; more complex designs have more shape to the handle and lip of the bowl. As the bowl dips further below the handle, all the curves become more exciting.

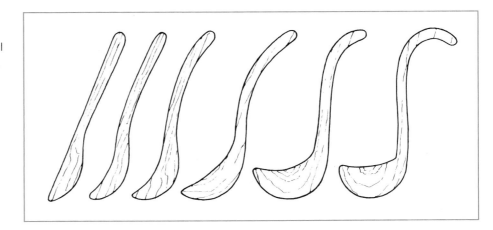

Kids can carve spoons without planning them first, but many need a structured approach. There's no reason to restrict children to conventional spoon shapes, but discourage the incorporation of sharp inside corners into the design; they look bad and are hard to carve.

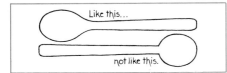

Like this...
not like this.

Occasionally, a spoon design is suggested by the shape of a piece of wood or by the way a chunk splits out of a log. Wood sometimes grows over an old knot in the shape of a bowl. If a kid comes across such a find, encourage him or her to use it in the design.

As you help the child design, always discuss how the spoon will be used; kids need help relating the spoon's dimensions to its purpose.

"Is it to stir oatmeal, dish out dog food or to eat your corn flakes with?"

"I don't know."

"You have to decide before starting your work."

"My mom likes to bake bread."

"A spoon to mix batter?"

"Yes."

"Well, that has to be pretty big and strong, doesn't it?"

"Mmmm."

"Okay. Let's decide how big."

A flat spoon is simple to make. Choose a knot-free, straight-grained chunk of wood, a few inches longer than the spoon, and plane its face smooth. Draw the top view of the spoon full size and trace the drawing onto the wood. Align the spoon handle parallel to the grain and sketch in the thickness of the bowl walls. For spoons with raised handles, the child will need to draw the side view. (After carving the bowl and sawing out the shape drawn on the top, draw the side view on the wood.) Some kids may prefer to work without a pattern; I usually ask children who propose free designs to draw the shapes directly on the wood.

Carve out the bowl first, holding the wood in a vise. I prefer a 5mm or 7mm veiner or a ¾-in. firmer gouge, which is a heavier tool. Driving the gouge with a light mallet, cut a series of shallow incisions around a small circle in the center of the bowl. The last cut should lift out a flower-shaped chip. Enlarge this little crater, pushing the gouge by hand, until you reach the lip of the bowl and the depth seems right. At the bottom of each cut, lower the gouge handle so the edge slices through the wood rather than chips it out. For deep-bowled spoons, you can use a spoon gouge (which is named for its shape, not its use). Its curved blade allows you to cut parallel to the bottom of the bowl and still lower the handle enough to cut without chipping.

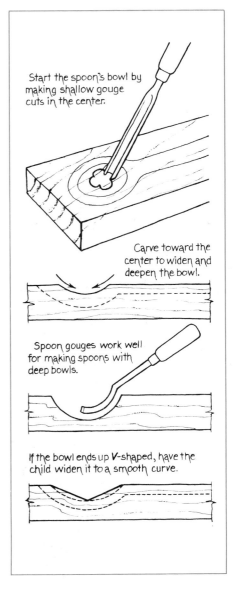

Start the spoon's bowl by making shallow gouge cuts in the center.

Carve toward the center to widen and deepen the bowl.

Spoon gouges work well for making spoons with deep bowls.

If the bowl ends up V-shaped, have the child widen it to a smooth curve.

Gouges want to cut in straight lines, so kids tend to make the spoon's bowl with straight sides and a tiny bottom. They must widen the bowl to a smooth curve without going deeper. Also, an enthusiastic kid may carve right through the bottom of the bowl if not careful; pinching the walls of the bowl frequently between thumb and forefinger will help keep track of depth.

The rippled surface left by the gouge can be attractive; if the child wants a smooth bowl, he or she can trim the tops of the ridges until they're even with the valleys. Use the gouge carefully: the better this job is done, the less sanding will be necessary later.

Now cut out the spoon outline with a bandsaw or coping saw. You can split out the handles for large, green-wood spoons with a froe, but first cut a saw kerf along each side of the bowl to keep the handle from splitting into the bowl. (Split near the edge of the board first to see if the grain runs straight.) This method leaves more shaping work for the drawknife, but it's the best way if you're trying to follow the natural pattern of the wood's fibers. If you have a chunk of wood whose shape suggests the curve of the spoon, this method works quite well. The drawknife follows the natural curve revealed by the froe.

The inside shape of the bowl governs the outside; the trick is to get the walls uniformly thick. You can carve the outside with a chisel, a shallow gouge, a drawknife or a spokeshave. We use several old, miniature drawknives (unfortunately, no longer manufactured), with comfortable, egg-shaped handles and straight-edged blades about 4 in. long. You might want to consider having a machinist make up a few of these little knives for you (p. 188).

Regular-sized drawknives work on large spoons, but kids tend to take off too much wood when using them on small spoons. If a big drawknife is all you have, it'll work fine if you take light cuts. Spokeshaves are easier to control than drawknives, especially for young kids.

When carving the outside of the bowl, work away from its centerline to avoid rough cuts and chips. (The rule for carving inside the bowl is just the opposite.) Be careful about this, because as the bowl gets thinner, carving in the

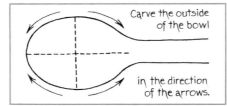

Carve the outside of the bowl in the direction of the arrows.

wrong direction can split off the whole side of the spoon. Eighth-grader Susie White reverses the direction of her drawknife in order to cut with the grain on the outside of her spoon. Hold the bevel of the drawknife down and take short, slicing cuts. End each cut by turning up the handle of the knife: this keeps the edge from digging in. Fair the bowl into the handle, but don't let this section get too thin because it's where spoons are most likely to break in use. If the curve is too tight, you can use a whittling knife or a file.

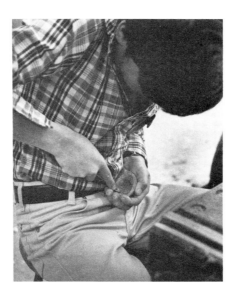

When Susie finished the outside of her bowl, she liked its shape better than that of the inside. So she reworked the inside, holding the handle of the spoon in the vise and resting the bowl atop the vise jaws, far left. The hollowed-out bowl of a spoon is fragile and easily split; never hold the bowl in the vise. Try holding it in your hand as you carve. Your hands will be safe if you carve only toward the bottom of the bowl, as eighth-grader Mike Kelly does here.

Next, shape the handle. Susie fixed the neck of her spoon in the vise. She supported its end on her leg—a clever idea for working long spoons—reversing the arrangement to work near the neck. She took just enough wood off the top surface to smooth it. Kids who take off too much wood wind up with the handle lower than the bowl, which looks odd.

When satisfied with the shape, go over the whole spoon with a square-edged cabinet scraper to further shape and smooth it. It's safe to hand-hold the spoon while scraping. Look at your work from every angle; these finishing steps make the difference between a crude and a refined spoon.

If the child has worked the surface of the spoon very carefully, he or she can start sanding with 220-grit sandpaper. Most kids, however, need to start with 100-grit paper, especially to smooth the inside of the bowl, where even coarser paper is sometimes useful. Be careful: sandpapering can soften or change the shape of an intentionally sharp edge.

When the spoon feels velvety smooth, immerse it in warm water for about five minutes. This process is called raising the grain. Most woods will come out feeling fuzzy, for the water releases little fibers, which spring up from the wood's surface. Let the spoon dry, and then sand again with 220-grit paper. After two or three cycles of this, the spoon should stay smooth when wet. To finish, rub on heavy mineral oil (which won't leave any taste or contaminate the food) and sand the wet spoon with 400-grit wet/dry paper. A spoon that's been finished like this will be glassy smooth and glowing with color. You can reoil and resand the spoon every now and then to keep it looking its best. Here's Susie's finished salad set.

There are any number of variations on the basic spoon. Eighth-grader Victoria Layman added decoration by inlaying a butterfly of exotic wood in her carefully shaped, asymmetrical, cherry spoon.

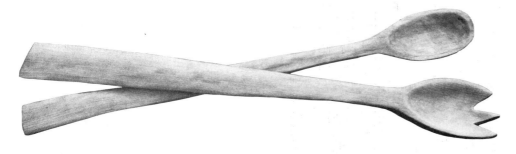

Mike Brown made a dipper by lowering the lip of the bowl and raising the handle. He drew the side view on the wood, making sure the handle paralleled the grain, and I roughed-out the shape on the bandsaw. Then Mike sketched the bowl on the blank and carved it out with a gouge.

Scoops are handy for serving up flour, berries or what have you. You can think of a scoop as an open-ended spoon, but it's actually easier to make than a spoon because the outside shape has fewer curves to carve. Start with a full-size, top-view pattern; the child can develop the sides during carving, but the type of handle—stick or loop—should be decided in advance.

Transfer the pattern to the planed wood and carve the scoop's bowl with a ¾-in. firmer gouge. For an open-ended bowl, start carving at the front end and work back toward the handle, as sixth-grader Philip West is doing in the photo at right.

Bandsaw the handle or split it out with a froe. If you bandsaw, make sure the scoop rests securely on the table—if necessary, support it with a wedge. For a stick handle, you'll need to bandsaw once more, using one of the pieces sawn off the side to support the handle.

If you're making a loop handle, draw the pattern for the loop on the handle blank, then bore and counterbore with a large auger bit to clear as much waste as possible from the inside of the loop. Clamp across the height of the handle to keep the wood from splitting.

Shape the handle and fair it into the bowl with a small drawknife. The inside of a loop handle is best worked with a sharp knife, though some kids might prefer to use a file and sandpaper.

A carved scoop can be as delicate as the bowl of a spoon, so be careful when clamping it to work on the handle. The safest way is to place the scoop on its side in the vise, with a block of wood inside its bowl so the vise jaws bear only against the bottom of the scoop and the top of the block.

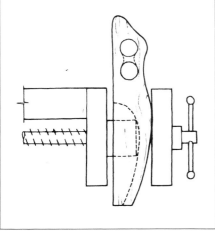

Hold the scoop vertically in a vise while shaping the handle. Place a wooden block in the scoop to avoid damaging the walls.

Eighth-grader David Barlow made this oak scoop, shown in the photo at right, with a large loop handle. He used spoon-making techniques to carve out its enclosed bowl. Alex Daniel added extra shape to the looped handle of his open-ended, butternut scoop, far right.

Using spoon-making and scoop-making techniques, kids can also make bowls and plates. These projects require a lot of carving and can be time-consuming and frustrating, so I won't let a child go ahead with one unless I see a whole lot of determination.

Green wood is good for deep bowls because it's easy to carve and easy to find in large dimensions. Sixth-grader Melinda De Chiazza chopped her bowl out of green butternut. She carved the outside with a shallow fishtail gouge and smoothed it with a spokeshave.

Fifth-grader Heather Gert carved her bowl out of butternut.

Plates are best made from seasoned wood; green wood might warp and the plate won't be flat. Use a soft, easy-to-carve wood like pine, basswood or butternut, and carve with wide, shallow gouges. Fifth-grader Cindy Surprenant, below, carved the inside of her pine plate, then began to work on the outside. A circle marks the base; working right up to this line, but not beyond it, takes a great deal of care. Notice how thin the edge is.

Stools

Chapter 12

here's something really special about making furniture directly from a log of green wood. It's an adventure for a child to help choose a fine log, and to split and shave the pieces into legs and stretchers. Splitting wood is easier than sawing it, and because the pieces follow the grain, split wood is stronger than sawn wood. Kids also learn about the structure and properties of wood when they work it this old-fashioned way. Stick furniture projects—stools, tables, benches and chairs built from green wood—are among the sturdiest and most enduring projects built in my shop.

One of the reasons these are good projects for kids is that the joinery is easy to do—round mortises and tenons wedged together. The mortises are simply holes bored with an auger bit. The tenons can be cut quickly and accurately using a hollow auger, a sort of inside-out auger bit. Though these are no longer made, they're pretty easy to find at flea markets. Kids can also whittle the tenons by hand or turn them on the lathe. I'll explain all three methods.

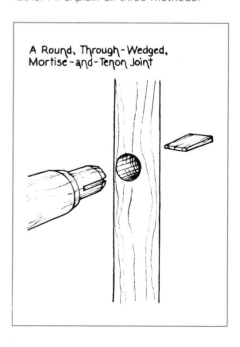

A Round, Through-Wedged, Mortise-and-Tenon Joint

Green woodworking is best suited to kids over ten years old, but I've helped even second-graders like Brant Nicks make perfectly creditable three-legged

milking stools. Handling and splitting heavy logs takes muscle, and adults will need to do this part of the job for small-sized children of any age. Every kid will need plenty of adult attention at crucial stages, but there are long stretches of independent work. A three-legged stool with stretchers will take at least twenty hours of shop time. Be sure kids understand the kind of commitment they are making—stools are perfect projects for self-motivated, persistent children.

Green wood is wet wood, still containing the sap of the living tree: over half the weight of a newly felled oak is water. When a tree is severed from its roots, the wood begins to dry out. Soon it begins to shrink and harden (the whole process is called seasoning), until its moisture content equals that of the surrounding air—about twenty percent by weight if outdoors, and as low as six percent indoors. The thinner the wood, the faster it will season; a whole log can take years to dry out. Green wood feels cool and damp and is heavier than dry wood. To tell them apart, clap two pieces of wood together: dry wood will ring, green wood klunks.

The advantage of using green wood is that it's much easier to work than dry

wood. In most parts of the country, it's cheaper to buy logs than it is to buy lumber, so working green wood can also save you money. Logs for green woodworking can often be purchased from firewood dealers, loggers or sawmills. Harvest your own if you have access to a woodlot. If you can't get green wood, you can use sawn, dry lumber to make your stool parts.

The legs and stretchers of a stick stool should be made of a sturdy hardwood. Oaks, hickories and white ash (ring-porous hardwoods) have traditionally been preferred for green woodworking because they split and shave easily. But many other hardwoods, including maple, birch, cherry, walnut and beech, can be used with good results. Whatever hardwood you use, it should be fairly straight and knot free. Curved pieces will split into curved legs, but this can add charm to a piece of furniture.

I'll describe how to make a three-legged stool with a round seat and two stretchers, the ones most often built in my shop. To begin, I ask the child for a drawing showing height, number of legs and stretchers, and seat diameter. The child makes decisions about leg position and splay as he or she goes along.

How to Keep Logs Green

Green woodworking requires green wood. Here are some ways to keep logs green until you get a chance to work them.

1. Stack wood in the shade. I store our logs on the north side of the building. Storage in a closed shed is okay as long as the building isn't exposed to direct sunlight. Don't store logs in a heated area unless you're looking to increase your firewood supply.

2. Coat the ends of the logs with melted paraffin, aluminum paint or a commercial end-grain sealer, because wood loses most of its moisture through end grain.

3. Leave logs whole as long as possible, because split wood dries faster. Lay halved logs flat side to the ground — the surfaces in contact with the earth may get moldy, but the wood inside won't be damaged. Smaller pieces may be kept in a tub of water, a stream or a closed, plastic garbage bag.

Getting Out the Wood

To split a log, you'll need two steel wedges and a light sledgehammer (6-lb.). For splitting the log into smaller pieces, you'll need a froe and a club. To trim these pieces to size, a broad hatchet is handy; you'll need a hatchet of some kind to separate the halves of uncooperative logs.

Seventh and eighth-graders may be strong enough to split out their own wood. Most kids can at least use the froe on smaller pieces.

Either the splitting wedge or the hammer may chip when they're struck together and send a steel shard through the air at tremendous speed. Always wear eye protection when doing this job, and keep observers back. (This hazard is reduced somewhat by grinding off the mushroomed lips that form on the top of the wedge. While at the grinder, sharpen the edge of the wedge to about 60°, so that it will enter the wood easily.)

To get out the wood, bowsaw the log 3 in. or 4 in. longer than stool height. Then split it into leg and stretcher blanks. I like to stand the log on end for the first split, as eighth-grader Tracy Wallace does here, though some kids lay it on the ground. The wedge will enter easiest if you start it at a slight angle on an edge of the log. Split open an existing crack to save sound wood. Holding the sledge near its head in one hand and the wedge in the other, tap the wedge to seat it in the wood. If the wedge won't stay put, check that it's sharp and its bevels aren't ground too steeply. If the wedge is okay, have the kid hit harder. If stubborn woods repeatedly spit out the wedge, cut a notch in the log's edge and start the wedge there.

Drive the wedge in until its head is almost flush with the wood, then put the log on its side and start a second wedge in the gap that opens down the side of the log, as shown below. Leapfrog two wedges until the log opens wide.

If the halves are tied together by straps of wood (called feathers), sever these with a hatchet, as shown at right. I use an old one in case I hit a wedge. Follow the same procedure to split each half in two. Check for knots and other defects and toss all useless pieces on the firewood pile. If you're not able to shave the posts the same day you split them, store them in a closed plastic bag.

The quartered pieces (called billets) are split into leg blanks with a froe. The froe is driven by hitting the blade with a heavy club; you can turn a club on the lathe or drawknife one from green wood.

Set the billet, end up, on the ground or on a low chopping block and place the froe blade where you want the split to begin; try to split the blanks close to finished size. When you place the froe on the billet, leave just enough blade beyond the wood to hit with the club. Lower the froe handle slightly so the blade touches only the edge of the log; strike directly over this point and drive the blade completely into the wood. Now strike the blade near its end, pushing down on the handle to keep the blade level. If the handle comes up, strike the blade between it and the wood to level it. When you're far enough into the wood, try pushing and pulling on the handle to lever the wood apart. You can also chop downward to sever feathers when you're almost through.

Large billets may yield more than one blank. Beware of the wood within an inch or two of the center of the log (called the pith) because it will check excessively as it dries. In some woods, the sapwood (the outer, living portion of the tree) will shrink faster than the heartwood (in oak, for example), so if a blank contains both sapwood and heartwood, it may crack badly. You may want to test-dry a piece containing both kinds of wood to see if you can use it. (Sapwood/heartwood combinations are okay in ash, birch and cherry.)

Most wood will split right down the middle if both pieces are equally stiff, but if one is more flexible, the split will wander toward it. This is called runout and it results in a tapered blank. There isn't much you can do about this when taking a thin piece off a thick one. When both pieces are equally flexible, however, you can control runout by pushing or pulling the froe handle in the direction opposite to the runout. Or try turning the wood over and splitting it from the other end. The resulting thick section in the middle of the blank can be removed with a broad hatchet or a drawknife.

After splitting, oversized billets may be trimmed with the broad hatchet before drawknifing. Chopping hatchets have cutting edges beveled on both sides; these are designed to chop across the grain of a log. The broad hatchet's cutting edge is flat on the side that swings parallel to the wood, allowing a smooth cut and easy control.

Broad hatchets are the only hand tools in my shop that can cause sudden and catastrophic injury. I use one to speed a child's work and only rarely do I allow a kid to try it. No child should be allowed to use a broad hatchet without constant adult supervision.

A chopping block is a must with this tool. I use an elm stump, 20 in. high, left behind by a crew that was cutting blighted trees. Hold the blank at the center of the block, not near an edge. This way if the hatchet misses, it will strike the block rather than your leg. Your hand should be near the top of the blank, with plenty of wood between it and the hatchet. Never lift the hatchet higher than a few inches below that hand. If the top of the blank needs to be trimmed, turn the piece end for end.

Hold the hatchet where it feels most comfortable; holding it near the head will give easier lift and better control. Swing the hatchet easily, letting the weight of the tool do most of the work, and lean the wood back a little so the edge of the hatchet takes a skew cut. To take off a lot of wood, make a series of relief chops into the blank at an angle before swinging parallel to the wood.

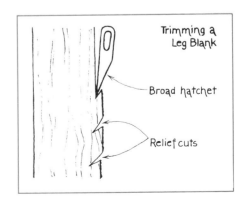

Shaving the Legs

The rough blanks are then shaved to shape with a drawknife. The drawknife is an effective tool; though it can waste a lot of wood quickly, it can also work delicately in small areas. It's one of the few woodworking tools in Western culture that is pulled toward the body. Some people shy away from this tool because it looks dangerous—a long, razor-sharp edge headed directly for the gut. But your arms loose their strength as they approach the torso and can't pull the tool close enough to do any harm.

Drawknives come in many sizes and shapes (p. 188). The ones we use have blades about 10 in. long and handles in the same plane as the blade—not offset below the edge or tipped slightly down.

A shaving horse (p. 196), also called a shaving bench, is the traditional complement to the drawknife. The work is held securely and can be released instantly. In the photo, seventh-graders Geoff Arend (left) and Fred Smith (right) are comfortably seated, with the wood held at just the right angle. By pushing on the foot of the central post, the child wedges the leg or stretcher blank between the horse's heavy wooden head and the table. The height of the head above the table is adjustable; use the lowest position the blank will allow.

Using a Drawknife Safely

Accidents do happen with drawknives, but you can prevent them by establishing a few simple rules.

1. Your hands are safe while on the grips of the drawknife. During rests or while pausing to adjust the wood, if one hand is off the tool, that hand is in danger. Most drawknife injuries happen to the back of the hand: make sure that when only one hand is on the tool, the other is moved far away from it.

2. Put the tool down in a safe place. Drawknives left in a pile of tools are accidents waiting to happen, so put the tool down where its exposed edge can be easily seen and avoided. Store the drawknives safely when not in use. A good drawknife rack is shown on p. 189.

3. Very small drawknives may be hazardous to thumbs. If your thumb can reach the blade while the hand is on the grip, round off the blade corners.

4. Make sure that the path of the drawknife is clear, so that its edges won't hit anything. And make sure no part of the body is in the drawknife's path. While seated at work, watch out for your knees.

If you'd rather not make a shaving horse or if the child would prefer to stand, the leg blank can be held in a bench vise for drawknifing, as demonstrated by seventh-grader Michael Schruben. Make sure the end of the blank points at the child's stomach.

There are several schools of thought about the best way to use a drawknife. Here's my tried-and-true method.

To take off heavy shavings, work with the bevel of the drawknife down against the wood. This lets you control the depth of cut by simply raising or lowering the handles.

For finer cuts, use the tool with its bevel up. If there's a counterbevel (a small bevel ground on the back of the cutting edge), you can still control shaving thickness without digging in. Some people prefer using the bevel up for long, straight power strokes because the handles are level with the pull, and the flat back of the blade guides the tool along. Use it if it works for you.

Always place the drawknife askew to the wood and take a slicing cut. I tell kids: "Start the cut at one end of the blade and slice to the other end. Start at the end of the blade nearest your body so you pull toward yourself as you slice. Keep one hand closer to your body than the other." The child won't have to pull as hard using a slicing cut and therefore will have more control over the tool; a slice also distributes wear over the entire blade. A pronounced slicing cut made with a very sharp edge can be used to clean up rough surfaces.

Children who have difficulty at first should take short strokes, bevel down, and turn the handles up at the end of each stroke so the blade cuts out of the wood and doesn't stick.

Little kids who can't handle a drawknife can spokeshave the legs, holding the blank in a shaving horse or a vise. I help youngsters along by giving them pieces that I've chopped close to finished size with a broad hatchet. Using a spokeshave is easy, because its blade can't dig in and get stuck. Any straight-edged, flat-bottomed spokeshave will work. For shaving legs, my preference is a cooper's spokeshave; this tool is big, easy to grasp and heavy enough to stick to the wood.

In our shop, we use two methods of shaping legs and stretchers. The first is easiest to explain to kids.

Onto each end of the blank, draw a circle having the same diameter as that estimated for the finished leg, and shave the wood to that shape. Turn the piece regularly to keep it round (about a third the circumference each time), and sight along its length to keep it straight. Turn the piece end for end several times during the work.

The second method is quite rigorous, just right for kids with lots of discipline. Start by drawknifing the stick to a square section, then shave off the corners so the piece is octagonal and all facets exactly the same width. (Less patient kids can work from square to octagonal without fussing over keeping the facets even.) Then shave the corners again until the piece is round. With practice, this method is faster and more accurate than working directly to round. And it's especially good for tapered legs: you can keep the legs straight by making sure the facets around any given section are of equal width.

The shape of the legs is a matter of taste. Most kids prefer simple, cylindrical legs, for they're easiest to imagine and to make. Some children prefer the legs to be quite thick for extra strength (usually this is unnecessary), while others shave them so thin the stool flexes when it's sat upon. Legs can taper toward the top or bottom, or be double-

tapered so they're thickest at the stretcher joint. I like to leave the legs octagonal. Smooth, even facets give a leg extra vitality, but sloppy facets look awful and should be shaved off.

Stretchers should complement the rest of the piece. Where legs are tapered or double-tapered, consider using double-tapered stretchers; for octagonal legs, make octagonal stretchers, too.

Legs that split out curved will also shave curved: it's very difficult to shave them straight. Go with the natural shape and let it add grace to the stool.

The child should rough-out one leg and use it as a pattern for the rest of the legs. Then all the legs are worked at the same time, so the child can refine them until they are exactly alike. When you're ready to shape the stretchers, do them all in a batch. You won't know the exact length of the stretchers until later; cut the blanks to about two-thirds the length of the legs before shaving them.

After drawknifing the legs and stretchers, do the final shaping and smoothing with a spokeshave. This tool allows better control and, in the hands of a beginner, will leave a smoother surface than a drawknife. On round legs, a half-round spokeshave works well. Get the shape right, but there's no need to be too fussy about the surface of the legs at this point—smooth, green wood becomes slightly rough as it dries, and the stool will be scraped and sanded before finishing, anyway.

Shaving green wood is an incredibly satisfying experience. The shavings come off in long strips, leaving an eye-pleasing, wet surface. After half an hour, the child is surrounded by a huge pile of shavings—a delightful mess in testimony to his or her good effort.

The Seat

After the legs and stretchers have been shaved to size, set them aside to dry and make the seat. Seats should be made of dry wood and can be almost any size and shape. I'll describe how we make a round one, 9 in. to 12 in. in diameter. We like to use 1-in.-thick cherry or maple to contrast with the oak legs; if you use pine or another weak wood, it should be at least 1¼ in. thick.

We usually have to glue up boards for the seat (p. 192). When the glue is dry, plane the board on both sides, then scribe the circle on the side that will be the bottom. Poke a good center mark; you'll need it later to position the legs.

I bandsaw out the seat, and the child smooths and shapes its edge with a spokeshave. The child must shave in the right direction, or else the tool will tear the edge. I illustrate the problem to kids using a softcover book. I fan out the pages and ask: "What happens when you push your fingernail the wrong way over this surface?"

"The pages separate."

"Right. If you spokeshave the wrong way, you get a rough surface, because the blade separates the wood fibers."

I have the child divide the seat into quadrants by drawing one diameter parallel to the grain and another at right angles to the first. Then we decide which way to shave, drawing an arrow in each quadrant as a reminder.

Where the wood fibers are exactly perpendicular or parallel to the direction of cutting, cut either way, taking short, fine shavings. Use a straight spokeshave with a flat bottom, as seventh-grader Laura Moorman does here. Always chamfer the arris (the intersection of the edge and the face) first, so it won't chip while you work the edge. Skew the spokeshave toward the center of the edge. The child can shape the edge profile, too. Most kids simply chamfer

the edge, but some get pretty fancy.

When the edge of the seat is smooth, turn the seat over and position the legs. For strength, they should be at least an inch in from the seat edge. Hold a leg at different distances from the center of the seat to find an eye-pleasing position, mark it, then set the dividers from the center of the seat to the mark and scribe a circle. Two legs placed along a single grain line will weaken the board, so each leg should be on its own grain line.

To position the first leg, draw a radius on the scribed circle, parallel to the grain of the seat. The intersection of the radius and the circumference locates the leg. Then set the dividers to the radius and walk two steps along the circumference from the first leg to locate the second. Two more steps locates the third and two more should bring you back to the first. (I learned this method from Geoff Arend, one of my students. Explained geometrically, one facet of an inscribed hexagon is equal to the radius of the circle.)

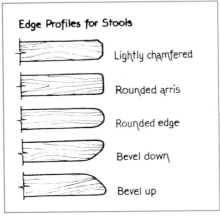

Divide the seat into quadrants and spokeshave in the direction of the arrows.

Edge Profiles for Stools

Lightly chamfered

Rounded arris

Rounded edge

Bevel down

Bevel up

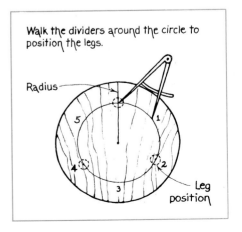

Walk the dividers around the circle to position the legs.

Radius

Leg position

Boring the Holes

The legs on our stools are not perpendicular to the seat and the floor, so the mortises in the seat must be bored at an angle. Splaying the legs out at an angle increases the stool's footprint on the floor, that is, it gives the stool a broader base and makes it more stable. How can you determine the right splay angle? Eyeball and instinct are the best guides.

Start by drawing lines (called splay lines) from the center of the seat to the leg positions around the edge. Imagine a plane intersecting the seat at a right angle along one of these lines: the leg must lie within this plane. Have the child stand back as you put a leg in place and move it through various angles to the seat, keeping it within the imaginary plane. When the child thinks the leg looks right, set a sliding bevel gauge to the angle, as sixth-grader Phil Cate does at right. The gauge acts as a guide while the child is mortising the seat.

The mortises should be at least ¼ in. smaller than the diameter of the legs; this allows for a ⅛-in. shoulder on each tenon to keep the leg from forcing its way through the seat. Put the seat, bottom-face up, on a piece of scrap wood and clamp it to the bench. Clamps on both sides of the hole will ensure good contact between seat and scrap, and keep the bit from chipping out the seat. We use pine scrap under hardwood seats because the contrasting colors of the shavings signal when the hole has been completely bored.

Most kids need help boring angled holes. The child should stand directly in front of the bevel gauge so that its edge appears vertical. The helper should stand to the side where the gauge's angle setting is visible. The child keeps the brace vertical from his or her point of view, while the helper gives instructions to raise or lower the brace to follow the angle. With young children, an adult can help steer by placing a hand on the head of the brace. Some kids can bore the hole without help, but they must keep track of both views by peeking at the auger bit from the side and making necessary adjustments after every two or three turns of the brace. Try to keep the brace and bit from wobbling, because the spiral part of the bit can catch the edge of the hole and lift out a large chip. (If this happens, save the chip and glue it back.) Be fussy about boring: crooked holes make a crooked stool.

Tenoning

After all the seat mortises are bored, you're ready to tenon the legs. Make sure they're completely dry: tenons cut in green wood will shrink and loosen in their mortises. In my shop, we use a hollow auger to make the tenons, but there are two alternative methods.

Whittling tenons isn't difficult, but requires a template, which is just a tenon-sized hole in a piece of scrap. Whittle the very end of the leg with a carving knife until it just begins to fit the hole. Twist the leg in the hole and the template will leave a mark showing where to remove more wood. Repeat this, whittling and checking, until the tenon is long enough to protrude through the hole in the seat.

Kids adept at turning can cut tenons quickly and easily on a lathe. Mark the length of the tenon and chuck the leg in the lathe. Set calipers slightly larger than the diameter of the finished tenon. With a parting tool, make a plunge cut at the shoulder and two or three other places along the tenon so that the calipers just slip over the tenon at these points. Then remove the wood between these cuts. Trim this oversized tenon to exact size with a skew. Check the size with a template. (Make one by boring a mortise-sized hole in a piece of scrap wood; cut through it so that just slightly more than half of the hole remains.) Using a small gouge or skew, shape the shoulder. Be careful: it's easy to turn the tenons too small.

The hollow auger is a handy tool; as the name implies, it's an inside-out auger bit that cuts a tenon rather than a hole. Used by chair makers and wheelwrights, hollow augers were probably first manufactured in the early nineteenth century, though homemade varieties go back further. I doubt if any were made after 1920, but they must have been popular in their heyday because they're common at flea markets and antique-tool stores. (For how to select, repair and set up a hollow auger, see p. 155.)

To make tenons with a hollow auger, first cut the end of each leg to a cone shape. The apex of the cone should be centered on the leg and just small enough to fit into the tool's throat. The throat will settle on the part of the cone that matches the hollow-auger's setting and will cut the tenon to that size. Sixth-grader Jessica Menezes, right, used a dowel pointer in a brace to make the cone, but she could have whittled it.

Check the hollow-auger setting by tenoning a piece of scrap and trying the tenon in the seat. When the fit is right (snug but not too tight), tenon the legs. Fix a leg vertically in the vise; it's difficult to cut the tenon true to the axis of the leg if the leg isn't straight up and down. I tell kids to step back about four feet to check this.

As when boring the mortises, the hollow auger must be held true in two planes. A helper can guide the child, verbally or with a hand on the brace, while viewing from another angle.

It takes a lot of force to turn a hollow auger, especially when cutting large tenons, so use a brace with the widest sweep you can find—14 in., if possible. Keep all the surfaces of the auger that come in contact with the wood well oiled to ease the work. I keep a squirt can of mineral oil on the bench and lubricate the throat profusely two or three times during the cutting of each tenon. Be sure to cut the tenon long enough to fit through the mortise, so that the tapered end clears the seat and can be trimmed off after assembly. Many hollow augers have adjustable depth stops, but I prefer to cut to a mark drawn on the leg.

Make the tenons long enough to be trimmed off after assembly.

Seat

Leg

The Stretchers

Now assemble the legs and seat to see how things look. If the legs are perfectly straight, their tenons cut exactly on axis, and the seat accurately mortised, you can put any leg in any hole and the stool will look just fine. But most hand-tenoned legs aren't perfect, so the child will need to judge in what positions the legs look best. If you've used curved legs, this is the time to position the shapes to work harmoniously.

Most children need help making the subtle judgments required in setting up a stool, but if adults go through this procedure with them, they can tune in to the fine points.

Invert the stool on a bench (use thick pieces of scrap wood to keep the protruding tenons clear of the benchtop). Have the child walk around the stool—does any leg seem to splay too far or too little? Look between every pair of legs; on a perfect stool, the middle leg will look centered.

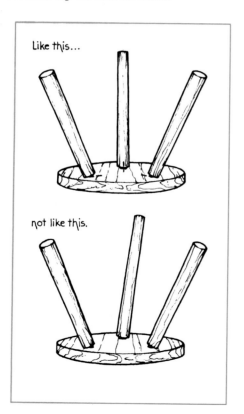

Like this...

not like this.

If things don't look right, rotate the legs in their holes or switch them from hole to hole. Sometimes errors cancel each other out; a crooked hole and a skewed tenon can combine to give an accurately splayed leg.

If the legs are not straight, find where they look best. In the stool at right, all three legs were split from the same log and have similar curves. By turning each leg 180° in its hole, the whole shape of the stool changed. You may find that your stool won't look perfect no matter what you do, but three-legged stools are amazingly forgiving—even crooked ones have great appeal.

When you've decided on the final positions, mark each leg and its mating hole, and witness-mark the leg and the seat. Now locate the stretchers on the legs. We most often use a *T*-pattern for stretchers, which joins all three legs using only two stretchers. It's a strong configuration, too: every part of the stool is joined to at least two others. The further the stretchers are from the seat, the more strength they add to the stool; if they are close to the floor, they can be used as footrests. I suggest to kids that stretchers be no higher than halfway up the leg. Both stretchers should join the legs at the same distance from the seat.

Clamp the upside-down stool to a corner of the bench with a piece of scrap wood between, and mark the position of the stretchers on the inside surface of each leg. The first stretcher fits between two legs; the second stretcher between the first stretcher and a leg. The first stretcher should run at a right angle to the grain of the seat, as shown in the drawing, in order to keep the legs from spreading apart when under weight and splitting the seat. Extend the stretcher marks around the legs; these marks should be approximately parallel to the floor (rather than perpendicular to the axis of the legs). Make sure that both of the legs are in their correct positions, and their witness marks are lined up with the marks on the seat.

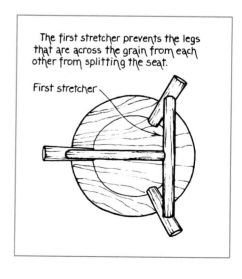

The first stretcher prevents the legs that are across the grain from each other from splitting the seat.

First stretcher

Mortises for stretchers shouldn't be larger than one-half the diameter of the legs or they'll weaken the legs. We usually make them ⅝ in. or ½ in. in diameter. To bore them, you'll need an extra-long drill bit (called an electrician's bit) or a common auger bit in a bit extension. The extra length allows the child to bore out one leg while lining up the drill-bit shaft with the mark on the adjoining leg. The long drill bit almost duplicates the position of the stretcher, so the mortise can be bored at the correct angle.

Boring for stretchers is a two-person job, and it's best if one of them has done it before. The stool maker (in this case, Geoff Arend) handles the brace, lining up the shaft of the long bit with the mark on the near leg. The helper (Henry Stout) places the point of the bit on the mark on the other leg, aiming for the leg center. (Carelessness in positioning the bit can result in a hole having very little leg on one side of it, which will severely weaken the stool.) Pressure is needed to start the bit, so the helper must support the leg to resist this initial pressure.

Once the bit is started, little support is needed and the helper should watch for the point of the bit to appear on the far side of the leg. (I do this by putting my thumb on the wood and waiting for the point of the bit to tickle—perfectly safe.) When the point appears, the stool maker and helper exchange places to counterbore the hole. (Boring all the way through from one side will split the wood.) Counterboring requires extra pressure and support.

Some kids don't have the muscle to push hard enough at the beginning and end of the cut. When I'm the helper, I hold the leg with one hand while I reach over to press on the head of the brace. If this is awkward, ask another kid to help with the brace.

Now tenon the first stretcher: it must be in place before you can mortise and tenon the second. Hold the stretcher beside the mortises with one end protruding about ½ in. beyond a leg. Mark where the stretcher crosses the inside faces of the legs and where the stretcher protrudes ½ in. beyond the other leg. Saw off any extra length. Tenon the stretcher in the same way that you tenoned the legs.

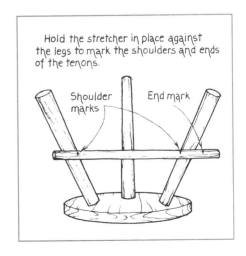

Hold the stretcher in place against the legs to mark the shoulders and ends of the tenons.

Shoulder marks   End mark

Now put the first stretcher in place; try to fit both of its tenons at the same time, and lightly tap the joints home with a wooden mallet. There's usually enough flex in the legs to spring them apart far enough; if you can't, pull the legs almost free of the seat to start the stretcher tenons, then drive all the tenons home at once. If a tenon is too large, use a cabinet scraper to reduce its diameter, working from the shoulder toward the end. Rotate the piece after each scrape.

The second stretcher fits between the remaining leg and the first stretcher. The mortise for the second stretcher is centered between the shoulders of the first. Mark the point and bore the mortise, lining up the long drill-bit shaft with the mortise mark on the remaining leg. Now mortise the leg, passing the bit over the mortise just cut in the stretcher, as Tracy Wallace and Jessica Menezes are doing below. The bit will angle down slightly, so the helper should pull back on the leg while the hole is bored.

Measure, tenon and install the second stretcher. The legs and stretchers are pretty flexible and they can be pushed together to fit. In fact, by using slightly longer or shorter stretchers than are needed, you can add a little splay or pull in a leg that sticks out a bit too far.

Assembly

Before final assembly, the child must take the stool apart to chamfer the shoulders of the tenons and saw a kerf in each tenon for a wedge. First, make sure all the parts are marked to go back together the same way. Then draw a line for the wedge across the end of each tenon, at a right angle to the grain of the mortised piece. If the child does this incorrectly, the mortised piece will likely split when the wedge is driven home.

Now take the stool apart. If the pieces stick together, gently tap them apart with a wooden mallet. Use a backsaw or fine dovetail saw to kerf each tenon to within ⅛ in. of the shoulder.

We chamfer the shoulders of the tenons with a spokeshave or knife to give the stool a finished look and to allow the pieces to fit closely together. The photo at right shows the difference between them: the spokeshaved tenon, left, requires less skill but results in a more mechanical-looking chamfer.

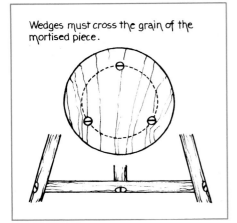

Wedges must cross the grain of the mortised piece.

Whittling

Grasp the knife in the right hand and the wood in the left. Hold the knife's edge across the arris of the shoulder, inclined about 45° to the axis of the leg. Take a slicing cut, pulling the blade toward you (by turning your wrist) while rotating the wood against it, using your right thumb as a pivot. Take short, thin cuts, and work around the shoulder until the chamfer looks pleasant.

Children have difficulty whittling; it takes good coordination and they usually aim the blade at the shoulder instead of toward the end of the tenon, so the knife gets stuck and it chips instead of shaves. Kids also tend to take too thick a shaving, which makes the knife harder to pull and leaves a rough surface. The best way to teach whittling is to demonstrate with a second knife so the child can watch and work at the same time.

After chamfering, make the wedges for the tenons. The wedge should be as wide and as long as the tenon; halfway up the length, it should be about half again as thick as the saw kerf. (A loose tenon may need a thicker wedge.) Use a straight-grained hardwood to make wedges; I use dark wood, like walnut, to contrast with stools of light woods.

Adults can make wedges easily on a bandsaw. First, cut a small block of wood equal in thickness to the width of the tenons. Then cut a series of wedges, as shown below. You can also split out wedges and shape them with a drawknife and a neat little jig.

Bandsaw wedges from a block of straight-grained wood, equal in thickness to the diameter of the tenons.

Length of the tenon

Width of the tenon

Don't use wedges with short grain, like this one.

Another Way to Make Wedges

Split pieces off the block with a wide chisel.

Width of the tenon

Length of the tenon

Thickest end of the wedge

Then drawknife the wedge to shape, holding it in a jig made from scrap wood.

Before gluing up the stool, it's a good idea to have a final dress rehearsal so the child is sure how it goes together. Then spread glue in every hole; it may seem easier to put glue on the tenons, but white glue swells wood quickly, and glue-covered tenons may become too large for the mortises or get stuck halfway in. Assemble the stool, driving every tenon home up to its shoulder.

I prefer to wedge the seat tenons first. Put a small dab of glue on one face of a wedge near the tapered end, and insert it in the kerf. Holding the leg perpendicular to the floor, drive in the wedge gently with a wooden mallet (a metal hammer could crush the wedge). When the wedge is firmly in place, pound a little harder until it's home: the mallet blows will sound solid and the wedge will resist travel into the kerf.

Wedge the stretchers with the stool on its side, resting the far end of the stretcher on a wood block while you work on the near end. Clean up excess glue with a wet paper towel. The photo shows the wedge from the inside.

Driving wedges requires a sensitive touch. I usually demonstrate the first one or two. Most kids need supervision, but I like to let them try while I watch carefully for broken or crooked wedges. Still, there are often problems. You can usually correct a crooked wedge by tapping it sideways with the mallet. If a wedge breaks, add glue to the broken piece, place it in the kerf and drive it the rest of the way in. If you can't get a wedge started, chisel a chamfer in the kerf and drive in a thick-ended wedge. If the tenon is still loose after one wedge is in, chamfer the kerf beside the first wedge and drive in a second.

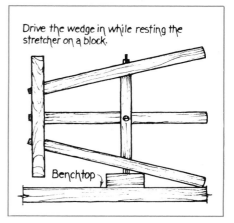

Drive the wedge in while resting the stretcher on a block.

Benchtop

Now come the details of finishing up the stool. Kids will be glad they invested the time and care in these details when they see the results. Trim the protruding ends of the tenons first. Kids in a hurry can do this right after gluing, but the glue dries quickly, so we usually wait to avoid a gummed-up saw. Use a fine-toothed crosscut saw (we use a 10 point or 12 point) to trim tenons. (Don't use a backsaw; its thick back makes it impossible to cut flush to the seat or legs.) To trim the stretcher tenons, grab each leg in the vise and push the upper portion of the sawblade against the leg so the saw won't cut into it.

It's tricky to saw the leg tenons flush without marring the seat. Ken Varnum, below, demonstrates how we do it. With the seat in the vise, saw a notch in the tenon about 1/32 in. from the seat surface. Holding the saw by the handle and the end of the blade, bend it so the teeth touch the tenon and the back of the blade touches the seat (p. 196).

Use a crosscut saw to trim the tenon stubs.

Push here to keep the blade against the seat top.

Seat top

Never use a backsaw. The back will aim the blade into the seat.

Seat top

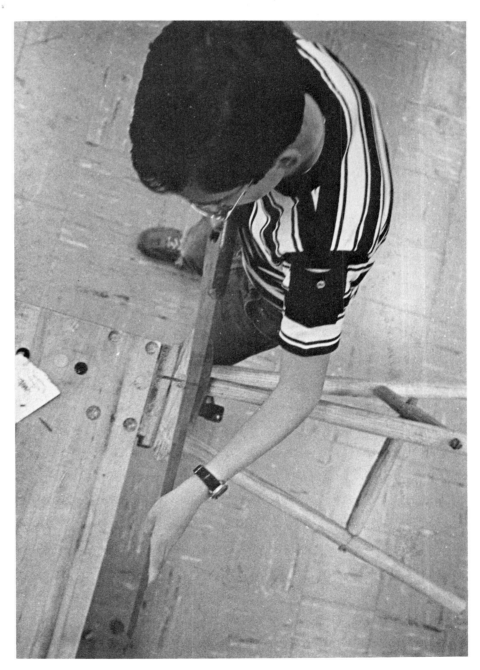

Now clean up the top of the seat with a sharp, finely set plane. Grab one leg in the vise while another bears against the edge of the workbench, as demonstrated in the photo below by seventh-grader Rusty Brigham. Work over the entire surface to keep its thickness uniform; when the seat is smooth, check to see if the edge chamfer needs to be touched up.

The ends of the stretcher tenons should be blended into the legs so you can't feel them with your fingers. Trim them with a finely set, flat-bottomed spokeshave. If the kid has sawed into the leg, he or she may need to do a lot of spokeshaving, working up, down and around the leg for some distance to hide the error. Check over every bit of the legs and stretchers, and shave off any rough spots or bumps. Then go over all the leg and stretcher surfaces with a cabinet scraper. I'm fussy about this step: the chips and tears left by the spokeshave may seem inconspicuous at this point, but they really show up when the stool is oiled.

One of the advantages of a three-legged stool is that it will never rock on the floor. If the seat is not level with the floor, however, you may want to trim the ends of the legs to level it up. If the legs seem evenly splayed, simply measure down the inside of each leg from the seat bottom and saw them all to the length of the shortest one.

Stools whose legs don't all splay at the same angle are harder to level. Turn the stool upside down on a table and mark the height of each leg on a long stick held at right angles to the tabletop. Transfer the mark of the shortest leg onto the other two and cut them off to that length. (This technique works with any splay-legged furniture.)

Sawing the end of a leg at a right angle to the leg's axis gives a pleasant shadow where the leg meets the floor. If you prefer the ends of the legs to be flush to the floor, first saw them at right angles to the axis. Then, place the stool on a benchtop and set dividers just slightly wider than the furthest distance between the end of the leg and the benchtop. Rest one point of the dividers on the benchtop and scribe a line around all three legs, then saw on the lines.

After the seat has been leveled and the ends of the legs trimmed, whittle or spokeshave a narrow chamfer on the ends of each leg. The chamfers keep the legs from chipping and reduce the chances of marring a floor. Though a dowel pointer produces a rather mechanical-looking chamfer, young children may be more comfortable

chamfering with it. Make sure the child doesn't go too far and make the end of the leg pointed.

Before sanding and oiling the stool, the child can carve his or her name and the date in the bottom of the seat, a historical record and, like a signature on a painting, a sign of accomplishment.

Sand the stool with 100-grit paper on a sanding block, then go over it again with 220 grit. If the legs are octagonal, be careful not to soften the edges of the facets as you sand. Now the stool is ready to be finished. Coat it with oil and sand it while still wet with 400-grit, wet/dry paper. For thirty to forty minutes, apply more oil to wherever the wood has absorbed it. Then wipe it dry; dispose of oily rags or paper towels properly by soaking them in water and putting them outdoors in a closed trashcan, or by burning them. After a couple of hours, oil and sand again. Repeat the process the next day.

In my shop is a stool I slapped together from abandoned parts. It's full of mistakes: the stretchers are too high, the mortises are at different levels, the grain of the seat isn't oriented properly with the stretchers. Wedges go every which way, and thick wedges fill undersized tenons in unevenly splayed legs. And yet, this stool has stood up to over six years of everyday abuse and it's still tight. Its top has developed a warm polish from constant use, and in spite of many bruises, the stool is attractive and useful. Give stool making a try; do your best and you won't be disappointed.

For legs flush to the floor, first saw each at a right angle to its axis.

90°

Set the dividers slightly wider than the distance between the high edge and the benchtop.

Scribe around all three legs and then saw along the scribed mark.

The little stool made by seventh-grader Ben Quick is charming to look at and handy to have around the house. Three-legged milking stools are easy to make—just leave out the stretchers. They'll stay sturdy longer if the seats are made of thick stock—at least 2 in. if you're using a softwood, 1½ in. if you're using a hardwood.

Eighth-grader Mary Snell made her stool with curved legs and curved stretchers. Putting the stretchers at different levels makes them seem to be walking up the stool.

Three stretchers, like the ones in Geoff Arend's stool, stiffen a stool better than two, and all the stretchers can be used as footrests. To avoid having tenons intersect in a leg, the stretchers must be staggered at least two tenon diameters away from each other. The child should bore holes for the stretchers and install them one by one with previous ones in place. Don't rely on witness marks, for a few minor errors will quickly turn into a major one, and the last stretcher will probably miss its leg by several inches.

Children can design their stools with additional stretchers for strength or convenience, if they wish. Eighth-grader Robert Plante's six-stretcher stool, with pleasantly curved legs, is used as a stepladder in his kitchen. The extra-wide splay keeps the stool from tipping over. Robert made his stool before we started using through tenons; he glued each of his into a blind hole. Extra stretchers reduce the likelihood that these less-reliable joints will fail because there's less stress on each joint.

Stool-making techniques come in handy for projects other than stools. This sled, made by seventh-grader Jeniffer Kleck, is a good example. The crosspieces are split and shaved red oak, tenoned on each end and wedged through the side of the sled.

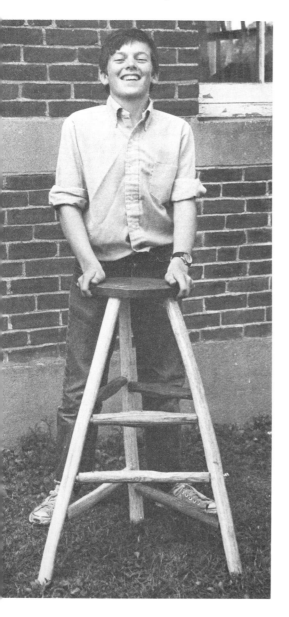

Four-Legged Furniture

Four-legged stools are less likely to tip over than three-leggers, but they're also less likely to stand steadily on uneven floors. The holes through the top of a four-legger shouldn't share the same line of grain, or else the seat will be weakened. The drawing below shows how to locate the legs. Scribe the circle on which the center of the legs will fall and imagine a diameter that follows the grain of the seat. Rotate that diameter about 22½° and mark it across the circle. Then draw another diameter at right angles to this line. The legs go where the diameters cross the circumference.

Pieces of four-legged furniture often have their stretchers laid out in a box pattern or an *H*-pattern. To make an *H*-pattern, first install stretchers between opposite pairs of legs, then add one or more stretchers to connect them. All the stretchers should be the same distance from the seat.

The box pattern requires at least four stretchers. Adjacent stretchers are installed at different heights, with opposites usually (but not necessarily) at the same height. Opposite pairs, if they are at the same height, should be equal in length from shoulder to shoulder so as to keep the legs evenly spaced. Install one pair of opposite stretchers, then the other, rather than working around the stool. While boring each mortise for the second pair of stretchers, try to keep the long, drill-bit shaft at right angles to the already-installed stretcher. This might require a slight twisting of the legs being bored. In the box pattern, any number of extra stretchers can be added to give strength or to use as footrests.

It's not hard to make benches and tables with green-woodworking techniques. They're like elongated stools, but the rectangular top requires that leg placement and splay be considered differently. Position the legs by marking a spot that looks right for one of them. Use a square to project the mark out to both edges of the top; reproduce these lines at the other corners for the other three leg positions.

If you are working with an odd-shaped slab, draw a centerline down it, decide how far from the ends the legs should be, and mark this distance on the centerline. Draw lines through these marks at right angles to the centerline. Position the legs on these lines, the legs in each pair the same distance from the centerline. (On three-legged benches, one leg should be on the centerline.)

Use dividers set wide to establish the splay lines. (You may need extra-large dividers; see p. 37.) Swing an arc toward the center of the bench from each mark. From the intersection of the arcs, draw a splay line to each leg mark. Lean the legs out along these lines and see if they look right. If not, reset the dividers and try again. Then, strike arcs and draw splay lines at the other end.

Determine the splay angle as previously described for a three-legged stool: place the bevel gauge on the splay line and hold a leg against it, trying a number of different angles until you find the one that you like.

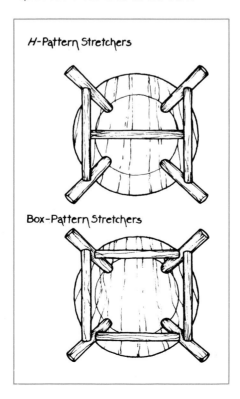

H-Pattern Stretchers

Box-Pattern Stretchers

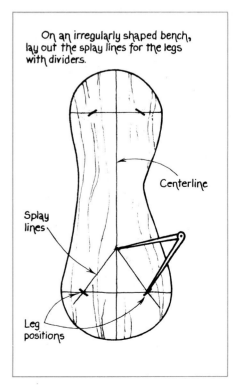

On an irregularly shaped bench, lay out the splay lines for the legs with dividers.

Centerline

Splay lines

Leg positions

Eighth-grader Heidi Sokol's 2-in. cherry benchtop is joined to neatly tapered, oak legs, which have tenons a full 1¼ in. in diameter. At about 16 in. tall, it's plenty solid without stretchers.

Eighth-grader Kathy Quinn made her bench of an irregularly shaped, 2-in. pine slab, the edges of which she carefully smoothed with drawknife and spokeshave. Rather than tying the ends together with a long stretcher, she ran stretchers diagonally up into the slab. To allow the stretcher tenon's shoulder to butt up against the hole, Kathy chiseled a housing in the underside of the slab. Wedging the tenon through might have lifted a chip from the top, so Kathy pinned the tenon in place with a dowel from below.

Chris Schell's bench, made in seventh grade, is built of lighter parts; the top is just over 1 in. thick and the legs have tenons 1 in. long.

Greg Norman's table is 24 in. high and has a ¾-in. pine top. Because his table is so high, he needed the stretchers for extra stability.

Windsor Chairs

When kids ask to make Windsor chairs of green wood, I tell them that the hardest part of making a chair is getting the proportions right, and that they should measure a favorite chair for every dimension they can think of. This includes the height of the seat (front and back), the length and width of the seat, the height of the back, the angle at which the back meets the seat, the height of the arms from the seat, and the distance between the arms. If the child isn't discouraged by all that fussy measurement, I figure he or she can find the patience to make a chair. This long-term, complex project requires a good deal of adult supervision, and any adult who embarks on chair making with a child should understand the concepts behind chair design.

The geometry of the Windsor-chair undercarriage is a little more complicated than that of a simple, four-legged stool or bench. The front legs are usually set a little further apart than the rear ones and usually spread wider. The seat is slightly lower at the back because the rear legs are shorter, have more splay angle, or both.

To lay out a chair, mark out the leg centers on the bottom of the seat, draw in what seem to be appropriate splay lines, and choose splay angles by eye, as when making a stool. Have the child stand back while the helper holds legs in the two front positions, then a front and a back position and, finally, the two back positions. If the chair looks good, the child is ready to mortise.

Eighth-grader Tom Kendall's chair has oak legs, *H*-stretchers and a round, butternut seat. The fancy, crested back is supported on four oak spindles, which are located on a circle, concentric with the shape of the seat.

When seventh-grader Fred Smith said he wanted to build a Windsor bench as his first project, I had doubts, but decided to let him try it. After a full school year of careful work, he had his bench. The back spindles are parallel to each other, but the spokes under the arm lean away from the seat. A hole in the arm fits loosely around the outer rear spindle. The joint could be tightened by running a small wooden pin through it.

This doll chair, which measures about 20 in. high, was made by eighth-grader Amy Gagnon. The arms are fitted around the outer spindles and held in place by a wedged dowel from behind.

The spindles on Leslie Watts's chair, below, which she made in eighth grade, are in one plane across the back. Her modified *H*-stretcher has two cross rungs and leg-to-leg stretchers at the front and back, convenient for use as a footrest and for a storage shelf.

Daphne Bien made this rocking chair over a period of about a year during seventh and eighth grades. It has arms, a dished seat and a seven-spindle back. The stretcher system is a modified box pattern: the rockers substitute for side stretchers. The leg ends are tenoned and wedged through the rockers. The end of the arm is fitted to the back spindle and secured with a wood screw. Rocking-chair geometry is subtle, and designing a good chair is an art. Your best bet is to copy the layout of a favorite chair, being careful to accurately reproduce the curve of the rockers, the length of the legs, their position on the seat and rockers, and the angle of the back to the seat.

Games

Chapter 13

I t's a satisfying experience to watch a youngster finish building a game and immediately begin to play. Seeing a couple of kids whacking knock-hockey pucks or hearing the musical bounces of a marble down an elegantly designed marble roll makes me feel successful with the students I teach, and you'll get similar rewards with your own child. Most of these games use skills that have already been covered in previous chapters or in the Tools and Techniques section (pp. 146-201), but refinements and special techniques are described below.

Knock Hockey

This classic game is one of the favorites in my shop. It requires a skill similar to pool to calculate rebounds off the wall or to carom shots from *x* to *y* to *z,* but even first-time players find it exciting and easy to play. Knock hockey introduces various woodworking techniques, particularly mitering, that kids will find useful in later projects. It's a good beginner's project, too, because the tasks are simple and straightforward.

The game can be any size your child likes. My standard size is 2 ft. by 4 ft. — big enough for an energetic game — and the plywood board is economically and easily cut from a 4x8 sheet. (Kids can even put legs on this project and make it a table, as described on p. 122.) Kids sometimes prefer mini-games. We have made knock hockey as small as 6 in. by 12 in. (we use a coin as a puck).

Here is a cutting list for the parts of the frame for a full-size game:

2 pieces of ¾-in. pine, 3½ in. wide by 54 in. long;
2 pieces of ¾-in. pine, 3½ in. wide by 30 in. long;
2 pieces of ¾-in. pine, 1 in. wide by 54 in. long;
2 pieces of ¾-in. pine, 1 in. wide by 30 in. long.

The exact lengths are not critical, since the pieces will be cut off at both ends when mitered. These measurements are extra long because the 2-ft. by 4-ft. measurement is for the inside of the frame formed by the wide boards. Even after they are mitered, the boards will be about 1½ in. longer than required. Also, extra length is necessary because you need a little wood on the waste side of the saw as the cut is made. That's why it's okay to make the pieces a little longer than the measurements I give, but don't make them too much shorter (p. 48).

I like to explain the structure of the game board when I supply the materials so that the child will understand the first mysterious steps. The drawing above shows how the bottom of the knock-hockey game is supported by a strip of wood nailed to the bottom edges of the walls. Show this drawing to the child, and describe how the sides will be mitered like a picture frame after the ledger strips are nailed on. Point out that the wide piece and the narrow strip are cut at the same time.

The first step in building the frame is to nail the ledgers to the walls. Demonstrate the whole process. First run a small bead of glue down one edge of a wide piece. Then show the child the rectangular ends of the narrow strips and explain that the narrow side (¾ in. wide) should be showing. Next, point out that the piece is longer than it has to be since both ends will be cut off later. Since it's unknown exactly where the cuts will be, none of the nails should be hammered in all the way. Later, if a nail is in the saw's path, it can easily be pulled out.

The ledger strip must be flush with the edge of the wall along its full length. Skinny strips of wood are often crooked, but they are flexible enough that they can be straightened out as they're nailed from one end to the other. Starting at one end of the board and working toward the other end,

demonstrate how to hold the strip flush to the edge of the board with your thumb as you hammer each nail, as sixth-grader David Christie is doing above. Hammer 1½-in. (4d) nails about every 4 in. (about the width of a child's fist between the nails). If there are any knots in the strip or the wall, suggest that the child nail around them. A knot is much harder than the surrounding wood, and it is difficult to nail through one.

When all four walls have ledger strips and the glue is dry, each side is ready to be mitered. This is a good opportunity to teach or review the concept of mitering, using a finished object like a picture frame or a box as an example. Remind the child that the angles aim toward the center of the frame, so they go in opposite directions on the ends of each board. Some children have difficulty remembering this concept, so you may have to set up the cuts for them (p. 49).

To miter, cut one end of each of the four walls—let's make it the right end as viewed from inside the frame. Set the miter-box saw at 45° with the handle swung toward the left. The wall is placed in the miter box with the wide board vertical, the ledger strip facing out and the bulk of its length on the left. Slide the board into position under the saw about 1½ in. from the end. (If there is only a thin amount of wood on the waste side of the cut, the saw may curve away from its line.) Check to see that there are no nails in the path of the saw by looking at the board directly above the cut. Pull obstructing nails with the claw of the hammer.

Now clamp the board in place, making sure it is flat on the table of the miter box. A long board might have to be propped at its end to keep it from pivoting on the edge of the miter box table. The child can also have a friend hold it while it's being sawn. Placing the

clamp close to the saw blade helps prevent pivoting too. Cut the right ends of all four walls.

Now it's time to measure for the second cuts. This distance is marked on the inside faces of the wide boards. We want the frame to fit loosely around the 2-ft. by 4-ft. plywood board, so add ¼ in. to each measurement. Measure from the obtuse angle of the diagonal sawcut to the starting point of the obtuse angle to be cut on the other end of the board. The placement of these 45° cuts

is important because that's how the inside dimensions of the frame are determined.

Have your child hold the end of a tape measure against the obtuse corner of one of the boards, and make the mark at the other end. Be sure to indicate the direction of the mitered cut. Cut one long wall and one short wall from these measured marks.

Now mark the opposite walls using these cut pieces as templates. Place them back to back and even up the

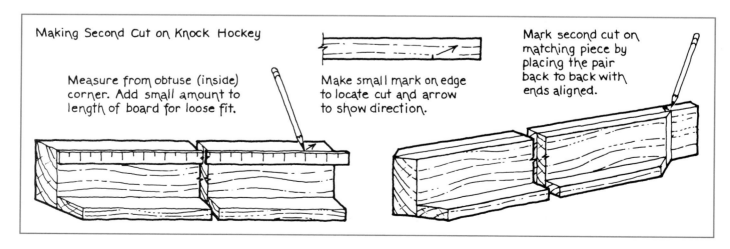

Making Second Cut on Knock Hockey

Measure from obtuse (inside) corner. Add small amount to length of board for loose fit.

Make small mark on edge to locate cut and arrow to show direction.

Mark second cut on matching piece by placing the pair back to back with ends aligned.

pointed ends (p. 50). Mark and cut the other two ends.

Next, lay out the goals on the two end walls. Your child can decide how wide the goals should be. On a full-size hockey board, I like 5½ in. to 6 in. Measuring along the inner, upper edge of the wall, mark the center, then mark half the width of the goal on either side of the center. Project these outer marks down to the ledger strip with a square. Cut along these two lines with a crosscut saw and remove the wood between these cuts with a coping saw. (You may wish to do this job for your child on the bandsaw or with a jigsaw or saber saw.)

Make the top of the goal from a scrap of the same wood as the ledger strips, cut to extend at least 1½ in. beyond the

goals (see the photo at left on p. 122). Kids sometimes like a sloped end on these pieces; cut them on the miter box. Glue the goal tops on and fasten them with two nails at each end.

When the goals are done, it's time to assemble the frame. I like clamping with a large band clamp, as described on p. 51. Spread glue on all eight ends of the frame and make sure the edges are lined up properly before running the clamp up tight. Since these glued joints will soon be reinforced with corner blocks, there is no need to nail them after the glue has dried. If there's no band clamp in the shop, just nail the corners together. Clamp two adjacent sides to a corner of the top of the workbench with their glued ends tight together. Nail in from both sides.

If you measured and cut correctly, the board will drop easily into the frame. Do not force the board into the frame. If the fit is tight, trim the plywood edges with a plane. If you used a band clamp, you can drop the plywood board into the frame as soon as the clamp is tight; if you nailed, wait an hour or so until the glue begins to bond. Now remove the board and run a thin bead of glue around the top of the ledger strip where the plywood sits. Drop the board back in and tack it down with ¾-in. brads about every 6 in. Remind your child that the ledger strips are about 1 in. wide, so the brads don't need to be right against the wall. Sink the brads with a nailset until they can't be felt with a finger, so they won't snag the puck.

Next, make the corner blocks and the goal blocks. These should be 1½ in. or 2 in. thick, so a piece of 2x4 stock will do just fine. Place the 2x4 flat on the table of the miter box, and saw one end off square. Set the saw at 45° and cut off a corner block. If the miter box is built to pivot directly under the edge of the board, as most are, leave the board clamped in place to cut two more corner blocks simply by swinging the saw. Move the wood over to cut off the last corner. To make square goal blocks, set the saw at 45° and clamp the board with a corner under the saw blade. Swing the saw to 90° and cut a perfectly square block. Sand the rough edges off the corner blocks and glue them in place. Be sure to glue the bottom and the surfaces that touch the walls of the game. There's no need to clamp the goal blocks in place; just leave them on a level surface until the glue dries.

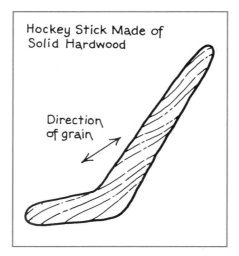

Hockey Stick Made of Solid Hardwood

Direction of grain

It's easy to make large knock-hockey or foosball games into game tables by installing legs. First decide the height of the table, usually 28 in. to 34 in. Next cut four pieces of ¾-in. by 6-in. pine board to length. Rip each of the boards diagonally at a moderate taper, but leave an extra ¾-in. margin on one of the edges so that when you glue and nail them together, the legs will appear proportionate. Apply glue to the inside surface of the leg, clamp and then nail or screw the leg to the game.

To position the goal blocks, mark the center of each goal and project a line down the middle of the board with a square bearing on the outside of the wall, as eighth-grader Amy Jacobson demonstrates in the photo above. Two diagonal corners of the goal blocks must sit on this line, the same distance from their respective goals. Glue the blocks in place, leaving the board horizontal until the glue is dry.

Cut pucks from any hardwood, using the method I described on p. 19 for making wheels. For a full-size board, 1½-in.-thick pucks of ½-in. diameter work well. Or you can purchase a hardwood dowel from a hardware store and cut off ½-in. slices with the miter saw. For small knock-hockey sets, checkers or coins work well.

Kids like two different kinds of hockey sticks. To make the ones that look like real hockey sticks, have your child draw a full-size pattern on paper and cut it out with scissors. Trace the pattern on 1-in.-thick hardwood, with the grain running as shown in the drawing above. After sawing it out, cut each stick in half lengthwise to get two sticks. Sticks cut from ½-in. plywood stand up well too.

A simpler stick can be made from a 3-in. pine or hardwood disc with a ½-in. dowel glued in a hole in the middle. Ask the child to scribe the circle with a compass and drill the hole before you cut it out on a bandsaw. Sand off any sharp or rough edges on the game board, sticks and pucks. Apply a light coat of furniture wax to the board, and the puck will fly.

Most kids will already know how to play knock hockey in one form or another. I have seen two basic forms of the game. In one, it's played like real hockey, with the players frantically pushing the puck around. I don't encourage this kind of play because bruised knuckles are almost inevitable. I prefer the other version, in which players take turns shooting for the opponent's goal, rebounding the puck off the walls and the goal block. When one player scores, the other starts the game again from the top of the goal block. No blocking is permitted.

Foosball

Foosball, also called table hockey, is an action-packed game that keeps kids involved for hours. Each player needs quick reflexes to keep the ball moving toward the opposition's goal and to defend the home team's net, the rows of kickers banging side to side and spinning all the while. The game is easy to build, though it takes a little longer than knock hockey, and you and your child will have to put a little extra thought into the design.

I like to build this game around a 2-ft. by 4-ft. piece of ¼-in. plywood for the same reasons I use this size for knock hockey; It's big enough for action and sensible to cut from a 4x8 sheet. Scale the project down to 8 in. by 16 in. or less if your child is a miniaturist.

The structure of the game is similar to knock hockey in that the plywood floor is supported on the walls by ledger strips. In foosball, the ledgers are

arranged to bend the corners of the board up, which rolls the out-of-reach ball back into play. The walls of the foosball game are much higher than those on knock hockey. Mitering wide boards is inconvenient, so we rabbet them instead (see p. 31 and p. 165).

After deciding on the proportions of the game, consider whether it will have six or eight rows of kickers. Fewer rows makes it easier to play, although eight rows will allow two children to play on each side of the board, the handle for a row in each hand.

If six rows, the kickers should be taller than if it's an eight-row game. Explaining the reason for this may help your child understand how important mathematics can be, even when designing something for fun. Here's why: each wooden kicker can swing forward and backward a distance equal to its height from the floor to its waist, where the dowel passes through. So to find the optimum height, divide the number of rows into the length of the board and divide the result by two. If there are six rows on a 48-in. board, for example, the kickers should be 4 in. tall from the dowel to the floor. If there are eight rows, each kicker should be 3 in. tall from the dowel to the floor. Use this method to work out the height of the kickers if your game is shorter or longer than mine.

Once the height of the kickers has been worked out, figure the height of the walls. The ledger strip will be ¾ in. thick, plus ¼ in. for the plywood floor. The walls should be at least 1½ in. above the kicker's waist on a large game. If you are building a 48-in.-long game with eight rows of kickers, make the walls at least 5½ in. high.

Now figure the lengths of the sides. The inside dimensions of the frame should allow the plywood to drop in easily, so add at least ¼ in. around the 2-ft. by 4-ft. plywood-board dimensions. The rabbet joints will be cut on the end boards, so add ¾ in. to each end of the short boards. Therefore, the end boards on a 2-ft. by 4-ft. game would be 25¾ in. long. The rabbets go about halfway through the thickness of the boards, so add ⅜ in. to each end of the long boards, which makes the sides 49 in. long. Work out the cutting list for your child's size game with a similar method. On a very small game, mitered corners may be convenient. Figure the lengths of stock needed with the guidelines I describe on p. 119.

After cutting the rabbets on the end boards, mark out the goals, as described on p. 121, but this time center them on

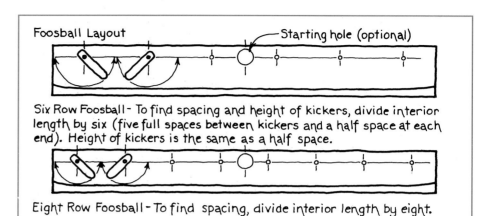

Foosball Layout — Starting hole (optional)

Six Row Foosball – To find spacing and height of kickers, divide interior length by six (five full spaces between kickers and a half space at each end). Height of kickers is the same as a half space.

Eight Row Foosball – To find spacing, divide interior length by eight.

the bottom edge of the board. Your child will want to decide what size the goals will be on the 2-ft. ends. I like goals about 6 in. wide and about halfway across the width of the boards. Cut them out on a bandsaw or by hand using a crosscut saw and a coping saw, as described on pp. 147-149.

You'll need enough ¾-in. by 1¼-in. stock for ledger strips to go all around the frame, about 12 ft. for a 2-ft. by 4-ft. board. Measure 1½ in. to either side of the goal on the bottom inside edge of the end boards and cut ledgers to fit the distance between the marks. Glue and nail these strips in place, flush with the bottom edge of the board, narrow edge up. Glue generously, and hammer at least two nails on each end because this strip is heavily stressed as the plywood is bent.

Cut four ledger strips to fit between the rabbets and the ends of the goal ledgers. Set one in place as shown in the photo at right, at an angle that looks reasonable—on a 2-ft. by 4-ft. game, about 2 in. from the bottom of the wall to the top of the ledger is good. If the angle is too steep, it will be difficult to bend the plywood, especially on smaller games. Glue and nail the strip in place, then measure the distance up the rabbet and mark it on the other three edges so all the corners are raised the same amount. Make sure the strips don't intrude into the rabbet. If one does, trim it with a dovetail saw.

Hold a side board against an end board in its final position in the rabbet. Trace around the end board's ledger strip where it meets the side. These marks on the side boards determine where to begin the side ledgers. Those side ledgers will slope downward to meet the bottom of the wall under the first row of kickers. Mark that distance on the bottom edge of the sides. (On a 2-ft. by 4-ft. board of six rows of kickers, for example, mark 4 in. in from the ends.) Cut ledger strips to fit between the traced marks and the measured marks, then nail and glue them in place. Be sure these strips don't cross the traced marks or they will hit the end strips, preventing the board from going together. Check the fit of each corner after the strips are nailed on. If a ledger is too long, trim with a dovetail saw.

Next, lay out the holes in the sides of the game. With a marking gauge, scribe a line the correct distance above the ledger strip. Make it a little farther above the top of the board than the height planned for the kickers to give them room to swing. If they are to be 3 in. from foot to waist, allow ¼ in. for the thickness of the plywood above the ledger and add about 3¼ in. for the player, for a total of ⌢½ in. Measure and mark this distance above the ledger strip, then set the marking gauge on that point with its fence against the top edge of the wall. Scribe the full length of the side walls.

Measure and mark the center of the scribed line. Set the dividers, or a compass that locks tight, to the height of the kickers. Starting at the center mark, walk off this distance in both directions along the scribed line with the dividers. Circle the two marks closest to the center with a pencil. Working toward each end, circle every other mark until the end of the board. Count them—there should be the required six or eight rows.

Clamp the board and a piece of scrap wood to the workbench and drill on the circled marks (see p. 152). Drill with a bit that is slightly larger than the kicker dowel so that it will spin and slide easily. I bore ⁹⁄₁₆-in. holes for ½-in. dowels on a full-size game or enlarge ½-in. holes slightly with a coarse round file.

Some kids like to have a hole to start the ball on one or each side of the game. Drill on the marks at the centers of the side boards with an expansion bit (p. 153) set to a diameter slightly larger than the ball.

After drilling, nail and glue the frame together like a rabbeted box or bookcase (p. 32). Once it's together, check to see if the plywood board fits loosely in the frame. If it doesn't, trim the edges with a plane. Now run a healthy amount of glue on the top surfaces of the ledger strips all the way around the frame. To begin bending the

plywood, pull the board down to the ledgers under the goals. Cut two scraps of wood the length of those ledgers and place them on the plywood. Push the board down and finish pulling it into contact with the ledger by tightening the clamp.

Short pieces of 2x6 serve as cauls to clamp the sides of the plywood down.

Place a block on each end of the straight ledgers where it meets the angled ledger. A third caul at the center of each side may be needed if the plywood doesn't sit flat. Let the clamped structure dry overnight to allow the glue to reach its full strength. Gluing the board down is sufficient; there's no need to nail it.

Laying Out Holes on Foosball Game

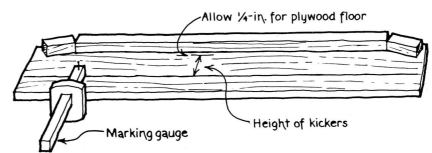

1. Scribe line parallel to top edge of side wall.
Set marking gauge to length as shown.

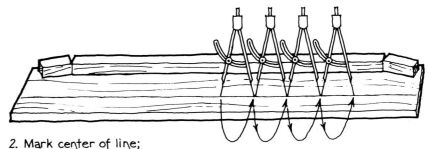

2. Mark center of line;
Set dividers to height of kickers, and walk off marks along line in both directions starting at center mark.

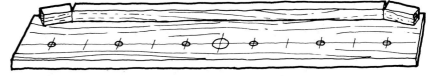

3. Circle the marks closest to the center, then skip a mark and circle, etc.

Here's how you can help your child design the kickers. The distance from foot to waist, where each kicker is drilled for the dowel, is already determined by the length of the game board. How far above the waist each player will go depends on how the row is to be balanced. If short players are designed, they will be bottom-heavy and their feet will fall to the floor when the grip is released. Rows of bottom-heavy players are hard to spin quickly, especially if they have a lot of kickers on them. The kicker may be as long above the waist as below it; rows of such players are easy to spin, but will stay in any odd position when the handles are released. That means kickers may not be on the defensive when they are at rest, and they may be in the up position just when the ball is shot. Somewhere between tall and short might give the best results. I suggest experimenting with different proportions before making the whole set.

Kickers can be any shape, from simple sticks to three-dimensional representations of soccer players, especially if you have access to a bandsaw. To make simple kickers, rip out some strips of wood the width and thickness desired. I like ¾ in. by 1½ in. for a full-size game. Along the length, mark out the heights of the players and the positions of the holes. Drill the holes, then saw the strip into pieces.

Simple shapes work just fine, but kids sometimes get a kick out of designing imaginative teammates. These may be shaped as seen from the sides, when viewed from the front, or both. Work out a pattern with your child, for both views if necessary. Mark the position of the hole on the pattern and drill the holes before cutting out the shapes. There are a lot of kickers; you'll probably want to cut them out for your child on the bandsaw.

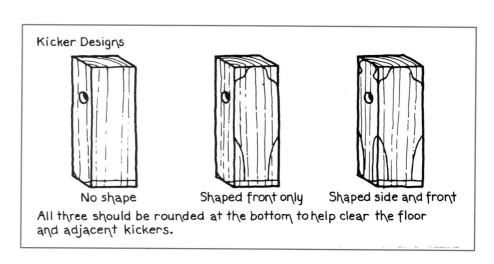

Kicker Designs

No shape   Shaped front only   Shaped side and front

All three should be rounded at the bottom to help clear the floor and adjacent kickers.

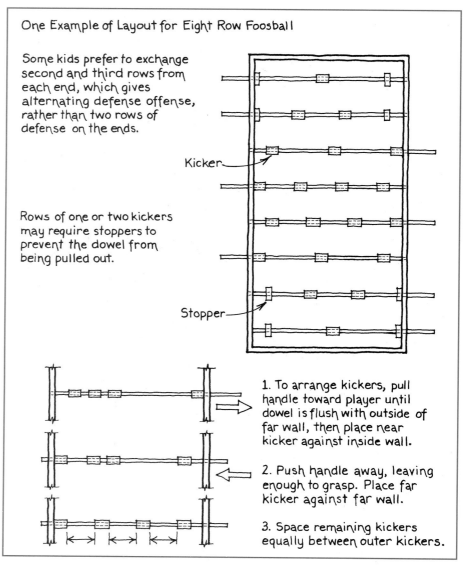

One Example of Layout for Eight Row Foosball

Some kids prefer to exchange second and third rows from each end, which gives alternating defense offense, rather than two rows of defense on the ends.

Kicker

Rows of one or two kickers may require stoppers to prevent the dowel from being pulled out.

Stopper

1. To arrange kickers, pull handle toward player until dowel is flush with outside of far wall, then place near kicker against inside wall.

2. Push handle away, leaving enough to grasp. Place far kicker against far wall.

3. Space remaining kickers equally between outer kickers.

Kids seem to have their own ideas about arranging kickers in rows. There is always a single goalie, but there may be two or three players in the next row in. Usually that second row is defending the goal, with the row after as offense. The third row in will usually have three players, while the fourth, if there is one, can have three, four or even five. Keep in mind that rows with many bottom-heavy players can be hard to operate quickly, and having too many kickers can block active play. It's easy to change the configuration if it doesn't work well.

My foosball games require 30-in. dowels on a 2-ft.-wide board. With those proportions it is possible to pull the dowels right out of the board on rows with one or two kickers. You'll need to make stoppers to limit the dowel's travel. These are like little wheels with center holes drilled to fit tight on the dowel (p. 177). Treat these stoppers as though they were players as you establish their positions on the dowels.

To find the permanent positions of the pieces, slide the kickers and stops onto the dowels, facing in the correct direction. Pull each dowel so it protrudes from the side of the game where its operator will stand, with its far end flush with the outside of the opposite wall. Slide a player or stopper against the inside wall on the handle side to prevent the dowel from traveling any farther. Mark that position on the dowel with a pencil on both sides of the player or stopper. Now slide the dowel inward until just enough of it sticks out the operator's side of the game to grasp as a handle (3 in. or 4 in.). Move a player or stopper against the far wall to prevent the dowel from moving any more in that direction. Mark its position on the dowel too. Now space the remaining kickers evenly between the outer players or stops. Mark these positions and fix the kicker onto the dowels, as shown in the bottom drawing on the facing page.

Skewer each kicker in place on its dowel with ⅛-in. dowels. First collect a bunch of small pieces of scrap wood, thick and thin, to stack under a kicker to hold it horizontal and steady. Bore a hole through the supported kicker or stopper, aimed through the center of the dowel with an ⅛-in. bit in an eggbeater drill, as seventh-grader Carter Gaffney is doing in the photo above. Drive a short piece of dowel through the hole. Boring right through the other side of the kicker makes it easy to drive the dowel out the other side for later repositioning.

Here are a few refinements that make the game a little smoother to play. Make

handles on the ends of the rows from sections of ¾-in. dowels drilled to fit the row dowels. Bore the end grain with a twist bit or a modified auger bit. Kickers or stoppers make a sharp noise as they bash into the walls in the heat of play. Cushion the crash and give the row a pleasant rebound by slipping hose washers or wrapping rubber bands around the outside end kickers or stoppers. It helps clarify play to paint kickers in team colors. Some kids enjoy painting faces and shoes on each player. This can be done after the game is finished, but it is easier to paint them before they are mounted on their rows.

Marble Rolls

Even in this age of radio-controlled cars, computer games and VCRs, kids still delight in making simple marble rolls, which use gravity to propel marbles in ingenious and amusing ways. In the process, they learn the value of patience and care, which results in pride of accomplishment as well as the ability to deal constructively with the frustration of things going wrong.

Building a marble roll is an enjoyable trial-and-error exercise in engineering and physics, a painless way to learn about motion, friction, gravity and momentum. Your child should experiment with dimensions, making adjustments as necessary. Shapes and sizes aren't critical. The point is not to follow a plan, but boldly to roll where none has rolled before.

The easiest-to-build marble roll is the traditional zigzag, like the one shown in the photo above, which Laurel Bernini made in the sixth grade. Sloping U-channel tracks are made from thin strips of pine ripped from the edge of a ¾-in. board and then are glued and

This section first appeared in a slightly different form as an article in the March/April 1989 issue of Fine Woodworking *magazine, published by The Taunton Press.*

nailed at each end to L-shaped uprights. A ¾-in.-dia. hole is drilled near the bottom end of each track section and sawed through to the end so the marble can drop through to the track below. Or you can just stagger the tracks so they end short, the way Laurel did. The uprights support the tracks and redirect the rolling marbles onto the top end of the lower track segment. At the bottom of the zigzag, marbles are collected in a scrapwood corral. For additional support, the uprights are fastened to a flat base. To decide how many tracks, how high and how wide the roll will be, a child can sketch the project full-size and take measurements directly from the drawing.

A nifty variation is the double-track marble race shown in the drawing below. Make your upright posts exactly as wide as two tracks side by side. Lay out the first set of tracks and then place the second set of tracks alongside the first, but tilted in the opposite direction so the tracks cross in the middle.

You can add to the excitement and validity of the marble race with a simple mechanism for starting two marbles at the same time. This automatic starter is made from three ¾-in.-thick pine boards that fit between the uprights. Drill them as shown in the top drawing on the facing page so the holes in the top piece are the same distance apart but offset from those in the bottom and middle pieces. The top and bottom pieces fit between the uprights, with the middle piece, which is ¾ in. shorter, trapped between them. When the middle piece is slid side to side, its holes line up either with the top holes, letting a marble drop into and be trapped in the center section, or with the bottom holes, which causes the trapped marbles to drop simultaneously onto the track. Carve sloping channels on the top board, directed toward each hole, so several marbles can be lined up and fed to the tracks. It's amazing to see dozens of colored glittering balls clunk and zoom down the tracks on their way to the finish line.

The chutes-and-ladders style marble roll is a simpler way to get the little spheres rolling and offers much more freedom of design. It is built on a piece of plywood mounted vertically in a simple stand like the one built by Becky Brayman. Although they begin as two-

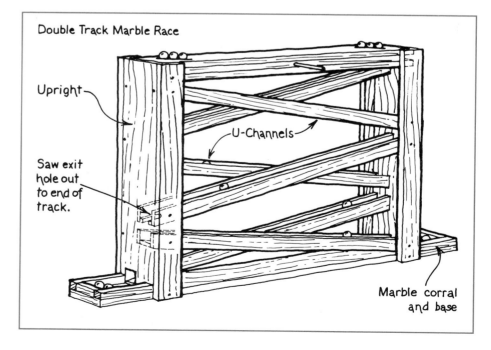

Double Track Marble Race

Upright

Saw exit hole out to end of track.

U-Channels

Marble corral and base

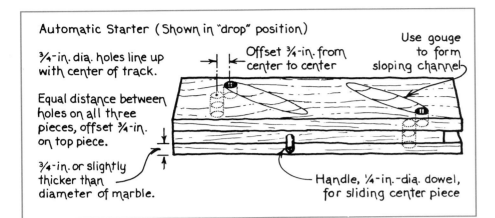

Automatic Starter (Shown in "drop" position)

¾-in. dia. holes line up with center of track.

Equal distance between holes on all three pieces, offset ¾-in. on top piece.

¾-in. or slightly thicker than diameter of marble.

Offset ¾-in. from center to center

Use gouge to form sloping channel

Handle, ¼-in.-dia. dowel, for sliding center piece

dimensional constructions, paths often run out from the board and sometimes bore through it. The backboard is a less restrictive structure than the uprights of the zigzags, offering more opportunity for experimentation. You can miter the *U*-channel track for the zigzag rolls into curves, steps and even spirals by gluing segments end to end and using masking tape to hold the pieces until the glue dries.

With imagination running rampant, your child may raid the bandsaw scrap box for odd-shaped pieces that can be glued to the backboard to alter the marble's path. A gouged path in a block of wood or a guardrail in just the right place may help keep the marble on track, and a small wedge at the start will

add to the marble's speed, enabling it to overcome obstacles farther down the line.

A neat variation is to tip the plywood board back 10° or so. That way the marble hugs the plywood, and any chunk of wood glued to the board can guide a marble with no need to carve a track in it or to add a guide rail.

If a backboard marble roll is like a quick and amusing scherzo, three-dimensional rolls are a symphony. There is less structure to fasten things to, but room for much more to happen. The framework is four upright ½-in.-dia. dowels glued in holes bored at the corners of an *H*-shape base (p. 138). We use *U*-channel tracks mitered and glued into various shapes and doweled to the

uprights. Begin at the top and work down. Think of the strange things the marble could do. To encourage kids, I built the marble roll shown in the photo below. It is 3 ft. high, with three separate paths. Several different events cause the marbles to accelerate, slow down, spin wildly, rumble or fall abruptly along the way. An automatic switching system feeds marbles to the various paths in sequence, and at the bottom, a marble pulls a lever that starts another at the top. The major events on this machine can be choreographed together or alone on rolls as simple or complex as desired.

Any marble can be directed to a variety of paths by using intersections and automatic switches. Furthermore, several switches can be married together to introduce an element of surprise. A simple switch gate is shaped like a three-point star and swivels on a dowel inserted in the track floor where two tracks intersect, as shown in the drawing below. The gate swivels until

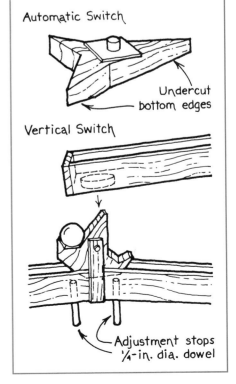

Automatic Switch

Undercut bottom edges

Vertical Switch

Adjustment stops ¼-in. dia. dowel

its long leg hits the sidewall, opening one path and closing the other. A marble rolling by the gate hits a short leg in the open path, causing the switch to swivel to its alternate position. Undercutting the bottom edges of the gate will keep it swinging free of the track surface. A small scrap acts as a nut to hold the gate on the dowel.

The basic principle is the same for a vertical switch. When a marble drops onto a vertical switch through a hole in the track above, it is directed to one of two paths, and the position of the switch is simultaneously reversed. Dowels located in the floor of the track limit the gate's tilt. To ensure that the marble doesn't roll off the side of the switch, you can either hollow out the edge of the switch slightly with a gouge and cup the lip where the marble exits, or add guards to the sides of the track to contain the marble.

A spiral length of track accelerates the marble dramatically, making a whirring sound. A spiral is an unusual shape for wood, but it's easy to make. Select an 11-in. square of ¾-in.-thick white pine with clear, straight and flat grain. Bandsaw this square by eye, with successive loops about 1 in. apart, leaving a straight tongue tangent to the circle and parallel with the grain as an entrance (see the drawing above right). Then decide which side will be up, thus determining whether the spiral will be left-handed or right-handed when stretched open. On the bottom surface, draw a line perpendicular to the grain and drill ¼-in.-dia. holes almost through the board, on the line at each turn of the spiral. Glue an 8-in.-long piece of ¼-in. dowel in each hole. Allow the glue to dry thoroughly.

On a ¾-in. by ¾-in. strip of pine, which will support the spiral, mark the position of each dowel and drill ¼-in.-dia. holes clear through. Position the strip with each hole lined up with its matching dowel. With a hammer, gently push the strip down so each dowel protrudes slightly.

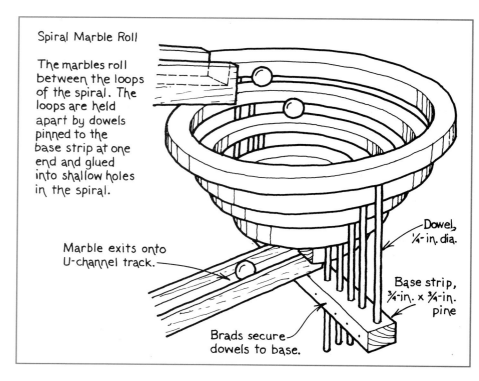

Spiral Marble Roll

The marbles roll between the loops of the spiral. The loops are held apart by dowels pinned to the base strip at one end and glued into shallow holes in the spiral.

Marble exits onto U-channel track.

Dowel, ¼-in. dia.

Base strip, ¾-in. x ¾-in. pine

Brads secure dowels to base.

To expand the spiral to its funnel shape, grip the strip in a vise with the spiral right side up. Use a short section of 1x1 driven by a hammer to persuade the dowels farther through their holes. Start at the center and drive the first pair of dowels through the base strip about ½ in. Moving outward, drive each successive pair of dowels through a little less than the previous set. Return to the center and repeat this process until a funnel shape is fully formed. The loops should be spaced so a marble is just barely retained by the next track up. The wood is stiffer near the bottom and can't be spread as far without breaking. On approaching full depth, test the track. Start a marble at the top with a little push so it'll cling to the rim. If it slows down anywhere along the path, drive that section of the spiral down slightly and try it again. When you are satisfied with the run, pin each dowel in the base strip with a small brad.

A spiral makes a fine beginning for any marble roll. If the spiral is installed some distance from the starting point, the marble may need an entrance ramp

to ensure that it has enough speed to take the long, sweeping, ever-accelerating path, instead of walking down the funnel's steps.

Tilting ramps provide a rhythmic, cascading motion that contrasts nicely with the faster, swirling motion in a spiral. Short ramps give a rapid, jerky motion; longer ones dip and rise more slowly in a less frantic way. The top drawing on the facing page shows how these tilting ramps are made. At the end of section of U-channel, where the marble enters, a ¼-in. dowel is inserted to hold an adjustable wooden counterweight. Another small dowel is installed to prevent the marble from escaping. The bottom of the other end is beveled to increase the distance the ramp can tilt. The ramp pivots on a dowel about one-third the distance from the counterbalanced end. When a marble drops onto the inclined ramp, it rolls toward the exit end, tilting the ramp more as it rolls. When it falls off the ramp, the counterweight causes the ramp to snap back to its original position. I call the tilting raps "click-

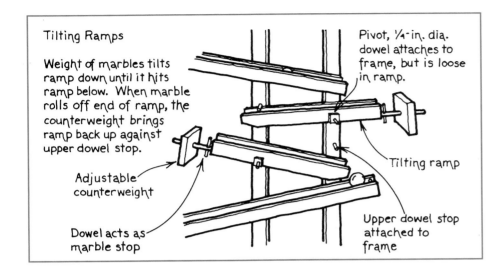

Tilting Ramps

Weight of marbles tilts ramp down until it hits ramp below. When marble rolls off end of ramp, the counterweight brings ramp back up against upper dowel stop.

Adjustable counterweight

Dowel acts as marble stop

Pivot, ¼-in. dia. dowel attaches to frame, but is loose in ramp.

Tilting ramp

Upper dowel stop attached to frame

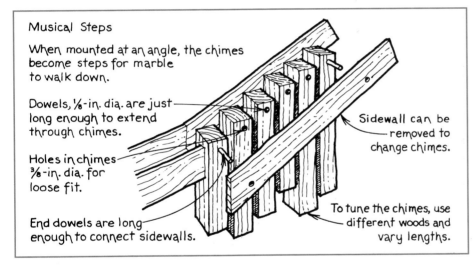

Musical Steps

When mounted at an angle, the chimes become steps for marble to walk down.

Dowels, ⅛-in. dia. are just long enough to extend through chimes.

Holes in chimes ⅜-in. dia. for loose fit.

End dowels are long enough to connect sidewalls.

Sidewall can be removed to change chimes.

To tune the chimes, use different woods and vary lengths.

Bongo Board

Here's a game that builds coordination and strength, and it's an enjoyable project, too. Learning to balance takes only a few minutes, then children compete for who can stay up longest.

Bongo boards are as safe as any piece of athletic equipment if proper precautions are taken. Use the board in an area where a fall is unlikely to hurt—I prefer a carpeted floor away from any furniture. Your child should take care to round all the edges of the board and roller, making sure they are smooth and free from splinters.

The game consists of a cylindrical roller with a groove that engages a guide strip screwed to the bottom of a board. At each end of the guide strip is a stopper strip screwed across the board to keep the player from flying off the roller. The stoppers also act as battens to reinforce the board.

Here's how I make bongo boards with the bandsaw. The roller is built of three units assembled along a central dowel, which aligns the parts and reinforces the structure. The outer sections should have a radius of 2¼ in. to 3 in. (4½ in. to 6 in. in diameter). Increasing the size of the roller makes the board harder to

clocks," because of the regular beat they produce as they dip, hit the underlying ramp and then rise and hit the upper dowel stop.

Musical steps are one of my favorite events (see the drawing above). Marbles march down a set of stairs, creating an entertaining percussive sound. To make the steps, mark out and drill equally spaced holes (one for each step) in a ½-in. by 1-in. strip of wood, which will be one of the sidewalls. On the other sidewall, drill just the two end holes. Glue a ⅛-in. dowel in each hole on this sidewall. The dowels at each end should be long enough to run through and support the other sidewall.

For the stairs, which will be the chimes, cut various lengths of ¾-in.-thick pine, drill a hole near the end of each strip and hang one on each dowel. They should fit loosely. Drill two ⅛-in.-dia. holes in the other sidewall, and install it in place on the long end dowels from the first sidewall.

Finally, hang the stairs on the framework of the marble roll at an angle that allows a marble to drop from step to step. You will find that different kinds of wood give different tones. The chimes can be tuned by adjusting their lengths, and the scale can be changed by removing the sidewall and rearranging the chimes.

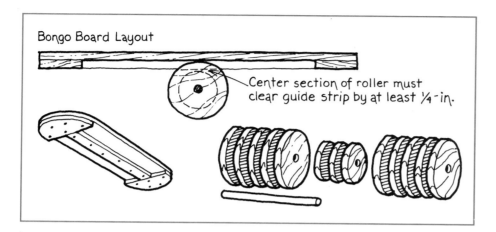

Bongo Board Layout

Center section of roller must clear guide strip by at least ¼-in.

control, which can be challenging, but a diameter above 6 in. is just too tricky. The center section of the roller must not touch the guide strip under the bongo board or it will lift the board off the outer sections of the roller. To find the radius of the center section, add ¼ in. to the guide strip's thickness, and subtract that sum from the radius of the large sections of the roller. So if the larger radius of the roller is 2¾ in. and the guide strip is ¾ in. thick, the radius of the roller's center section will be 1¾ in.

The three sections of the roller are built up from discs cut from ¾-in. pine stock. Make the center section three layers, or 2¼ in. thick. That means the guide strip on the bottom of the bongo board will have to be about 2 in. wide to fit loosely in the groove. The outer sections can be built of five or six layers, depending on how wide the board will be. A 10-in.-wide board would require five layers on each side of the roller; the outer sections would be 3¾ in. wide and the center section would be 2¼ in. wide, for a total of 9¾ in.

Set a pair of dividers or a compass to a radius about ⅜ in. larger than the finished radius of the roller. Poke the point of the dividers into a possible center position and swing the scribing end into any position where it might overlap an edge, another circle, a bad knot or a crack: check all four quadrants of the circle. Reposition the center and try again until the circle fits in the most

economical place. By checking first, you can avoid messing up the board with a useless circle. Mark out the required number of discs on a board or scraps of wood. (Don't be fussy about knots or small cracks because a laminated structure is forgiving of minor imperfections in the wood.) Remind your child to leave about ¼ in. between circles for the saw cut. Be sure the center of each circle is clearly marked, because you'll need to find it again. Now set the dividers for the finished radius of the roller sections and scribe this circle on each piece on the same center as the bigger circle.

The roller has a central dowel running through it longitudinally for alignment during gluing, and for additional strength. Once all the circles are marked, bore a hole at the center of each one for the central dowel. I like a dowel ¾ in. or bigger because it strengthens the roller, but match the auger bit to the dowel size you are using. (Boring methods are described on p. 152.) Then bandsaw the discs along the large-diameter circles.

Glue up each of the three sections of the roller separately, using the dowel to align the discs as they are glued. Spread white glue on the first disc, leaving a little dry area around the dowel hole, since we don't want it glued in yet. Slide the next disc down the dowel onto the first and rotate it so the grain runs 90° to the one under it. Spread glue on it

as above and continue this procedure until the last disc in the section is added. Make sure that the scribed inner circle of the last disc is facing out so it can be seen. Equally space three clamps around the perimeter of the disc to pull all the glued surfaces tightly together. After the glue has set for ten minutes or so (when it has a grip but isn't firm), punch the center dowel out of the hole using a mallet and a smaller-diameter dowel. Glue all three sections this way.

When the glue has dried, bandsaw each section to its finished size along the scribed inner circle. Put a sharp blade on the bandsaw and work slowly to get a smooth, accurate circle.

Now glue the sections of the roller together. First spread glue on both sides of the center section. Cut a dowel that is about 2 in. longer than the width of the roller. Chamfer the ends of the dowel with sandpaper or a knife to help it enter the hole easily. Make a puddle of glue on scrap paper, then roll the dowel in it to coat its surface lightly but completely. Push the dowel through one of the outer sections of the roller, then slide the other two sections on. The fit may be very tight since the glue can cause the dowel to swell; try driving the dowel through the holes with a wooden mallet. Allow the dowel to project 1 in. or so past both sides of the roller. Squeeze the assembly together with three clamps equally spaced around the perimeter of the discs. Tighten the clamps a little at a time, trying to keep the pressure equal to avoid bending the cylinder. Leave the assembly clamped at least a couple of hours.

Trim the ends of the dowel flush with the roller. Soften the sharp edges of the roller with 50-grit sandpaper on a sanding block. The roller doesn't have to be perfectly smooth, and light sanding is adequate. If your child wants to get the roller extra smooth or get the work done quickly, you can chuck the roller in a lathe or even a drill press. This is work you should do, unless your child is ready to tackle lathe work (see pp. 197-201). Make sure the roller is centered and is securely mounted in the machine. This is a heavy piece of work, so don't turn on the machine until you're sure it's set to run at the lowest speed. Click the lathe on and off a few times before letting it reach full speed to assure yourself that the piece is safely fastened to the machine. Follow the additional precautions described on p. 201.

A good size for the board is ¾ in. by 10 in. by 30 in., though a big child or an adult might prefer one a couple of inches longer. If it's less than about 9 in. wide, the bongo boarder will have

problems with the board and roller tipping over; wider boards are fine. Choose a piece of straight, flat ¾-in. stock, free from large knots, cracks and other defects. Have your child design the corners of the board on the corner of a piece of paper; any shape will do as long as it isn't pointed. Scissor out the pattern and trace it on all four corners of the board. After you've bandsawn the shapes, your child can sand or spokeshave all the edges of the board to a gentle chamfer or curve.

Cut the guide strips as shown in the the drawing on the facing page and bore the screw holes with a twist drill in a zigzag pattern. Most boards are slightly

cupped, that is, warped across the grain. You can see cupping by sighting along an end of the board. If there is any noticeable cupping, put the hollow side of the board on the bottom so that its outer edges will run on the roller. Place the board along an edge of the workbench, bottom side up, and center the guide strip both end to end and side to side. Clamp the guide strip to the board and the workbench and run screws into each hole.

If you are using hardwood for the board, be sure to drill pilot holes into the board through the holes in the guide strip to ease entry of the screws. Screws don't require pilot holes in softwood. Use flat-head screws, and tighten them until the heads pull themselves slightly below the surface of the guide strip. (If the board has hardwood guide strips, countersink the head of the screw.) I like to use a screwdriver bit in a hand brace. Phillips-head screws make it easier to keep the bit centered.

Softwood boards require wide stop strips to strengthen them across the grain. These can also help flatten a cupped board and keep a flat one from warping. Shape the stop strip to fit the shape of the end of the bongo board. Screw it in place like the guide strip.

The finished board can be painted, oiled or stained. Some kids like to put skateboard grip tape on the ends of the board to help keep their feet in place.

To use the bongo board, place the roller at one end of the board and step on the low end. Now place the other foot on the high end and press it downward. To balance the board, press down on the end that is coming up. Some kids like to have you hold both hands when they first try the bongo board. First they will learn to balance without movement, then they'll begin to roll the board back and forth. After a while, they'll start inventing tricks and time trials. Again, carpet is one of the safer surfaces for a bongo board, away from furniture with sharp edges.

Pinball

The fun of making marble rolls comes from careful observation and intuitive engineering, and from the added problem of designing a challenge for the player. Pinball is the mechanical equivalent of a video game, but it's one that your child can whimsically design and modify. A true pinball wizard has the body language of a dancer, but it's the builder who makes the rules. So anything, within the laws of physics and fun, is possible.

Building the game is much like building the other table games. First you have to decide on the dimensions of the pinball game, including the depth of the sides. Add 1 in. to the depth to get the width of the side boards. Rip out the four sides from 34-in. stock, 3 in. to 4 in. longer than the dimensions of the sides. Rip out four strips of pine 34 in. by 34 in., equal to the lengths of the sides. Glue and nail a strip along an edge of each side board. Leave the nails standing proud of the surface so that they can be pulled if they're in the way of the miter saw. Cut the sides to size in the miter box. Assemble the frame with

a band clamp and glue. (If there's no band clamp, nails and glue work fine.) Cut a piece of ¼-in. plywood to fit, then tack it in place with glue and brads. (Build with ⅜-in. or ½-in. plywood to make it is easy to mount dowels, nails and other obstacles in the floor of the game. Thinner plywood may have to be backed up with gluing blocks on the underside where the flipper's shafts come through.)

To make the shooter, glue a block of wood to the wall of the game in the lower right-hand corner (inside or outside) to double its thickness. While the glue is drying, create an alley for the shooter by gluing a strip of wood (⅜ in. by ¾ in. on edge will do) to the right side of the board about 1 in. from the wall. Leave room for the marble exit at the top, and if the design calls for a ball return with automatic feed, leave an opening about 3 in. from the bottom.

Drill a ⁷⁄₁₆-in. hole in the doubled wall at the end of the alley to give a loose fit for the ⅜-in. dowel that will be the shooter shaft. The hole should be at least ⅜ in. above the floor and centered on the alley. The hole will have to be drilled from the outside, so help your child eyeball the position of the hole or lay it out by projecting around the wall with a combination square.

The shooter block is cut from a piece of ¾-in. by ¾-in. stock that fits loosely in the alley with its grain pointing up the alley. Drill a ⅜-in. hole in its end grain and glue it to the dowel. Make the handle a comfortable shape, also with the grain parallel to the alley. The handle should be removable so that the spring can be adjusted. Drill its end for the dowel and cross drill it for a ⅛-in. dowel to pin it in place. Push the pin out with a 1½-in. finishing nail driven head first through the hole. If the game needs an automatic ball feed, build the pusher block so that its top end can be pulled slightly below the opening in the alley wall. Cut a shallow V-notch in the end of the shooter block to center the marble, as shown in the drawing.

Power the shooter with a stretched-out spring that fits loosely around the dowel. Hardware stores carry a selection, or a try section of old screen-door spring. Experiment with the length of spring and degree of stretch to get the right kind of power and control.

The bottom end of the pinball game should be raised a couple of inches off the table to allow the shooter and any hardware beneath the board to clear the table. Half-inch dowels in holes bored in the edge of the wall work well for legs. The top end of the board is higher and needs more substantial support. Play with the angle by stacking blocks under the top end. A steeper board gives a faster game, and guides on the board need not be angled as much to keep the marble rolling. A slower marble is easier to control with flippers. I find an angle of between 10° and 20° is about right. When it's decided how high the top of the game should be, cut a "legboard" as shown in the photo at left, and glue and nail it to the game.

Now add the outer marble guides. The arcs in the upper corners are cut from ¾-in. pine stock and glued in place. The ball-return guide at the bottom may be a solid block or a ⅜-in. by ¾-in. strip glued on edge. The shooter should give smooth control so that the marble may be artfully controlled to drop into the center of the board. The ball return should feed the marble back to the shooter every time. Is the board too fast? Too slow? Now is the time to make adjustments. Make sure everything is working smoothly before going to the next step.

Flippers give the pinball player influence over the marble. They are easy to make and fun to use. First locate the position of the flipper on the board and drill a ⅛-in. pilot hole through the plywood to indicate this position under the board. Glue a 2-in. by 2-in. block of ¾-in. pine at that point under the board to act as a bearing for the flipper shaft. (You don't need the blocks if you've used thicker plywood.) When the glue is dry, bore a 7/16-in. hole through the plywood and block to allow a 3/8-in. dowel to move freely through it.

Make the swing arms of a sturdy hardwood for extra strength. Each should be about 2 in. long and 1 in. by 1 in. in section. On one, drill a 3/8-in. hole at one end for a tight fit on the flipper shaft; on the other, a 7/16-in. hole, so it can swing freely on its fixed shaft. Both get a 3/16-in. hole at the other end. Bandsaw the slot in the arm as shown in the drawing, making the slot wide enough to freely accommodate a 1/2-in. dowel.

Locate a point on the bottom edge of the game's wall opposite the hole for the flipper shaft and bore a blind 3/8-in. hole. Glue a dowel in place that protrudes about 1 1/2 in. and cross drill a 1/8-in. hole to retain the swing arm.

Draw the shape of the flipper on a piece of 3/4-in. board, bore a 3/8-in. hole, then cut it out on the bandsaw. Assemble the flipper, shaft and its swing arm in the hole. Mount the other swing arm on its shaft, retaining it with a 1/8-in. dowel through the hole. With both arms pointing toward the bottom end of the game, set a 1/2-in. dowel in place in the arm slots and mark the positions of the pins. Bore 1/8-in. holes in these marks, then trim the dowel so it protrudes beyond the side of the game far enough to act as a handle. Fasten the arm in place with 1/8-in. dowels and check to see that the assembly moves smoothly. Stretch a rubber band between the 1/8-in. dowel on the flipper arm and a peg in the side of the game. Glue the flipper dowel in the hole in its swing arm. Determine the resting position of the flipper and glue it in place on its dowel. Fashion a handle for the end of the pusher dowel, and the flipper is ready to run.

Brainstorm with your child for ideas for targets and obstacles in a pinball game. Shapes salvaged from the bandsaw scrap box can provide imaginative bumpers and catches for the marble. Create ramps to jump a marble shot to the top of the board or drill a target hole in a raised block. Make a maze of upright dowels. Stretch rubber bands between dowels stuck in the board to add extra bounce. Rig a ball-ejector system for marbles that land in holes with springs, or make a ball-return ramp under the board. Many of the tricks of marble rolls work well for pinball games, too.

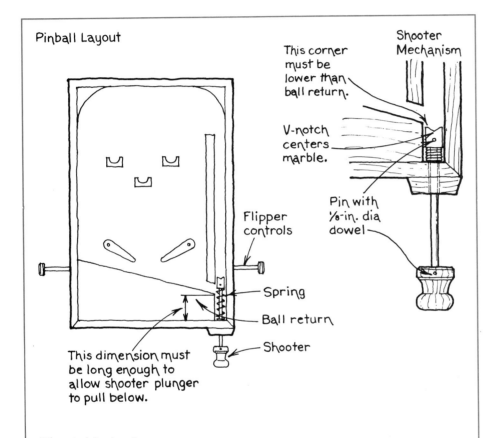

Pinball Layout

Shooter Mechanism

This corner must be lower than ball return.

V-notch centers marble.

Pin with 1/8-in. dia dowel

Flipper controls

Spring

Ball return

Shooter

This dimension must be long enough to allow shooter plunger to pull below.

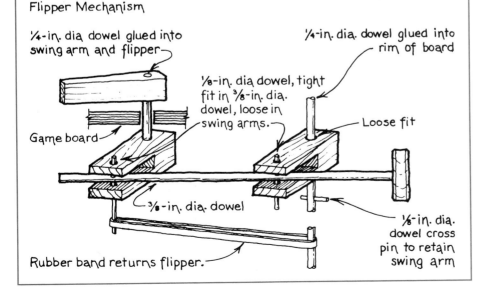

Flipper Mechanism

1/4-in. dia dowel glued into swing arm and flipper

1/4-in. dia. dowel glued into rim of board

1/8-in. dia dowel, tight fit in 3/8-in. dia. dowel, loose in swing arms.

Game board

Loose fit

3/8-in. dia. dowel

1/8-in. dia. dowel cross pin to retain swing arm

Rubber band returns flipper.

Gallery

Chapter 14

To give you an idea of what can happen when kids' ideas are given free rein, here's a selection of popular projects, including several unusual ones.

Our dollhouses are built like real houses; the studs are made of sticks, and the thin flooring and paneling are ripped from ¾-in. pine. We rip shingles from butternut for contrasting color.

Joy Clendenning, below, spent her entire middle-school shop career working on her enormous house with its mansard roof. It has interior walls and even a staircase.

The top of eighth-grader Jay Sailor's drafting table can be adjusted to different angles, and the height of the whole table can be adjusted, too. The halves of the table are held together by a removable wedge through the tenon; the locking mechanisms are tightened with 1-in. wooden screws. This table took Jay a full school year to build.

Eighth-grader Jeannie Perin's butternut lazy Susan spins on the dowel that fits under the peak of the arch. Jeannie cut the spiral on the dowel with a file while holding the work between the centers of the lathe.

The fishing-rod rack at far left was made by Tom Boswell, a sixth-grader. The horizontal pieces are dadoed into the sides, and the arched brace is rabbeted to fit a notch in the sides. Carved depressions in the bottom receive the rod handles.

Jon Runstadler made the trash can at left in eighth grade. It's coopered like a barrel; the stave edges are beveled on an upside-down plane (p. 57) fitted with an angled fence. Band clamps held the parts together during gluing.

Marble rolls take a good deal of imagination and engineering, but they're great fun. This one, built by Peter Ghirardini in seventh grade, is supported by four ½-in. dowels that are mounted in an *H*-shaped base. The base is leveled with ½-in. wooden screws in each corner. Peter made the ramps, which are glued and doweled to the uprights, by gluing together three strips of wood, ⅜ in. thick by ¾ in. wide. To cut the pieces for the curve, he used a miter box.

Michael Cohen made his Shaker step stool in eighth grade. The top is rabbeted at the front and mortised to allow the post to pass through. He shaved the rung from green wood (as in Chapter 12). It's tenoned and wedged through the front and back boards.

Susan Reeves, far left, a sixth-grader, carved a frog sitting on his toadstool and then hung pieces of wood from it to make wind chimes. Each of the chimes is made of a different wood and they are all of different lengths.

This flared, octagonal rosewood box, near left, was made by Molly Hanlon in sixth grade. Molly put a wedge between the wood and the back of the miter box to saw the compound-angled miters.

Young kids can make boats simply by sawing out a boatlike shape and sticking a dowel in it for a mast. Older kids can do much more, carving the hull from a block made of four or five ¾-in. pine boards glued together. Some kids hollow out their hull, using a cradle to hold the boat steady, as demonstrated by seventh-grader Jeremy Biesanz at right. Boats can get pretty sophisticated, like the almost-finished boat at far right, made by eighth-grader Stefan Richter.

Sixth-grader Scott King's paddle-wheel steamer rolls along the floor on its wheels; as they turn, the horizontal walking beam moves up and down, just as it did on the old steam engines.

Guitars take at least a full year to make and require patience and dexterity. Our instruments have solid sides, sawn out of stacked blocks of wood, instead of bent sides—a simplification that makes it possible for middle-school kids to make them. The sides are glued to a neck block and a tail block, and clamped using the waste pieces from the sides as clamping pads, as shown at right.

Seventh-grader Peter Ingram glued the back on his large, four-string ukulele, using threaded wooden clamps made from ½-in. dowel and two wooden nuts. Then he planed the back to a thickness of less than ⅛ in. (He planed the inside of the back before gluing.) The spruce soundboard is braced on the inside, then glued and planed the same way.

The notches in the fingerboard for frets are set out with a guitar-maker's ruler. Then the notches are cut and the fingerboard is glued to the neck. Its edges are trimmed flush to the neck with a spokeshave and the frets are hammered into place, as Peter is doing at right.

Here's a finished guitar, held by its maker, Darby Garrity, a seventh-grader.

Eighth-grader Emily Kucer took two years to make her elegant, cherry music stand. The height and the angle of the rest are adjustable and are locked by wooden screws.

Sixth-grader Cathy Greer, below, assembled her footstool with ½-in. dowels, after I cut out the parts on the bandsaw. For the dowels that go into end grain, glue was enough to hold them tight; for the dowels that pass through the face of the board, the end of each one was sawn and wedged for extra holding power.

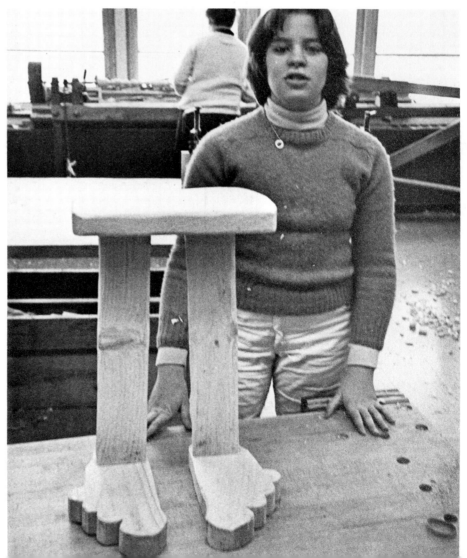

Darby Yacos made her two cherry boxes in eighth grade. To make the little drawer for Thing I, far right, she bored a hole through the board, then cut out the piece with a coping saw. Thing II, right, looks like it was turned on a lathe, but it was actually planed round. Darby bored a hole through the center and sawed the piece in two on a miter box. The cylinder ends are plugged with walnut; the lid is located by two dowels.

Jeffi Pattison made her clogs in seventh grade. She traced the outline of her foot, and I bandsawed the shape of the sole from 2-in. hardwood. Jeffi carved the soles to fit her heel, big toe and arch, then she scraped and sanded them smooth. The upper pieces are cut from leather; I nailed each one to the sole while Jeffi stood on the table with her foot in the clog.

Carol Hurd's marble maze, right, built in sixth grade, balances on a dowel fixed to the center of the bottom. Tipping the maze guides the marble past and around the holes.

Tools & Techniques

The Workshop

I've worked wood with kids in lots of different spaces: pushing a workbench from room to room, in a playroom set up as a shop, in a tiny *L*-shaped room with almost more bench space than floor space, and finally, in the spacious shop at the Richmond School. You can make any room work for you and your kids.

For young kids and simple projects, you need a workbench, or at least a stout table. Many nursery and early-grade classrooms have workbenches that are ideal for little kids—2 ft. high and built of solid maple. If you have one of these, tighten all the bolts to make sure it's solid. If you can cut down a sturdy table, that will do fine. Little kids can work at higher benches by standing on a block or climbing right up on the benchtop. A clamp-on vise can turn almost any table into a workbench; the Stanley vise below is a good one.

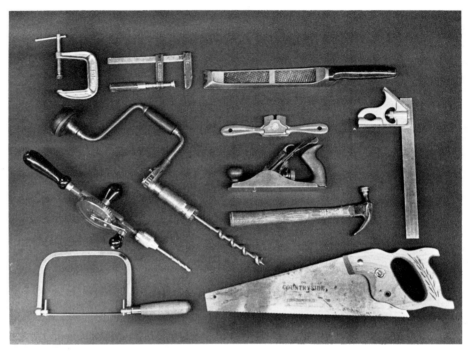

Older kids need a bench about 30 in. high; my design for one is included on p. 195. Even if you don't intend to build the bench, read the section for the notes on what makes a bench efficient.

A basic tool kit for little kids is shown in the photo, above right. In the top left-hand corner are two kinds of clamps: a *C*-clamp and a quick-set clamp. Below them is a brace and bit for boring large holes, and an eggbeater drill for small ones. A coping saw for cutting curved shapes is at lower left.

In the top right-hand corner is a Surform, which is useful for smoothing and shaping. It works like a file, but is easier to use. The spokeshave and the plane (below the Surform) are optional; they require sharpening, which means you would need a grinder and sharpening stones or a cloth wheel (p. 181). If you can keep these edge tools sharp, little kids can use them. If not, the Surform will do.

At right in the photo is a combination square, which can be used as a ruler or to mark out lines at right angles to an edge (as used in making the box in Chapter 4). The small Disston Countryside crosscut saw (its blade is about 18 in. long), is handy for kids; it's a real saw, not a toy. These can be special-ordered at hardware stores. In a pinch, a full-size saw will do. Also, get a small hammer (with a handle 8 in. or 10 in. long) and a bottle of white glue.

We use some specialized tools to make the more grown-up projects in the book. Some of them, such as the hollow auger and tongue-and-groove plane, are no longer in production. You may be able to find these (and more common tools at bargain prices) at flea markets or junk stores. If not, old-tool dealers should be able to locate them for you. The following sections about tools tell you what to look for in an old tool, and how to renovate it.

If you have sharp handsaws, you can get by without most power tools. I use a radial arm saw and a bandsaw to save kids the tedium of sawing wood to size or shape (which also takes considerable skill to do by hand). The radial arm saw is ideal for crosscutting wood to length. The bandsaw is useful for cutting shapes, such as round stool tops, odd-shaped signs and so on. It is also good for making two thin boards from one thick board (called resawing), as is done in making the little mitered box in Chapter 7. Bandsaws are designated by the size of the wheels on which the continuous blade runs; a 10-in. bandsaw, the smallest available, has 10-in. wheels. You probably won't need a bandsaw larger than 14 in.

If you want to buy just one power tool, I think the bandsaw is the most versatile. You can crosscut with it as well as rip (cut along the grain). And though a portable, electric circular saw or a handsaw can replace a radial arm saw for crosscutting, it is difficult to find replacement tools as versatile and convenient as the bandsaw. The proper and safe use of these power tools is beyond the scope of this book; there are many books on the subject and each tool comes with an owner's manual.

Wood—you can't woodwork without it. Little kids can make almost any small project from scrap wood. Lumberyards, sawmills, cabinet shops or your local school shop are usually pleased to give away softwood scrap. For advanced work, you'll have to purchase wood. To save money, I buy large quantities of wood each year directly from a sawmill. All our ¾-in. pine is kiln-dried, which means its moisture is removed in an oven under controlled conditions; its faces and edges are planed smooth on a power planer. I buy our 2-in. pine and various hardwoods rough (unplaned) and air-dried. For drawer bottoms, game boards and other odd jobs, I buy the cheapest ¼-in. plywood I can find.

I suggest using an ordinary white glue like Elmer's, which I buy by the gallon and distribute in the little squeeze bottles sold for mustard. White glue is very strong. It dries within an hour, which is convenient, but doesn't stick quickly, so kids can take their time when assembling their work. Unlike yellow glue, it mops up easily with a wet cloth or paper towel. Best of all, it is quite inexpensive compared to other glues.

The 1½-in. finishing nail is the standard nail in my shop. I buy a 50-lb. box of them, which lasts us several years. I purchase smaller quantities of other nails, brads and screws as they are needed. Dowels can be bought singly, by the dozen, or in larger bundles at a considerable saving.

Crosscut Saw

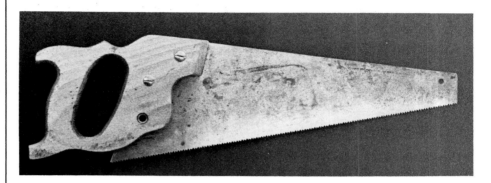

Given enough time and energy, even a very young child can saw through a piece of wood. The saw will usually follow the line if it is started accurately. Once the saw is seated in the sawcut, it's unlikely to cause the child injury. Careful kids, about seven years old or younger, can learn to start a saw safely, but an adult should start the saw for a child who is a beginning woodworker. Once the child is accustomed to the feel of the saw, he or she can learn some of the finer skills.

A crosscut saw, photo above, will cut across or with the grain of a board. Ripsaws, which we hardly ever use in the school shop, are designed for rapid cutting with the grain; they're unsuitable for cutting across the grain. Look for a crosscut saw that has eight or ten teeth per inch (an 8-point or 10-point saw). Standard 24-in. or 26-in. saws are fine, but shorter saws, 16 in. to 20 in., are better for small children to use.

Sharp saws are the easiest and safest to use. Saws that are worn or bent are difficult to push, require an excess of downward pressure and may wander off the line. For children especially, a sharp tool is a safe tool and one that will minimize frustration: take the time to keep your saws in good shape. To have a saw sharpened by a professional sharpener is inexpensive, and most sharpeners are able to recondition an old saw to perform like new. In busy shops, it pays to keep extra saws and rotate them for sharpening.

The simplest cut to make is at right angles to the edge of a board and perpendicular to its face, as shown in the drawing. Some cuts, like a miter, are perpendicular to one surface but not the other; a compound cut isn't perpendicular to either surface. Draw lines for all cuts on the face and edge of the board; these lines are essential for starting the saw correctly.

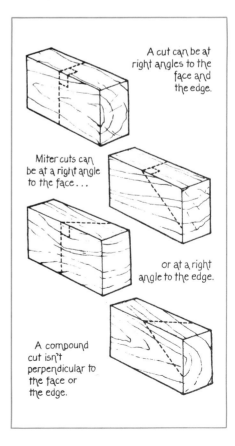

A cut can be at right angles to the face and the edge.

Miter cuts can be at a right angle to the face...

or at a right angle to the edge.

A compound cut isn't perpendicular to the face or the edge.

Hold the wood in a vise when sawing. Place the cut line close to the jaws to keep the wood from flexing; even a little movement can cause the saw to chatter. It's easier to saw straight up and down; even if the face is to be cut at an angle to the edge, chuck the board in the vise so the cut will be vertical (p. 11).

Starting—With the board in the vise, position yourself to start the cut. Stand so that your line of sight is in the plane of the sawcut. (Close one eye and focus on the lines on the face and edge of the board; when these lines appear as a single, straight line, you are standing in the right place.)

Teeth on a saw are set alternately left and right, so the sawcut (called the kerf) is slightly wider than the sawblade, and the saw is easier to push through the wood. The kerf must be in the part of the wood that you don't want to use. If it isn't, your piece will be one kerf width too short, so place the saw next to the line and in the waste wood. Remember that lines have thickness, too.

If you hold the saw with your right hand, rest the saw firmly against your left thumb and at a 45° angle to the edge, as shown in the photo at left. Pull the saw slowly backward across the arris (the corner formed where two surfaces meet) to make a shallow notch. Do this three or four times to deepen the notch, lifting the saw on the forward stroke so it doesn't cut. Now start sawing gently on the forward stroke.

Maintain the 45° angle so you make as much progress across the edge as down the face. Make sure that you are following both lines and that the kerf stays on the waste side of the lines. Once the cut crosses the edge of the board, saw a bit faster and bring the saw closer to the horizontal. If the saw is dead perpendicular to the face of the board, however, it may chatter. The further you cut, the harder it is to alter the path of the cut. After an inch or two, it is usually safe to hand the saw over to the child to finish the cut.

Tell kids: "No hands on the wood while you're sawing, except when starting or finishing a cut." If the wood needs support, the vise isn't tight enough or the line is too far from the jaws. Kids who rest a hand on the wood while sawing are asking for an accident.

Encourage kids to take long strokes, using most of the saw's length. They can keep both hands on the handle, as kindergartener Rebecca Schlosser does below, if that's most comfortable. Saw slowly and easily; frantic movements can cause the saw to jump out of the kerf and cause an accident.

Don't push down hard on the saw: this makes it harder to push on its forward cutting stroke. A sharp saw should cut well by its own weight and just a little help.

A sawcut that has gone off the line was either started in the wrong direction (the kerf will be straight) or cut with a damaged saw (the kerf will be curved). It's almost impossible to steer a crosscut saw; to correct a wandering kerf, move back up near the top of the kerf and restart the cut in the right direction.

At the end of a cut, the weight of the waste piece can break a splinter off the good piece. Support the waste with your hand at the end of the cut; don't pull up on the waste or you'll pinch the saw.

Sometimes the saw kerf will widen or close as you saw, due to the release of tension in the wood. If a closing kerf pinches the saw, drive a screwdriver or small wooden wedge into the kerf to keep it open.

Check the wood carefully for nails or screws and make sure the metal parts of the vise are out of the saw's path. Sawing metal will ruin sawteeth; they'll require recutting and resharpening.

Coping Saw

A coping saw is designed for cutting tight curves. The blades are thin with lots of teeth (about fifteen per inch) and so fine that they would buckle if they weren't held in tension by the springy frame. The blades are cheap; you don't sharpen them, you just buy new ones. Coping saws come in handy for lots of odd jobs around the shop.

Coping-saw blades should be installed with the teeth pointing toward the handle, as shown in the photo above, so that the power of the stroke is transmitted directly from the handle to the blade. Installing the blade the other way makes the saw chatter, because the power is transmitted through the springy frame; this can cause the blade to jump out of the saw.

To replace the blade, you must hold the pin on the blade holder at the handle end of the saw and unscrew the handle to release the tension. Now insert the pins of the new blade in the notched blade holders, one at each end of the frame, and tighten the handle until it locks the blade holder against the fence. Make sure that the holders are adjusted so the blade is not twisted.

Here's a quick way to replace the blade. Clamp the far end of the frame in a vise, push on the handle to squeeze the ends of the frame together, then drop the blade in place and slowly relax the pressure on the handle.

Coping-saw blades can practically cut through a right-angle turn if worked properly, though they will break or bend if forced. The trick is to steer the saw on the pull stroke; don't try to twist a stationary blade. To cut a right-angle turn, saw in place while rotating the blade a bit on each stroke.

The sawblade should be held perpendicular to the face of the wood. Tell children, "Point the saw right at the wood, not up or down, or left or right," and demonstrate. Explain that "the cut in the back needs to keep up with the cut in the front." If the saw goes off sideways, and the child tries to twist the blade straight, it will break.

A coping-saw blade can be rotated with respect to the frame to allow the frame to clear obstacles (p. 4). Hold the pin and unscrew the handle a couple of turns. Turn both pins, making sure they both point in the same direction so the blade isn't twisted. When the frame is in the correct position relative to the blade, tighten the handle.

Miter Boxes

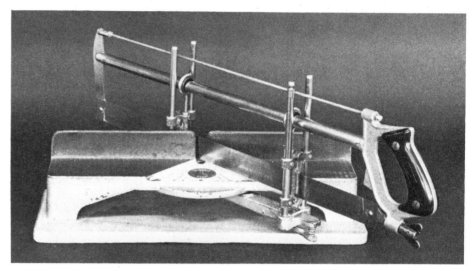

Manufactured miter boxes are expensive, but maintain their accuracy even under heavy use. Most can be locked at the angles necessary to make hexagons, octagons and squares, as well as at a precise 90°. Some models can be locked at other positions as well.

Miter boxes come in a variety of styles. The most common American miter box, photo above, uses a large backsaw held in guides. I've used a European miter box, photo right, for years; it has a special saw whose blade is made stiff by tensioning. I prefer to use this miter box with kids because it's safe. The blade has stops at both ends, so it can't be pulled out of the guide frame. The blades are inexpensive and are easy to replace, too; I keep half a dozen on hand in my shop and send them regularly to the saw sharpener.

A Miter Box

You can easily make a simple wooden miter box to use with a regular backsaw. Fasten three boards together with nails or screws and glue. The side boards should be wide enough so that the back of the saw will rest on top of them and stop the cut about 1/8 in. into the bottom board.

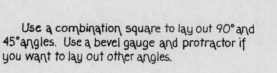

Use a combination square to lay out 90° and 45° angles. Use a bevel gauge and protractor if you want to lay out other angles.

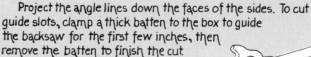

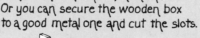

Project the angle lines down the faces of the sides. To cut guide slots, clamp a thick batten to the box to guide the backsaw for the first few inches, then remove the batten to finish the cut. Or you can secure the wooden box to a good metal one and cut the slots.

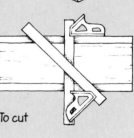

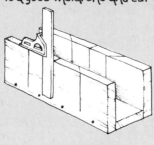

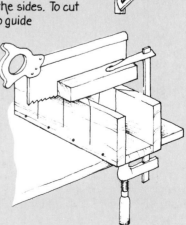

Eggbeater Drills

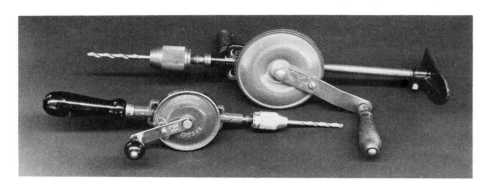

The two drills shown in the photo above are called eggbeater drills in my shop. This name makes it easier for kids to understand how the drill works. Eggbeater drills (the hand-driven predecessors of electric hand drills) use gears to speed up the hand's motion.

Eggbeater drills come in two basic sizes. Smaller drills are between 10 in. and 14 in. long and accept bits with shanks up to ⅜ in. The larger, 16-in. to 24-in. drills (which are called breast drills in most tool catalogs) accept shanks up to ½ in. Some models of both styles have two gears, so they can turn at high or low speeds. The larger drills have longer cranks, give more leverage and are best to use to bore large holes. (Using the slower gear on the smaller drill produces much the same result.)

Good, new eggbeater drills cost more than electric drills these days; cheap ones are usually stiff and frustrating to use. Look for a used one at flea markets; make sure all three jaws are positioned evenly inside the chuck, and the handles are intact. If the drill has two sets of teeth on the larger gear, it will have two speeds. (You may have to puzzle out how to change from one to the other.) An eggbeater drill should turn freely and easily; keep the bearings well-oiled and lightly oil the gear teeth.

Twist bits are used in eggbeater drills; the type common in hardware stores is designed for boring holes in metal, but is effective in wood, too. You need to dimple the wood so the bit won't wander as it's started, and the bit may tear the wood around the lip of a hole in softwood. Brad-point twist bits, which have a central point for easier starting and spurs for cleaner cutting, cost a little more and usually must be ordered from woodworking supply houses.

Kids in my shop most often use the ⅛-in. and ¼-in. bits because these are the sizes of the dowels I stock. I keep twist bits ranging from 1/16 in. to ⅜ in.; for anything larger, we use auger bits chucked in a brace.

Twist bits are made of hardened tool steel and retain their edges quite well. The smaller sizes are often lost or broken before they need sharpening; fortunately, they're inexpensive. Larger sizes are worth sharpening regularly, but this can be tricky: if not sharpened exactly right, the hole that the bit cuts could be oversized or oval. To sharpen twist bits, I use the Eclipse 39, shown in the photo, upper right. This little gadget uses sandpaper as an abrasive.

When using an eggbeater drill, make sure the chuck is tight on the bit; line the crank up with the frame of the drill, hold the crank and frame in one hand and tighten the chuck with the other. Adults will probably have to do this for little kids. To bore vertically into a piece of wood, place one hand near the top of the handle and the other on the crank. When boring horizontally, put one hand on the little knob opposite the crank, the other hand on the crank, and rest the handle against your body. Usually, the

handles of the breast drills are fitted with a curved saddle to lean against.

Sharp twist bits work best when turned quickly. But kids usually press too hard, and the bit takes too big a bite and stops dead. Tell the child to press lightly and to turn the crank quickly.

Brace and Bit

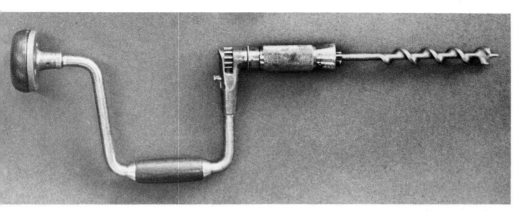

The brace is a crank with a chuck on one end and a pad-like head on the other. The chuck will hold most bits with a four-sided, tapered tang: auger bits (as shown in the photo), dowel pointers, hollow augers and even screwdrivers. These are all tools designed for slow speeds and high torque, which is a measurement of twisting power. Some two-jaw chucks on older braces will hold the round shaft of a twist bit, but not as securely as will an eggbeater drill's three-jaw chuck.

The brace is a powerful tool. It is direct drive, unlike the eggbeater drill, which uses gears to increase speed but reduces power. The power of a brace varies with its sweep, which is measured by the diameter of the circle in which the handle travels around the bit. I prefer braces with large sweeps because they make it easier for kids to bore holes 1 in. in diameter or larger. Sadly, modern braces only have 8-in. or 12-in. sweeps; some old ones have 14-in. sweeps, but these are almost impossible to find on the antique-tool market.

Bargain-bin braces are poorly made, and new ones cost an arm and a leg. Fine old braces, however, are quite common at flea markets; when considering one, see that the chuck opens and closes properly and that the crank handle and head turn freely. Squint at it, end on, to make sure the chuck is not twisted out of line with the head.

Modern braces come with a ratchet mechanism, though this is not an essential feature. The ratchet allows the bit to be driven without turning the handle in a complete revolution—handy for working in tight corners where only a portion of the sweep is possible.

An auger bit for a brace will have a little, tapered screw at its tip. This screw draws the bit through the wood, so that a properly sharpened auger bit requires very little downward pressure, except when starting. Most auger bits have two pairs of cutting edges. The spurs scribe a circle while severing the cross-grained fibers; the cutters follow, lifting wood out from within the circle. The spiral body draws chips up out of the hole and helps keep the bit straight.

Auger bits are available in diameters from ¼ in. to 1½ in.; the number stamped on the tang is the size in sixteenths of an inch. (A No. 12 auger has a ¾-in. diameter.) In my shop, we bore holes measuring ⅜ in. or more with auger bits; I've given up on ¼-in. augers because they are easily damaged and difficult to sharpen. Use twist bits for these small holes.

An auger bit will make a clean entrance hole, especially when boring at right angles to the wood, but it will tear the wood badly if allowed to burst out the far side of the hole. To prevent this, bore until the lead screw protrudes through the wood, then use that small

hole to center the bit and bore in from the other side. This counterboring takes extra pressure because the lead screw has nothing to bite into, but the cut is soon completed.

Another way to prevent a torn exit hole is to bore through the work into scrap. Perfect contact is needed between the underside of the stock and the top of the scrap. Clamp both pieces to the workbench with two clamps near the hole. Use a depth gauge to avoid boring through both pieces into the benchtop. Or clamp brightly colored paper between the two and stop boring when paper shavings appear. Boring from harder wood to softer may cause the lead screw to lose its bite, so extra pressure may be needed if you do this.

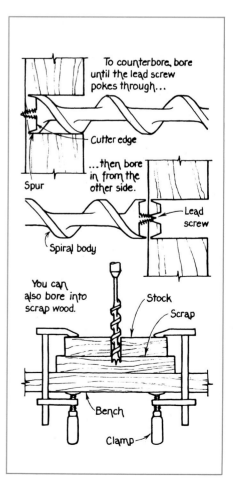

To counterbore, bore until the lead screw pokes through...

Cutter edge

Spur

...then bore in from the other side.

Lead screw

Spiral body

You can also bore into scrap wood.

Stock

Scrap

Bench

Clamp

You can wrap a masking-tape flag around the bit as a simple depth gauge, but the tape will wear out if you're boring a series of holes. Commercially made depth gauges are clamped to the shaft, and a flexible spring, which won't mar the wood, is set to the desired depth. (In the photo at right, a gauge is fixed to an expansion bit.)

The expansion bit, an adjustable variation of an auger bit, is a handy tool to have around. It will bore odd-sized holes or fill in if you don't have the standard bit that you need. Expansion bits come in two sizes: the smaller adjusts between ⅝ in. and 1¾ in., the larger between ⅞ in. and 3 in.

Unfortunately, expansion bits are awkward to use; having only one spur and cutter, the bit is unbalanced as it cuts, making it difficult to bore a straight hole. An expansion bit will stick in deep holes because there is no spiral shaft to clear the shavings. In hardwoods, the spur must be filed shorter or it will bend outward, increasing the size of the hole. And make sure the lock is tightened securely; the stress of boring in hardwood often causes these bits to lose their adjustment.

To set the expansion bit, estimate the size of the hole with the adjustment scale on the bit, but bore a test hole in scrap wood to be precise. Expansion bits won't counterbore; the screw loses its center before all the waste is removed. To bore through, always use a backing of scrap wood.

Here are a few hints for using a brace and bit:

Start the bit slowly, with enough pressure to seat the lead screw in the wood. Once started, steer the bit true; wiggling the head of the brace will enlarge the top of the hole and is likely to cause the screw to lose its grip in the wood. If this happens, press hard on the bit until the screw catches again. If it happens repeatedly, the bit probably needs sharpening.

Children may have trouble keeping one hand stationary on the head of the brace while the other hand turns the crank. Young kids may move both hands in a motion similar to pedaling a bicycle. You can help by holding the top hand steady; you can also help steer the bit in this way, especially when boring at an angle.

To supply extra pressure, put your hand under the child's hand on the head of the brace, but remember that the child must always have a hand at the top. If the child isn't strong enough to turn the brace alone, another child can help; but both of them have to keep a hand at the top, as second-graders Jessica Salvatoriello and Ben Foss are doing below. This counterbalances the force of each child turning the brace.

Extra steadiness and pressure can also be had by leaning the forehead against the hand at the top of the brace. A more powerful way, which is also more comfortable, is for the child to lean his or her shoulder against the hand—not as awkward as it sounds.

Accurate boring is easier if the bit is held vertically, at right angles to the work, but the brace can also be used horizontally. If boring horizontally, lean the body against the hand at the head of the brace for extra pressure and steadiness. Professionals sometimes don't hold the head, using the free hand to steady the work. Only calm, well-coordinated children should be allowed to do this. I usually have young children bore holes in the vertical position because they have trouble starting the bit horizontally.

Sharpening auger bits—New auger bits cut well across the grain in softwoods, but they need modification to cut efficiently in hardwoods or end grain. All bits need attention after heavy use or damage. Sharpening an auger bit is tricky business, requiring care, practice and an understanding of the way the bit works. It pays to practice on old bits until you get the knack.

In sound wood, a sharp auger will produce a pair of long, spiral shavings as it cuts. Fuzzy, short chips are a sign of a dull bit. A badly worn auger won't cut unless pushed very hard: the lead screw loses its bite and the bit turns easily without cutting.

When a bit won't cut, first check the lead screw to see if it is clogged with pulverized wood. Clean the threads with the point of a knife, then examine them for damage. Chase damaged sections with a very fine, V-shaped jeweler's file, removing as little metal as possible. Make sure that the end of the screw nearest the cutters isn't jammed; if blocked, the whole screw will clog up with wood.

Next, check the spurs. Their edges should be sharp and free of nicks. A sharp edge will be invisible; light will reflect off a blunt edge. Sharpen the bevel on the inside of the spurs with a flat auger-bit file or a small, triangular file. Don't file on the outside of the spurs except to lightly brush away the burrs that result from filing the inside.

To sharpen the cutters, poke the point of the bit into a piece of scrap and tip it until the bevel of the cutter is almost horizontal. File the entire length of the bevel (from the edge back), keeping the bevel at the same angle. Don't file the flat surface of the cutter, except to remove the burr.

After a number of sharpenings, I use a coarse file to reduce the angle of the cutter bevels to about 20°, then I sharpen just the leading edge at a 30° angle. This double bevel makes touch-up filing much easier: there's less metal to remove on the short bevel.

Take care to file the same amount of metal off both cutters. Imbalanced cutters cut poorly, if at all. Check the balance by boring, absolutely vertically, into a piece of scrap. Observe the thickness of shaving made by each

cutter. If one shaving is thicker, file the bevel of that cutter slightly. Repeat until the shavings are the same thickness.

Most new auger bits are designed to cut softwood. The spurs are too long and thick to penetrate hardwood without extra force; they may cause the lead screw to lose its bite. Such auger bits will work better in hardwood if you file down the inside of the spurs. In addition to reducing the thickness of the spurs, filing will make them shorter, but the spurs need only protrude beyond the cutter slightly more than the thickness of a shaving. Judge this by trial and error, and try to keep the length of the spurs equal. A bit tuned for hardwood will also work well in softwood.

There are no horizontal fibers to sever when boring in end grain, so spurs aren't needed. In fact, they add extra drag to the bit, causing the lead screw to lose its bite, which is weak in end grain, anyway. Remove the spurs and the auger bit will chew its way right through end grain. This is a good way to recycle bits with badly damaged spurs. I hide my end-grain bits so that they aren't used by mistake; they can tear an awful mess in cross grain.

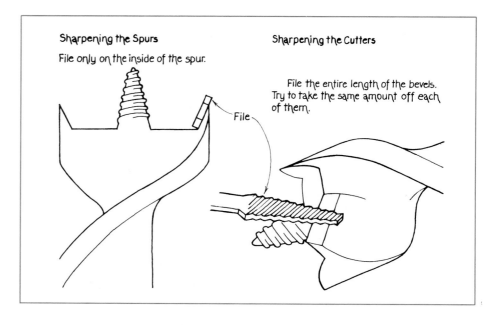

Sharpening the Spurs

File only on the inside of the spur.

Sharpening the Cutters

File the entire length of the bevels. Try to take the same amount off each of them.

File

Hollow Augers

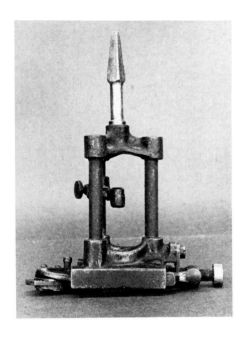

We use a hollow auger to make tenons on the legs and stretchers of stools, benches and chairs. I've explained how to use the tool in Chapter 12, so here I'll tell you specifically what to look for when purchasing one and how to maintain it. Hollow augers have not been manufactured since about 1920, but can usually be found at flea markets.

A hollow auger consists of a cutting blade (or blades), positioned in front of a throat that is sized to fit the tenon. (The photos above show a side view and a bottom view of an adjustable auger.) In all hollow augers, the blade or blades approach the wood at right angles to the tenon to cut a square, rather than a tapered, shoulder.

The throat can be either a fixed size or adjustable. The fixed-size models can cut tenons of only one size. The throats of most adjustable hollow augers are formed by a pair of V-shaped guides that may be moved apart or together to make tenons ¼ in. to 1¼ in. in diameter. (There is also a dial-type auger, which has a rotating plate with holes of different sizes, much like a wall-mounted pencil sharpener.)

I keep both fixed-size and adjustable hollow augers in my shop. (The photo below shows, from left to right, an A.A. Woods adjustable hollow auger, another adjustable auger, a dial-type auger, a fixed-size auger and a dowel pointer.) The versatility allowed by the adjustable size is invaluable, but these hollow augers take time to set accurately; a properly tuned, fixed-size hollow auger can be used right off the shelf.

Fixed-size hollow augers usually have two blades; before buying one, be sure that both blades are present or can be replaced easily. (Some blades have slots down the center, which make them more difficult to reproduce.) When considering an adjustable hollow auger, make sure that it has all its parts and that nothing is broken. This may take a bit of imagination if you're not familiar with the tool, but faults are usually obvious. On the other hand, sometimes moving parts are rusted or frozen, but they can be cleaned up and freed if not too far gone.

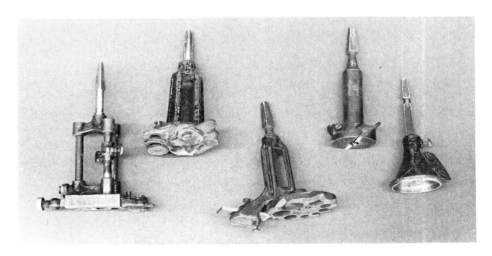

By far the best adjustable hollow augers were made by A.A. Woods and Sons. They're solid, beautifully made and easy to adjust. If you find one, it's worth paying a little extra for it.

Most fixed-size and adjustable hollow augers have a square, tapered tang that fits the two-jaw chuck of a brace; some have only a round shank for use in the chuck of a lathe. It takes a fair amount of power to turn a hollow auger, and round shanks will slip in a two-jaw chuck. Favor augers with square, tapered tangs; if you find a round-shanked one in nice shape, buy it anyway. The shank can be unscrewed and replaced with one from a junk tool having a square, tapered tang. Another option would be to cut the tang shank off an old auger bit and have it threaded to fit the hollow auger. I have had several shanks with square tangs made by a machinist from scratch for a reasonable price. You may come across hollow augers, permanently fixed to braces, and these are also worth having.

Many old hollow augers need a great deal of work to get them in shape, and even the superb A.A. Woods tools need a little attention. Some don't have enough room between the blade and the metal under it for chips to escape. If your tool jams, remove the blade and use a file to open up the chip escapement. Look for the point at which shavings seem most confined, and start widening the passage there. Keep testing the tool and removing more metal until chips escape freely.

Hollow augers that have seen a great deal of use often have worn, tapered throats. If your hollow auger becomes more difficult to turn as it moves along the tenon, the narrower part may be binding on the wood. To repair such a throat in a fixed-size hollow auger, you must bore the end of the throat to the same size as the opening—usually a job for a machinist, though you may be able to do it with a file. Take off as little metal as possible and hope that, by allowing

the blade to protrude a little more, you can still cut a tenon that matches your auger bit.

It's easier to recondition the throats of adjustable hollow augers. Wrap some 100-grit sandpaper around a dowel, holding it in place with a rubber band. Remove the blade from the tool, then adjust the throat to fit snugly on the dowel. Fix the dowel horizontally in the vise, mount the hollow auger in a brace and turn it on the dowel. Keep adjusting the throat to smaller sizes until the sandpaper takes metal off at the opening as well as the back of the throat. Be sure to hold the brace true to the dowel and not to wobble it as you turn. Do this with three or four different-sized dowels that correspond to the tenon sizes that you use regularly.

The leading corner of the blade must protrude slightly into the throat. If it doesn't protrude enough, the tenon will be slightly too large and will bind in the throat, making the tool difficult to turn. A blade protruding too far will cut an undersized, crooked tenon because the throat will fit too loosely to follow the tenon accurately.

Between these two extremes, there's a range of adjustment that allows you to make small changes in the diameter of the tenon for an easy or tight fit in the mortise. On adjustable hollow augers, such minor changes are more easily made by varying the size of the throat, but subtle adjustments of the blade are very useful on fixed-size hollow augers.

Some hollow augers have bevel-up cutters and an adjustment for the blade's angle of attack; others work with the bevel down and have no adjustment mechanism. In both cases, there should be about 10° of clearance between the cutter and the wood. If you can't adjust the angle, grind the bevel to get the correct clearance. With too much clearance, the tool will bite too deeply into the wood; with too little, it will take a thin shaving or no cut at all.

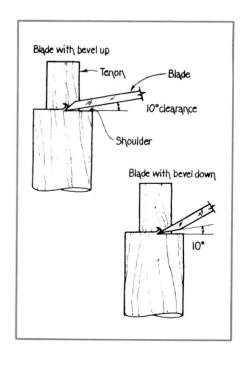

Trysquare

A trysquare, at center in the photo above, is used to mark out lines at right angles to the board edge. Its important parts are the blade and the stock. (In the photo, the blades are marked with measurements.) The combination or sliding square is a variation: its blade is adjustable in length and can be used to lay out 45° angles.

When children learn to use a trysquare, they are also learning what a right angle is—a difficult concept for most children to grasp. To teach a child to use the square, I say, "It's important that the line is straight across the board, not crooked, like this," and I tip the square one way, then the other. I point to the stock and add, "Squeeze this part of the square tight against the edge of the board." The child learns what a right angle is by experiencing what it is not.

When you lay out measurements along the length of a board, scribe the marks on the arris (where the face meets the edge), not in from the edge. To make a line across the board, slide the stock of the trysquare along the edge of the board until the mark appears against one edge of the blade; the blade's inside edge will usually be the most accurate.

When working with kids, I use a pencil to draw the line, though many craftsmen prefer to scribe the line with a knife. Hold the pencil against the blade as you slide it up to the mark; stop when the mark is under the pencil point rather than against the blade. Use a sharp pencil and keep the point as close to the blade as possible.

Bench Planes

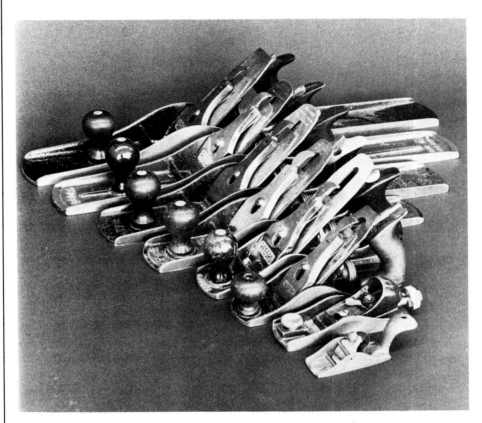

I keep a variety of bench planes in my shop. Bench planes come in sizes from about 7 in. to 24 in. and they can be used for many jobs—from reducing the thickness of a board to flattening and smoothing. You can tune and set a bench plane to take very fine shavings from fussy-grained wood or to hog off huge amounts of wood all at once. You can get along with one or two bench planes in a beginner's shop if you retune them for each different use. As your needs grow, you'll want to have more. You can use the following brief description as a guide.

The 7-in. smooth plane (No. 2 in the catalogs) is an ideal size for young hands. Tuned for medium to fine work, it is good for use on small projects (like planing the sides of the small boxes in Chapter 7). The No. 2 is hard to find, but an 8-in. smooth plane (No. 3) is a good substitute.

I keep several 9¾-in. smooth planes (No. 4) tuned for fine, medium and coarse work. These are general-purpose planes used for lots of different things.

The 14-in. jack plane (No. 5) is useful for planing surfaces almost flat. Our two No. 5's are tuned for coarse work. After a board has been roughed-out with a jack plane, we use an 18-in. fore plane (No. 6), tuned for fine work, to smooth and flatten the rough surface.

Cabinetmakers use the 22-in. jointer plane (No. 7) to prepare edges for gluing, but I keep ours set coarse so it can be used to rough-out large surfaces; then the surfaces are smoothed with the fore plane.

We use a 24-in. jointer plane (No. 8) to plane the edges of boards that are to be glued together. It's tuned to take a very fine shaving and is kept on a high shelf so that kids won't take it unless they actually need it.

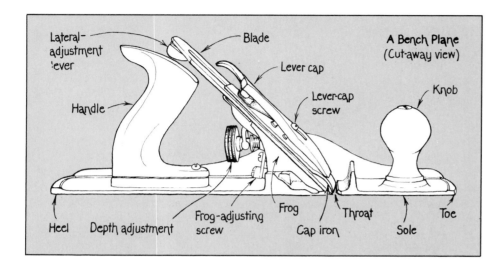

Lateral-adjustment lever
Blade
A Bench Plane (Cut-away view)
Lever cap
Lever-cap screw
Handle
Knob
Heel
Depth adjustment
Frog-adjusting screw
Frog
Cap iron
Throat
Sole
Toe

At least three companies make bench planes today, but I don't think any are as fine as the older planes. Many woodworkers share this belief, so good used planes often cost more than new ones and some are valued by collectors as well. Still, it's not hard to find an old plane that is a good buy. Make sure that it has all its parts and that the working parts are not too rusty. Rust-pitted blades can easily be replaced with new ones because the sizes have been standardized for over one hundred years. Parts are usually interchangeable between planes of the same size and manufacture, so you may be able to save money by combining several junkers. Though new planes lack the fine fit and finish of the old ones, they can be tuned to work just as well.

Dismantling the plane—Let's assume that you've just bought a new or an old bench plane of any size; here's how to go about tuning it to do good work. These instructions will be most useful if you have a plane in your hands as you read them.

To take the plane apart, lift the lever on the lever cap and pull the cap back and up to lift it off the lever-cap screw. Lift out the cap iron and blade. To separate these two pieces, loosen the

cap-iron screw (you can use the lever cap as a screwdriver), turn the cap iron at right angles to the blade and slide it toward the cutting edge until the screw head passes through the large hole in the blade.

Remove the frog from the body of the plane by taking out the two hold-down screws. Make sure the depth-adjustment knob runs smoothly on its screw: a drop of oil will help. Use a wire brush to clean up rusty threads. The lever-cap screw should turn easily with your fingers; if it doesn't, unscrew it and clean and oil the threads. The lateral-adjustment lever should also move easily.

Rusty surfaces on the body of an old plane can be cleaned up with 220-grit sandpaper. On both new and old planes, chamfer all the edges around the sole with a file; this helps keep them from becoming dented and then marring the wood's surface. Extra-large chamfers on the front and back ends help the plane ride up over sharp bumps, like the uneven edges of glued-up boards.

Tuning the plane—Now set the frog back in the plane body. The opening in the sole in the front of the frog is called the throat. If you're planing softwoods with easy grain, this opening can be roomy. For hardwoods and woods

where the grain goes every which way, a small throat will hold the wood down in front of the cutting edge and keep it from splitting.

The throats of most bench planes can be adjusted by moving the frog. A frog-adjusting screw in the body fits a metal fork, mounted on the back of the frog; make sure it's engaged before replacing and tightening the two hold-down screws. Now back these screws off just enough to allow the frog to move.

Turning the adjusting screw will move the frog forward and back (lacking this screw, you should be able to move the frog by tapping it gently with the end of a screwdriver handle). Place the leading edge of the frog so it just meets the end of the bevel of the back edge of the throat. Make sure the leading edge of the frog meets the throat all the way across its width.

Set the blade in place, holding it on the frog with your fingers, its edge flush with the sole of the plane. Now look at the bottom of the plane and you'll see the plane's maximum throat opening. If the plane is intended for rough work, the opening should be at least ⅛-in. wide, to keep thick shavings from clogging. Enlarge a small throat by filing its leading edge; scribe a line across the sole of the plane at right angles to the sides and file to the line. If you undercut the edge of the throat slightly, as shown below, you'll improve the chip passage, especially when the cap iron is set close to the cutting edge.

For fine work, the throat should be no more than ³⁄₃₂ in. or ¹⁄₁₆ in. wide. Slide the frog forward with the blade in place to reduce the opening. The cutting edge should be parallel to the leading edge of the throat and to the sole; twist the frog slightly until it is. When it's right, tighten the frog's hold-down screws.

Now check the cap iron and the blade. The front edge of the cap iron must fit tightly against the back face of the blade. Even a tiny space will catch chips and jam the plane. (Even new planes may have this fault.) Refit the cap iron to the blade, reversing the procedure used to remove it. When viewed from the side, only the front edge of the cap iron should be touching, as shown in the photo at right. A space at one end or the other indicates a twisted cap iron that has probably lost its tension and can't press down hard enough on the blade. Try correcting it by holding it in a vise and bending it slightly forward, as shown in the photo below.

If the leading edge of the cap iron isn't touching the blade, or if contact is uneven along the leading edge, you must refinish the edge of the iron with a file. Secure a wide, flat, finely cut file horizontally in a vise and move the edge of the cap iron carefully across it. Hold the tail end of the iron slightly lower than the file and try to work the whole edge at once so you don't take off more from one place than another. The job is done when the whole edge shows file marks. Try the cap iron in place; several tries may be needed before it fits properly. Hold the tail of the iron somewhat lower on subsequent filings. When the fit is right, use a very fine file to remove burrs from the leading edge of the cap iron, taking care to leave a sharp edge, without rounding it under.

Shape and sharpen the blade as described on p. 181. For certain planing jobs, you should grind and sharpen a crowned cutting edge on the blade. Blades used for rough work (such as removing large amounts of wood, which is called scrub planing) must be heavily crowned—¹⁄₁₆ in. or more across a 2-in.-wide blade. Use the blade in a plane with a wide throat.

For general smoothing, a very slight crown is desirable. The crown should be just visible as you sight down the edge. The blade will leave very few marks on the wood and produce a shaving that is slightly thinner at its edge and comes off the wood easily. Dub over the corners of these blades.

Jointer blades must be ground dead straight to produce a perfectly flat surface. Their corners can also be dubbed over.

If the cap iron is set close to the cutting edge, the shaving is curled as soon as it's severed from the wood, as shown in the photo below. The curled shaving is flexible and can't pull wood up ahead of the edge.

A very closely set cap iron (and a narrow throat) can produce a smooth surface on woods with pretty wild grain. For fine smoothing where the grain isn't fussy, set the cap iron back about $\frac{1}{64}$ in. from the cutting edge. For heavy-duty scrub planing, set the iron back as much as $\frac{1}{8}$ in. At any setting, if the plane is too hard to push or if shavings get caught in the throat, either the cap iron is too close, the throat is too fine, or both.

Now gently lower the blade and cap-iron assembly (called the cutter) back into the plane, taking care not to nick the cutting edge. Lower the back of the blade down on the frog, wiggling it slightly so that the depth-adjustment and lateral-adjustment mechanisms engage in their respective slots. With the lever up, slide the lever cap into place over the screw, pushing it forward as far as it will go. The lever should snap down easily

but firmly—if too loose, the plane won't hold its adjustment; if too snug, the adjustments will be stiff. Turn the lever-cap screw with your fingers while the lever is still up, and keep trying it until it feels right.

Setting the plane—Setting adjustments are made quickly and without taking the plane apart; set the plane every time you use it. Unlike the tuning adjustments explained earlier, setting doesn't require disassembly, but then you don't have to tune as often as you set.

The depth-adjustment knob, below left, which is just in front of the back handle, sets the depth of cut. This determines the thickness of the shaving. The knob moves the cutter up and down through a clever linkage that also locks the cutter in place so that it won't get pushed back while planing.

First adjust the thickness setting: I do this by feel, placing a finger of my left hand on each corner of the blade while twirling the depth-adjustment knob with my right hand, as shown in the photo below. Move the blade in or out of the sole until it feels right. The last adjustment should always be outward to take up their slack and to make sure the blade is locked in place. There's considerable play in the mechanism, especially in recently made planes.

Now move the lateral-adjustment lever until the blade feels like it protrudes through the sole by the same amount at each corner. For coarse work, this rough setting is all you'll need.

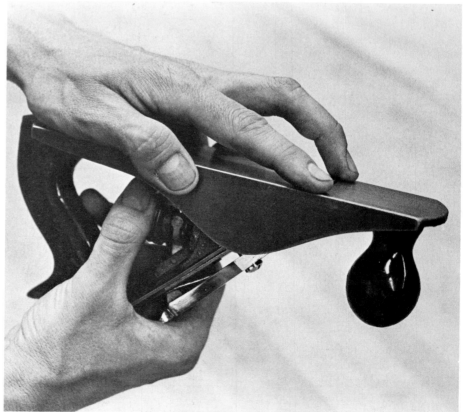

Most planing requires a finer setting. Turn the plane over and sight along the sole from the front of the plane to make further adjustments with the knob and lever, as my friend Bruce Curtis-McLane is doing in the photo at right. Some people prefer to sight with the plane held right-side up so that light coming through the sole illuminates the blade. Try it both ways and see which method works best for you. Finally, try the tool on the wood the child will be planing to make certain that it works easily and smoothly. With experience, you'll be able to make these adjustments quickly.

Kids in my shop usually choose a plane with my advice, and I check it out, sharpen and set it. Kids with a knack for mechanical things could easily learn to set a plane; if you are working with your own child or just a few kids at a time, it's worth letting them give it a try.

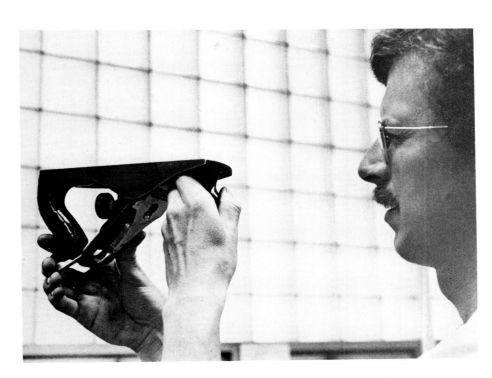

Planing Problems and Solutions

If the plane leaves a stepped track on the surface of the wood...

the blade is not taking shavings of even thickness. Correct the lateral adjustment.

If the plane leaves a rough surface that feels rougher one way than the other...

you are planing into rising grain. Plane in the other direction or across the grain.

If the plane leaves raised tracks...

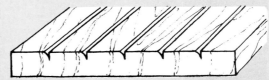

the cutting edge of the blade is nicked. Grind out the nicks.

If the plane leaves distinct tracks...

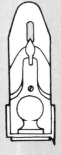

the edge of the sole is nicked. Chamfer the sole with a file.

Block Planes

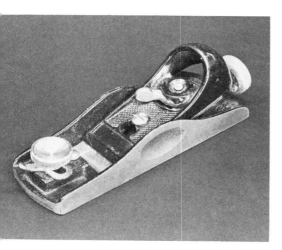

The first block planes may have been designed for smoothing the end grain of butcher's blocks and engraving blocks. Today, these small planes (usually about 6 in. long) have many uses.

Bench-plane blades work with their bevels down, cutting at the 45° angle created by the frog (the bed for the cutter). Most block-plane blades are set in the body of the plane at a 20° angle, but they cut with the bevel of the blade up. Add the 25° of the bevel to the 20° frog and you'll find that most block planes also cut at 45°. I prefer to use a low-angle block plane, like the Stanley No. 60½, photo above. In this plane, the blade is seated at 12°, so the cutting is done at about 37° (the 12° frog plus the 25° bevel). This lower angle gives a gentler cut. Block-plane blades are usually ground perfectly straight, with slightly dubbed-off corners.

Better block planes have an adjustable throat that can be set after the blade has been adjusted in the plane, photo left. They're very easy to tune for fine work.

Setting the plane

Setting the plane—On good block planes, the blade is held in place by a cam lever cap, which slides over a screw as does the lever cap of a bench plane. Tighten the screw just enough to hold the blade firmly when the lever is closed, but no more. If you tighten the lever cap too much, it can push the blade right through the bottom of the plane where the blade seat meets the sole.

Cheaper block planes have a screw that holds the blade in place. Loosen it slightly while you sight along the sole to position the blade, then lock it. Block planes with adjustment mechanisms can set the thickness of cut without loosening the cam lever cap. Set these as you would a bench plane, making the final adjustment outward to lock the blade in place. (The depth-adjustment knobs on recently made, low-angle planes will break off if dropped on their back ends. A machinist can repair or reinforce this for you in about twenty minutes by soldering a pin in a hole bored down the center of the screw.)

A few block planes have lateral-adjustment mechanisms, but on those that do not, move the blade from side to side by hand. This usually can be done without loosening the blade.

Palm planes or finger planes are also called block planes in some tool catalogs. They're smaller than block planes (3 in. long or less) and usually have the blade set at a 45° angle with the bevel down. They're handy for cleaning up board edges, and they can also trim end grain, as shown below.

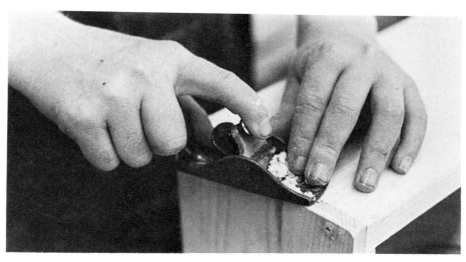

Plow Planes

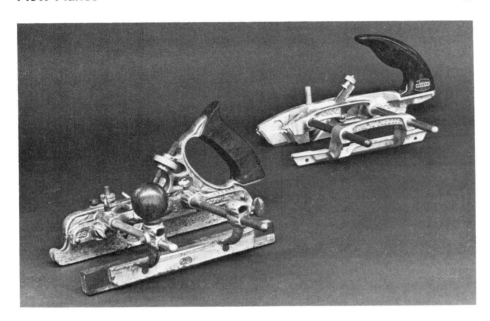

With a plow plane, you can cut grooves for drawer sides; it can also be set up to cut rabbets and moldings. Most plow planes come with a blade for cutting tongues, so a plow can also substitute for the tongue-and-groove plane used in Chapter 8. On the other hand, the tongue-and-groove plane can substitute for an expensive plow to cut a groove for a drawer bottom. But for versatility, there's nothing like a good plow plane.

There are several different styles of plow plane. The Stanley No. 45 combination plane (in the foreground of the photo above) and the simpler Stanley No. 50 are no longer made, but the English company Record produces copies of them. (The Record No. 50 can be seen in the background of the photo.) New plows are so expensive that it pays to check with old-tool dealers for a used one, especially the less-complex ones that are not popular with collectors. To save money, consider one of the older, wooden-bodied plow planes common on the antique market.

Plow planes work beautifully when cutting along the grain of the wood. They can be set to cut dadoes (grooves across the grain), but I think kids should learn to cut them by hand (p. 40).

Plow planes may look fearsome, but they are just a little bit more complicated than rabbet planes. They, too, have a fence to guide them along an edge and a depth gauge to stop the plane when the cut is finished.

Plow planes don't have a solid sole, but rather slide along on rails positioned in front of and behind the blade and within its width, as shown in the photo below. The distance between the rails is varied for each different blade. The mainstock of the plane, which forms one of the rails, also mounts the blade and the depth gauge, and secures the fence bars. The sliding section forms the other rail; it can move on the fence bars and is locked in place with a pair of thumbscrews. The fence itself is also moved on and locked to the fence bars.

Blades for plow and tongue-and-groove planes are ground to a 25° to 30° bevel. The cutting edge must be exactly at right angles to the sides of the blade because there is no lateral-adjustment mechanism to compensate for an off-square edge. Use a trysquare to check the edge as you grind.

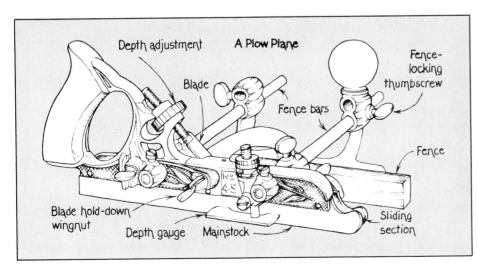

A Plow Plane

Depth adjustment

Blade

Fence bars

Fence-locking thumbscrew

Fence

Blade hold-down wingnut

Depth gauge

Mainstock

Sliding section

Setting the plane—Loosen the blade hold-down (which is usually a wingnut outside the mainstock or a screw above the cutter) and put the blade in place. If there is a blade-adjusting screw, engage the notch of the blade on it. A side of the blade should protrude just slightly beyond the mainstock rail; if it doesn't, remove it to see if there are any shavings in the way. Tighten the hold-down, then move the sliding section over so that the other side of the blade protrudes just slightly beyond the rail on the sliding section. Lock the sliding section in place with its thumbscrews.

Now back the hold-down off just enough so the blade can be moved to set it. With the plane held upside down, sight along the rails and move the blade up or down until the cutting edge protrudes below the rails just the thickness of the desired cut, then tighten the blade hold-down.

Set the depth gauge by measuring from the corner of the cutting edge to the bottom of the gauge. Adjust the fence, measuring from the edge of the blade to the fence. Be sure everything is locked tight before trying the plane on the wood.

Using the plane—Hold the wood in a vise, bench stop or clamp as you would for rabbeting. The board should overhang anything below it that would obstruct the fence of the plane. Hold the back handle in the right hand and push sideways on the fence with the left, as eighth-grader Heather Johnston is doing in the photo at right. This plow plane has a handle mounted above the fence, but it's hard to keep the plane level while using it.

Pull the plane back until you feel the cutting edge drop off the end of the wood. Now push it forward, holding the fence firmly against the edge of the board; keep going until you feel the cutting edge clear the far end of the board. Make sure that you hold the

plane level all the way across or else you'll damage the groove, especially if you are working near the edge of the board. Continue planing until the depth stop touches the board all the way along the groove. The plane will stop cutting

when this happens on a narrow groove; on a wider groove you might continue the cut beyond the stop if you tilt the plane outward, and this will ruin the work. It's best to watch for the gauge to touch the wood.

Rabbeting

A rabbet is a rectangular recess along the edge of a board. It's one of the simplest woodworking joints; don't believe my students when they tell you that rabbets have long, floppy ears and a fluffy tail.

Rabbets are cut with rabbet planes. They are designed to work right up against the vertical part of the rabbet (the shoulder), so the blade protrudes slightly beyond the plane's sole on one or both sides. On most other planes, the sole extends beyond the blade on both sides, as shown in the photo below.

The workhorse rabbet plane in my shop is the Record 778. This English-made tool has a fence to determine the width of the cut and a depth gauge to determine the depth. The fence runs the full length of the plane and is supported by two stout rods. Similar rabbet planes, such as the Stanley 78, have only one rod, which is easily bent, and a short fence, which is harder to use than a long one. The Stanley 278 plane is identical to the Record 778; look for this one in flea markets.

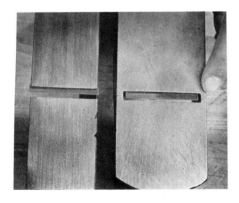

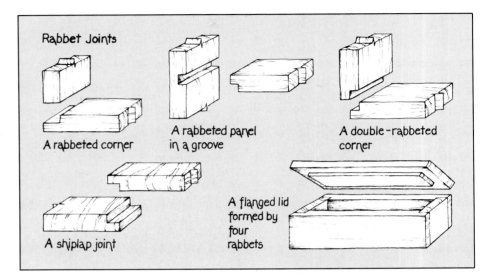

Rabbet Joints

A rabbeted corner

A rabbeted panel in a groove

A double-rabbeted corner

A shiplap joint

A flanged lid formed by four rabbets

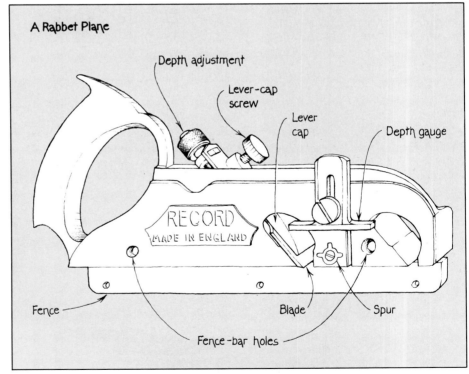

A Rabbet Plane

Depth adjustment
Lever-cap screw
Lever cap
Depth gauge
RECORD MADE IN ENGLAND
Fence
Blade
Spur
Fence-bar holes

There are other kinds of rabbet planes designed to trim rabbets that have already been cut. We use the side rabbet plane to trim dadoes (p. 42); the shoulder rabbet plane, used to trim the flanged box lid on p. 34, is discussed at the end of this section.

I usually sharpen and set rabbet planes for kids in the shop, as I do most planes, though advanced students are eventually introduced to these skills. Rabbet planes are a little trickier to set than bench planes, and it helps to be familiar with bench planes first.

The blade of a rabbet plane is locked in place by tightening the lever-cap screw. To adjust the blade, loosen the screw enough so the blade moves, but not easily. Hold the plane upside down and sight down the sole from the front. Now adjust the blade for thickness of shaving. (You'll learn the proper setting by trial and error on the wood.) The Record 778 has a depth-adjustment screw to move the blade forward or backward, but similar planes have a lever adjustment, or no adjustment at all. Be sure the same amount of blade is exposed across the width of the plane, and that the edge protrudes just slightly from the working side (the side with the depth gauge), about $\frac{1}{32}$ in.

Rabbet planes don't have the lateral-adjustment mechanism found on a bench plane, so you must make these adjustments by hand while the lever-cap screw is loose. I usually do this by grasping the sides of the blade just behind the edge with my left hand, while working the depth-adjustment screw and lever-cap screw with my right. Tighten down the lever-cap screw when the blade is set.

To remove the blade for sharpening, first loosen the lever-cap screw and pull the lever cap back and up to remove it. Then lift out the blade. The blade is sharpened in the same way as any other blade or chisel. Its edge must be ground straight across (no crown or hollow is permissible as with other planes) and at 90° to the sides of the blade. When I grind these in a hurry, I seldom bother to use a square; if the edge is not at right angles to the sides, the angle between the two should be acute, not obtuse. The plane can't cut a square rabbet if the angle is greater than 90°, but it can if it's less than 90°. Grind the blade slightly narrower where indicated in the drawing at right to give added freedom of adjustment.

Rabbeting is the first step in making popular, early projects like boxes and

bookshelves, so it's often the first skill children learn in my shop. Using a rabbet plane takes more coordination than most other basic woodworking operations, and the child must watch for several things at once: Is the plane level? Am I pushing sideways on the tool? Is the cut finished or am I going too far? Because it's important that a kid's early shop experiences are successful, it pays to take time to teach rabbeting carefully. As with other skills in this book, you must be familiar with rabbeting before you can teach it to a child.

I teach kids to rabbet right on their own projects, not on scrap. When they've received the wood for their box or bookcase, I mark out the positions of the rabbets on the pieces. "Boards are seldom flat," I tell them. "Can you see the hollow side of the cup on this board?" To see it, they must sight across the end of the board (p. 31). Rabbets on the ends of boards are best cut on the hollow side of the cup. It's easy to flatten a cupped, softwood board for planing: clamp it to a corner of the workbench with two clamps. Later, during assembly, the cupped board can be flattened by using a single clamp.

When clamping the board to the bench, be sure the corner of the bench doesn't protrude beyond the end of the

board or it will obstruct the fence of the plane. Narrow boards that have little cupping may be held in a vise. When rabbeting with the grain, you can hold the board between bench stops, but be sure the rabbeted edge overhangs the benchtop or the fence will hit the top.

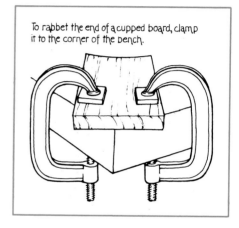

To rabbet the end of a cupped board, clamp it to the corner of the bench.

While setting the fence and gauge, I point to them with a pencil and explain to the child, "The width of the rabbet is from the corner of the blade to the fence, and the depth is from the corner to the depth gauge." I always add, "By the way, the corners of the blade on a rabbet plane stick out the sides of the plane. Watch out for them or they'll give you a nasty cut."

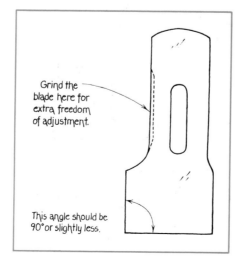

Grind the blade here for extra freedom of adjustment.

This angle should be 90° or slightly less.

Rabbets for corner joints on a box or cabinet should be about half the thickness of the rabbeted board. Measure from the corner of the blade to set the depth gauge; use a ruler, or eyeball the measurement. The rabbet should be as wide as or slightly wider than the thickness of the board that butts into it. Set the fence by loosening the locking screws, then place the plane on the end of the mating board, with the working corner of the blade even with, or slightly overhanging, one face of the board; slide the fence up against the other face and tighten the screws. This may sound complicated, but it soon becomes second nature and can be done in about thirty seconds.

After the plane is set, I demonstrate how to use it. I grasp the plane's handle in my right hand. My left fingers push against the fence at the front of the plane, with the thumb on the comfortable little curve on top of the plane, as shown in the photo, above right. The right hand pushes the tool forward and keeps it running level, while the left pushes the fence firmly sideways against the end of the board to ensure uniform width along the rabbet. Some kids will modify this grip once they've learned to use the tool.

Most woodworking hand tools are symmetrical, showing no favor to right-handed people. But the rabbet plane is a right-handed tool and it's good to anticipate a lefty's problems—the child will appreciate your concern. Though lefties can hold the plane the same way righties can, they usually find it easier to keep the plane level with their left hand. Others adopt another position: the left hand on the handle, the right hand reaching over the top of the plane to push it sideways. It may look awkward but it works.

When working across the grain, the plane is likely to split pieces off the edge at the end of the cut. To avoid this, pull the plane backward over the end a few

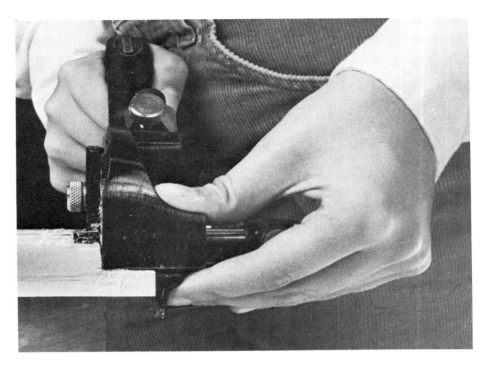

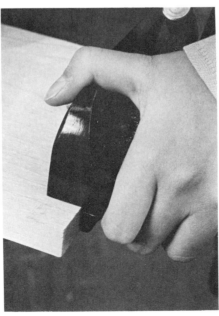

times (pushing firmly sideways on the fence). This will leave a shadowy impression of where the cut will be, as shown in the photo above. With a fine saw, like the dovetail saw used here, make a notch on the arris as deep as the rabbet will be, with the saw kerf on the waste side of the mark, as shown above. You will still get splitting, but it won't continue past the notch. There's no need to do this when you are working with the grain.

Now, start the cut. "Put the plane on the wood and, pushing sideways on the fence, pull it backward until you feel the blade bump off the near end of the board." I demonstrate while I'm explaining. "Now push forward, always pushing sideways too, until you feel the blade leave the wood at the far end. Pull the plane all the way back and make another cut."

After a few cuts, I tell the child to see if the rabbet is level. "Get your eyeball right down to the end of the rabbet to check. Is it tilted in or out?" I can't help tilting the plane slightly inward when I start, but I can get it right after I check a few times. Most kids can see a tilted rabbet, but you can make this fault clearer by setting a ruler on the board projecting over the rabbet, as Chrissy Chioffi does in the photo.

To continue, I tell kids: "Keep planing and checking for level until the depth gauge is almost touching the wood. Be especially careful now, because if the depth gauge touches the wood without your knowing it, you can ruin the rabbet. The plane will stop cutting, but you won't know why, and so without thinking about it, you'll tilt the plane outward to cut more. Then you have a tilted rabbet that's too deep. So watch that depth gauge and stop when it tells you to."

With these instructions, most kids can make a good, square rabbet, but some will require more attention. To help a child who has difficulty keeping the plane level, sit directly in front of the plane and watch it; tell the child when he or she is going off. Some children roll the plane outward near the end of a cut, particularly on long rabbets. Suggest that they walk a short step rather than extend their arms too far.

If the depth gauge touches the far end of the rabbet first, it simply means that the child has not started planing at the near end of the board on every stroke. Simply plane the high area until the depth gauge touches all the way across.

Should a child overshoot the depth gauge, the board can be saved by increasing the depth of the rabbet: raise the gauge enough to reach the deepest part of the rabbet while the plane is held level. If there are rabbets at each end of the board, be sure to deepen the other rabbet by the same amount.

If the rabbet is badly messed up, saw the ruined end of the board off and have the child try again. Be sure to shorten the opposite board by the same amount.

Certain woods, such as unseasoned pine, are stringy when rabbeted across the grain. The face of the board that is rabbeted will chip and tear, and the shoulder of the rabbet will be fuzzy. One way to prevent these problems is to sever the wood fibers with a marking gauge set to the width of the rabbet; the plane blade can then lift them out without tearing.

There is a spur on the rabbet plane that will sever the fibers. File the spur so it cuts only slightly deeper than the blade; it should be beveled on the side nearest the blade. Because the blade protrudes slightly, you need to add a shim between the spur and the plane; set the blade so it protrudes sideways no further than the spur. Setting up the spur is a nuisance, and most woods don't need it. Nicking the wood with a marking gauge is a good substitute and usually need be done only before the first few strokes.

It's easy to find the cause of most messed-up rabbets:

If the shoulder of the rabbet is stepped, the blade is not projecting beyond the side of the plane. Each cut is slightly less wide than the one before, because the plane can't reach all the way into the corner.

If the shoulder is vertical, then steps over at a certain depth, one of the fence bars is protruding through the side of the plane and is hitting the rabbet shoulder. This happens when the plane gets knocked around or dropped on the bar. Loosen the set screw that holds the bar in the plane body and the one in the fence, and slide the bar back in place.

If the rabbet is not at full width at either or both ends of the board, the child is not pushing sideways at the ends of the cut. At the beginning of the cut, this can happen if the handle of the plane is pulled away from the board, even if the front of the plane is against it.

If the rabbet becomes irregular partway through the cut, the fence could be hitting something projecting beyond the board's end—perhaps the corner of the bench or part of a vise or clamp. Be sure the board overhangs the bench.

If the plane won't cut a level rabbet despite your best efforts, check to see if the blade is taking a shaving of even thickness. The edge of the blade should be parallel to the sole.

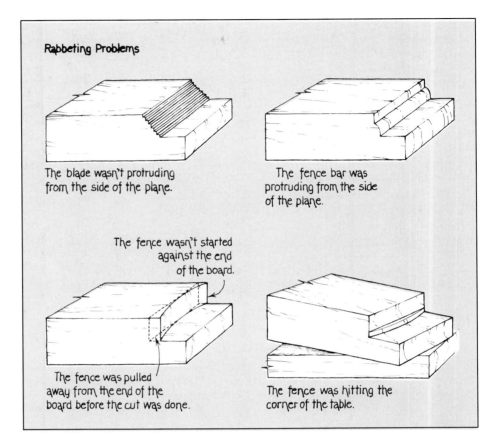

Rabbeting Problems

The blade wasn't protruding from the side of the plane.

The fence bar was protruding from the side of the plane.

The fence wasn't started against the end of the board.

The fence was pulled away from the end of the board before the cut was done.

The fence was hitting the corner of the table.

The shoulder of a rabbet can be cleaned up, or the rabbet can be made wider, with one of a variety of special rabbet planes. These planes have no fence, depth gauge or spurs, and most have blades set at a lower angle (20° rather than 45°). The Stanley 92, right, is also called a cabinetmaker's rabbet plane or shoulder rabbet plane. By resting the side of the plane on the ledge of the rabbet, the blade will trim the shoulder square and straight. The plane will chip the far end of the cut, so work three-quarters of the way across the rabbet and come back the other way. (Always work into the center of the rabbet, rather than off its ends.) When widening a rabbet with this kind of plane, it helps to mark a line across the wood and work up to it. The Record 778 plane can be used for this job if you remove the fence and depth gauge.

Nailing

Nailing is one of the easiest ways to hold two pieces of wood together. All you need is a hammer, some nails, glue and a nail set.

Nails come in many shapes and sizes. We use common nails and finishing nails. The common nail has a large head, which helps it grab the surface of the wood. Finishing nails have much smaller heads, which can be driven below the wood surface with a nail set. This lets you plane or sand over the nailhead and hide the head with wood filler or a small dowel plug. Common nails make a stronger joint, but we use finishing nails for most jobs in our shop.

Nails are sold by the "penny." A 1½-in.-long nail is 4 penny (indicated as 4d), a 2-in. nail is 6 penny (6d), and so forth, but they're often called by their actual length: 2 in. common, 2½ in. finishing, for example. We most often use 1½-in. finishing nails in our shop; they're just right for nailing together ¾-in. boards. We use thousands of them, so I buy 50-lb. boxes. I also stock a few longer finishing nails, but we rarely use them.

Nails shorter than 1 in. (2d) are usually described by their length and gauge number, a measure of thickness. For example, ½-in. nails are commonly sold in 16 gauge or the thinner 18 gauge. Small finishing nails are called wire brads, and small flathead nails are called wire nails. The ⅝-in., 18-gauge wire nail with its thin, flat head is ideal for nailing leather to wood, as for leather hinges or wooden clogs. We use ½-in., 18-gauge wire brads to nail flooring to dollhouse frames.

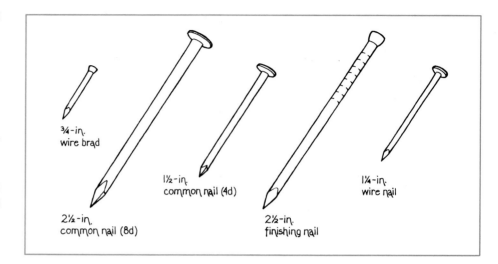

Hammers—The hammer most people have at home, a carpenter's 16-oz. claw hammer, is too heavy for most children to use; a hammer weighing 8, 10 or 12 oz. is much better. I drive 1½-in. finishing nails with the lightest hammer in the shop. Light-weight hammers are easier for small children to control. A light-weight claw hammer, however, can be difficult to find, so use a tack hammer or small ball-peen hammer instead; they'll work just as well.

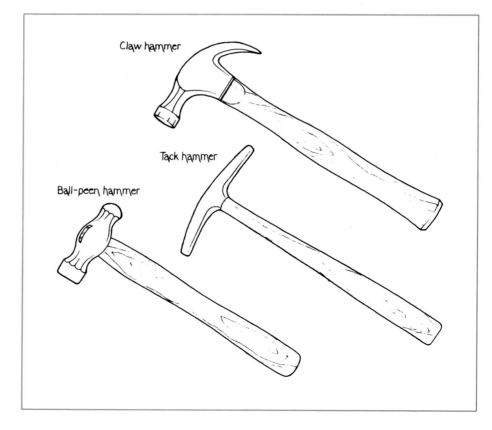

Nailed joints—Nails have two jobs in a joint: locating and securing. Locating means keeping the two pieces from sliding on one another. Pieces joined by two or more nails can slide on one another only if the nails bend or shear off. Securing means keeping the pieces from coming apart as a result of the friction between the nails and the wood. You can increase the strength of the joint by using longer, thicker, or a greater number of nails. Sometimes the primary job of a nail is to locate, sometimes to secure; often it's a combination of both.

When you choose nails for a project, you should always consider what job they will have to do.

It's easier to pull a nailed joint apart than it is to dislocate it. One way to increase the securing strength of a nailed joint is to apply glue to the pieces before nailing them together. We glue nailed joints in my shop as a matter of course. If you're concerned that nails and glue won't hold the joint together, you should use wood screws instead. The threads make it much more difficult to pull out a screw than a smooth nail.

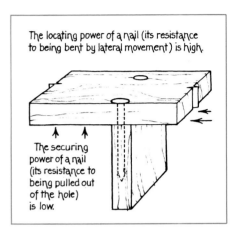

The locating power of a nail (its resistance to being bent by lateral movement) is high.

The securing power of a nail (its resistance to being pulled out of the hole) is low.

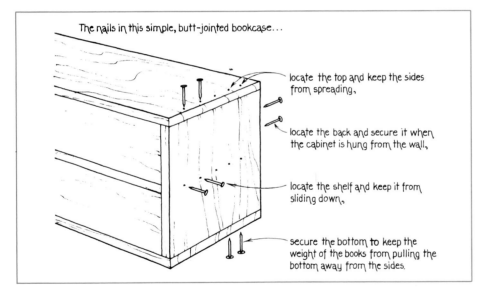

The nails in this simple, butt-jointed bookcase...

locate the top and keep the sides from spreading,

locate the back and secure it when the cabinet is hung from the wall,

locate the shelf and keep it from sliding down,

secure the bottom to keep the weight of the books from pulling the bottom away from the sides.

Teaching kids to nail—I often hear even older kids say, "I can't hammer a nail straight." Some kids seem to pick up the knack intuitively, while others need direction and practice. If you are patient and reassuring, you can teach anyone to nail. Here's what you'll need to know.

What makes a nail go in straight? A nail is steered into the wood by the angle at which it is struck by the hammer face. Small changes in the angle can bend the nail. Try striking at different angles to bend the nail slightly, then steer it back. Little adjustments in the angle come from the wrist or by slightly raising or lowering the elbow. (Most of the hammering action itself should come from the elbow, not the wrist.)

Once the nail is well started into the wood, its point will generally continue in the same direction no matter how you bend the top of the nail. So it's important to aim the nail properly during the first few hammer strokes. An improperly aimed nail cannot be redirected by bending it.

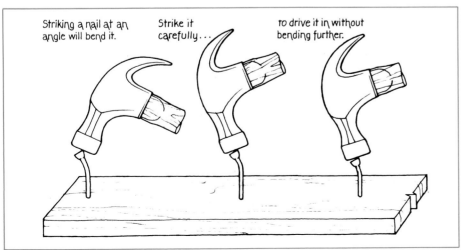

Striking a nail at an angle will bend it.

Strike it carefully...

to drive it in without bending further.

Sometimes kids are afraid to start nails for fear of bashing their fingers. With very young kids, start a bunch of nails in a scrap of wood and let the child drive them in. Having experienced the satisfaction of finishing the job, he or she will feel more confident about starting it. You may prefer to hold each nail for the new hammerer to start; you can do this safely with a pair of pliers. Eventually, you can let the kid hold the pliers; when this becomes tiresome, he or she will probably be willing to risk using fingers to hold the nail.

For young children, always mark the position of each nail on a project with a small *x*. This tells the child how many nails should be used and where—an extra bit of security a child will welcome.

A hammer is usually held in a fist without extending the forefinger (except for delicate work). There's no need to hold it at the far end of the handle; in fact, a novice may get better control by holding it a few inches back from the head. Don't let kids hold the head itself and also never let them hammer with two hands or they will never learn to hammer correctly.

Some kids just can't seem to hit the nail hard enough with the hammer. Usually, they hammer like this: *tap...tap...tap...tap*. They should be going *BANG...BANG...BANG*. The rapid rhythm of tapping has no power. Tell the child to lift the hammer high after each impact. Very young kids can establish a healthy rhythm if you ask them to say *BANG* at each impact. Start them off by saying it with them.

Support the pieces being nailed together on a sturdy benchtop, or hold the bottom piece in a vise. If the wood can move even a little, the hammer blow will bounce the wood rather than drive the nail. This is very frustrating, especially for a novice. If the piece you are nailing into is flexible, devise some method to support it against the bench or floor so it won't bounce (p. 45).

Some wood is just too hard to nail into. For nailed projects, use pine or other softwood, not hardwoods like maple, cherry or oak. Don't try to drive a nail into a knot. Though nailing into hardwoods and through knots can be done, it's not a job for a beginner.

Problems and tips—You may split the wood if you nail into short-grained wood, nail too close to an end, or nail through a knot or near a knot too close to the end. Wood will also split if you place too many nails in the same line of grain; zig-zag the nails to avoid this. If you can't avoid short grain, ends or knots, here are three things you can do.

Blunt the point of the nail with your hammer. A pointed nail acts as a wedge, pushing fibers apart as it enters the wood. A blunt end pushes fibers ahead of itself and exerts less sideways pressure. Blunting is not a guarantee against splitting, but it helps.

Clamp the wood firmly across the grain while nailing to help it resist the nail's wedging action. Hold the piece between the jaws of the vise, a bar clamp or a *C*-clamp.

Bore a little pilot hole for the nail to pass through. Use a twist bit just slightly smaller than the diameter of the nail. This method is the most reliable of the three and will allow you to nail into hardwood or through a knot.

If a nail keeps sneaking out of the side of the wood, pull it out and try again in a new hole. But never start another nail in the same hole because it will just follow the old path. Occasionally, the grain of the wood will bend the nail off its course. If several nails all bend the same way, try leaning a nail in the opposite direction to compensate.

A pointed nail pushes wood fibers aside as it enters the wood. A blunt nail pushes the fibers downward and exerts less sideways pressure.

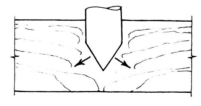 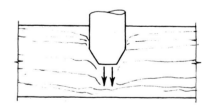

To guard against splitting, blunt the point of the nail by resting the nailhead on the metal part of the vise and tapping the point with your hammer.

Or clamp the wood firmly together so it can't split.

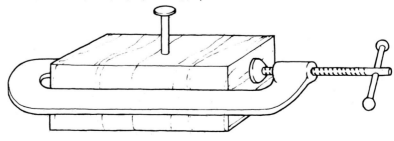

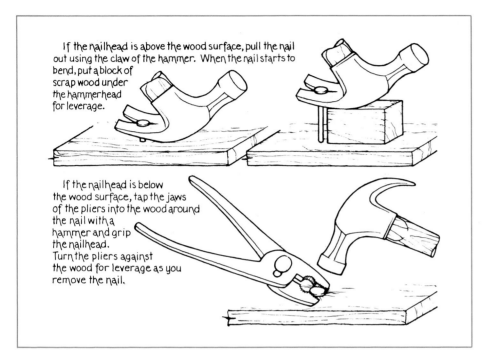

If the nailhead is above the wood surface, pull the nail out using the claw of the hammer. When the nail starts to bend, put a block of scrap wood under the hammerhead for leverage.

If the nailhead is below the wood surface, tap the jaws of the pliers into the wood around the nail with a hammer and grip the nailhead. Turn the pliers against the wood for leverage as you remove the nail.

Pulling a nail—You may need to pull a nail if it's bent, sticks out the side of a board, or is in the way of a tool. If the nailhead is above the wood, pull it out with a claw hammer. If a nail bends as you pull it, put a block of wood under the hammerhead for extra leverage.

If the nailhead is below the wood surface, try to grab it with a pair of pliers. If you can't get a grip, spread the jaws wide enough to fit around the head and tap them into the wood around the nail. Once you've gripped the head, twist the pliers sideways on the wood, bending the nail as you draw it out.

If the point of the nail is exposed, place a nail set on the point and drive the head out of the wood. The end of a nail set is slightly hollowed and will stay centered on the nail's point. Once the head is free of the surface, pull it with the hammer's claw.

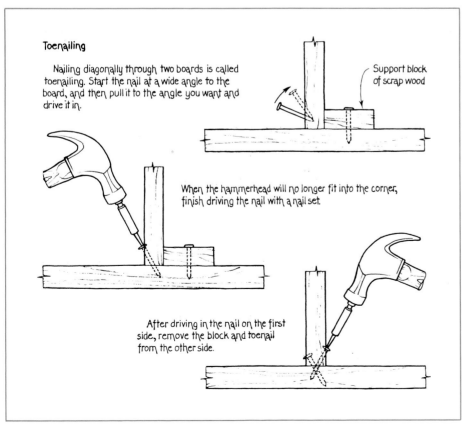

Toenailing

Nailing diagonally through two boards is called toenailing. Start the nail at a wide angle to the board, and then pull it to the angle you want and drive it in.

Support block of scrap wood

When the hammerhead will no longer fit into the corner, finish driving the nail with a nail set.

After driving in the nail on the first side, remove the block and toenail from the other side.

Toenailing—Toenailing, driving nails diagonally through two boards, is a useful technique to use if there is no other way to nail them: for example, when nailing rafters to walls (p. 66). Toenailing is almost always done with pairs of nails, one nail driven from each side of a board, so the opposite nails reinforce each other.

The nails must be angled so they don't come through the other side of the board. Start a nail at a wide angle to the board to seat its point (don't drive it in too deep), then pull the nail into the correct angle and drive it home. As you drive the first nail, the board will want to walk sideways off its mark. You can prevent this by tacking a block of scrap wood against the far side of the board, removing it when the nail is all the way in. The first nail will keep the board from moving while you drive in the second. Drive the nailheads flush with the board surface with a nail set, or sink them below the surface. Use nail sets whose ends match the diameters of the heads of the nails you use.

Drawers

A drawer is simply a box that slides out of a box. Adding a drawer makes a cabinet more useful and attractive; it also shows that extra care and effort went into a project.

Drawers appeal to kids because they move. Drawers transform cabinets into action toys, and also suggest that something is hidden or locked away—children love secrets. But kids usually underestimate the time and energy that is required to add drawers to a project. I discourage kids from adding more than one drawer in their early projects because I know there's a good chance that they will be overwhelmed by the detailed work.

The simplest drawer is a mitered or rabbeted box with a plywood bottom, as shown in the drawing above. Just size the box to fit the space in the cabinet, allowing a clearance of ⅛ in. in each direction. Add a drawer pull, or cut a recess in the top front edge of the drawer. The drawer may slide on its bottom on the cabinet shelf, or the drawer bottom can be recessed in a rabbet so that only the edges of the drawer sides sit on the shelf—a refinement that eases sliding.

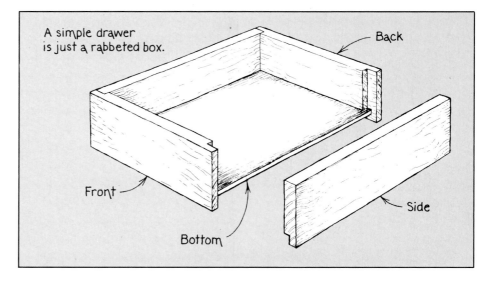

A simple drawer is just a rabbeted box.

Back

Front

Bottom

Side

In a typical cabinetmaker's drawer, the bottom fits in grooves in the drawer sides, as shown below. The drawer back is cut flush with the top edge of the grooves, so the bottom can slide into place after the drawer is assembled. The bottom is nailed or screwed to the drawer back, but pulling out the fastener allows the bottom to be removed for cleaning. Making this kind of drawer isn't difficult for kids, so this is the drawer I suggest for all but the tiniest cabinets.

Drawer fronts can be either flush or overlapping. In flush-front drawers, the drawer front nestles between the cabinet sides. A stop at the drawer back ensures that the front stays flush with the cabinet edges when the drawer is pushed all the way in. Overlapping-front drawers hide the space between drawer and cabinet. The front may overlap on the sides only, or at the top and bottom as well. The stop in overlapping-front drawers is the overlap itself.

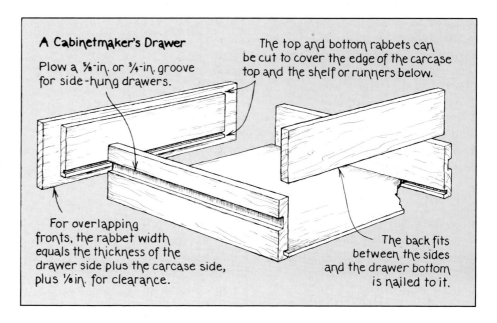

A Cabinetmaker's Drawer

Plow a ⅜-in. or ¾-in. groove for side-hung drawers.

The top and bottom rabbets can be cut to cover the edge of the carcase top and the shelf or runners below.

For overlapping fronts, the rabbet width equals the thickness of the drawer side plus the carcase side, plus ⅛ in. for clearance.

The back fits between the sides and the drawer bottom is nailed to it.

If you don't want the drawer to slide on the cabinet shelves, you have two options. You can support it between two sets of runners fixed to the cabinet sides above and below the drawer. Or you can groove each side of the drawer so it will slide on strips of wood fixed to each cabinet side; this is called a side-hung drawer, and is shown at the bottom of the drawing at right. I prefer the last method and will show how to build a side-hung drawer with a front that overlaps on four sides. You'll need a plow plane (p. 163) to make the grooves. Plow planes are expensive, but secondhand planes can be found; lacking one, cut the grooves with a tongue-and-groove plane. You can also cut grooves for a drawer bottom with a table saw or a radial arm saw.

Most drawers in my shop are made from ¾-in. pine. We cut the fronts of large drawers from thicker wood; the additional wood makes a stronger joint. For most cabinet drawers, the overlapping front will be as long as the cabinet is wide. Measure the outside dimensions so the overlap will cover the full thickness of the cabinet sides. On tables, measure the size of the opening in the apron and choose an overlap that seems suitable. The sides must be slightly shorter than cabinet depth so the drawer won't hit the back of the cabinet when it's pushed all the way in.

Rabbet the ends of the front first. These rabbets must be wide enough to include the overlap, the thickness of the drawer sides, and a clearance between the drawer side and cabinet of about ⅛ in. The depth of the rabbet depends on how thick you'd like the overlap to be; set the depth stop to leave that amount. If these rabbets are wider than your rabbet plane, cut them in two stages. You may wish to rabbet the top and bottom of the drawer to form upper and lower overlaps. Several side-hung drawers, placed one on top of another, won't need top and bottom overlaps.

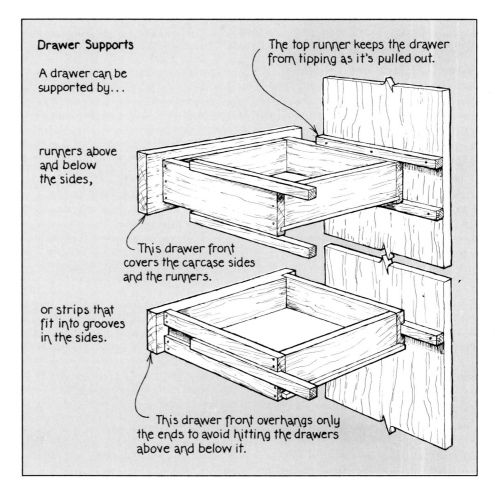

Drawer Supports

A drawer can be supported by...

runners above and below the sides,

The top runner keeps the drawer from tipping as it's pulled out.

This drawer front covers the carcase sides and the runners.

or strips that fit into grooves in the sides.

This drawer front overhangs only the ends to avoid hitting the drawers above and below it.

Cut the grooves for the drawer bottom with the plow plane. Do the drawer front first. The groove should be about ¼ in. above the inside edge of the bottom rabbet. (If you're not using a plow plane, just cut the bottom rabbet to accommodate the overlap plus the drawer bottom.) The groove must not be deeper than the rabbet; to be on the safe side, cut it slightly shallower. Plow the grooves in the drawer sides using the same cutter and fence setting, so that these grooves align with the groove in the drawer front.

Use a wider blade (⅝ in. or ¾ in.) in the plow plane to cut the grooves for strips in the drawer sides. Position these grooves about a third of the way down from the top edge.

Before assembling the drawer, take the time to smooth the arrises on the drawer front with sandpaper or a block plane. Then chuck the drawer front in a vise, end up, put glue on the rabbet and nail the side in place. Angle the nail slightly as when nailing on the bottom of a box (p. 33). Make sure that the grooves for the drawer bottom in the sides and front line up. Then turn the front end for end, and nail on the second side. Be careful that you don't damage the edge of the overlap while you are hammering. Use a nail set to drive the nails home.

Fit the back between the sides, lining up its bottom edge with the top edge of the grooves for the drawer bottom. Glue and nail the back in place.

Now make the drawer bottom from ¼-in. plywood. Measure its length by sliding a metal ruler down the grooves in the sides. Cut the plywood a little undersized, slide it into place and tack it to the bottom of the drawer back.

Make the strips on which the drawers are hung from a narrow, hardwood board that is the length of the sides and as thick as the grooves are wide. Remember to saw the strips a little thicker than groove depth so the drawer won't touch the cabinet side. Prebore five or six holes in the strips to make nailing easier. (If you don't have the right bit, nip off the head of one of the finishing nails you're using and chuck it into an eggbeater drill.)

Now position the strips. With the drawer front sticking out of the cabinet just enough to allow a pencil behind it, mark the position of the side grooves. Hold the drawer level from side to side, and leave sufficient clearance between the top edges of the drawer sides and the top of the cabinet (or the next drawer up). Tack the front of the strips in place and slide the drawer in partway. Holding the drawer level front to back, reach in to mark the positions of the backs of the strips. If there's no room to reach in, position the back ends by setting a square on the front edge of the cabinet and resting the runner on the square's blade. Tack down the backs of the strips and try the drawer. If it slides smoothly and appears level, front to back and side to side, keep nailing. If it's not level or binds, pull off one or both of the strips and try again. (You can position runners for a drawer using the same techniques.)

A side-hung drawer will bind if the strips are too thick or unparallel. If you can't slide the drawer side to side slightly, the strips are bottoming out in the grooves: plane them thinner.

Once the drawer runs smoothly, wax the grooves and strips (or the runners) for an extra-smooth glide.

Table drawers—It's not hard to add a drawer to a square-legged table. The drawer fits in an opening in an apron, and slides on side-hung strips fixed to slide boards nailed to the aprons.

Cut the opening before or after the table frame is assembled. The opening shouldn't be so big that it weakens the apron. Leave enough room beyond the ends of the opening for the corner braces and slide boards. Lay out the opening and bore holes in opposite corners; saw to the line with a keyhole saw, as shown at right; smooth the edges with a spokeshave and file.

Make sure the assembled table frame is square, then fit the slide boards, and

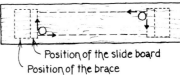

Bore two holes in the apron and saw out the opening with a keyhole saw in the direction of the arrows.

Position of the slide board
Position of the brace

nail through the aprons into them. The slide boards should be perpendicular to the apron with the drawer opening.

Make a drawer with an overlapping front and grooves for side-hung strips; fit the strips to the slide boards. The photo below shows the finished assembly.

Wheels and Rolling

For our purposes, wheels are just wooden discs with holes in the middle. Simple—but they're a problem for adults who work wood with kids, because there is no straightforward way for kids to make them. Here are several ways we make wheels in my shop.

Bandsawn wheels—I make wheels on the bandsaw as described in Chapter 3. The child scribes a circle on the wood with dividers, bores an axle hole, and hands it to me to saw out. This method lets the child decide the size of the wheel and do some of the work. (If you don't have a bandsaw, though, this method isn't much good.) Why not have the child saw out the wheel by hand? This is slow work, and most kids just don't have the skill with a coping saw to produce a round wheel. (And lumpy wheels don't roll well.)

Closet-rod wheels—Using closet rods—softwood dowels about 1¼ in. in diameter—the child can do most of the work of making the wheels. Punch a dimple in the center of an end of the rod and have the child bore a hole for the axle just deeper than the thickness of a wheel. Then he or she can cut off the first wheel with a crosscut saw. Repeat the process for the next wheel, using the shallow hole left in the end of the dowel to start the bit. If the hole has wandered too far off center, cut off the end and start again.

This method makes fine wheels and is well suited for working with very young children. But the wheels can only be the diameter of the closet rod, which isn't a useful size for large toys.

Hole-sawn wheels—When I shuttled between classes at a nursery school and a primary school, I would carry a supply of wheels of various sizes. I made dozens at a time, using scrap wood and a hole saw chucked in an electric drill. A hole saw is a hollow cylinder with teeth

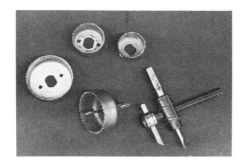

on its edge, centered on a twist bit. (The photo above shows four different sizes of them.) It's made for cutting holes in boards, but in wheel making, we throw away the boards and keep the holes.

Hold the wood securely in a vise and grasp the drill firmly in both hands. The hole saw may suddenly stick in the wood, and this can wrench a wrist. Use a drill press if you can; it's safer and quicker. Just be sure that the wood is clamped securely to the table. Whatever drill you use, either back up the piece with scrap wood or counterbore, so that the back face of the wheel won't splinter as the hole saw comes through the wood. Usually, the wheel will stick in the hole saw; if it does, pry it out with a screwdriver, but make sure the drill is disconnected before you do. The central twist bit on a hole saw is usually ¼ in. in diameter, or less. You can use a twist bit to enlarge this hole in order to fit a bigger axle.

Hole saws require plenty of power behind them and they cannot be used in braces or eggbeater drills. I tried modifying a tool called a circle cutter to be used in a brace, but the brace turns far too slowly. Though the circle cutter works fine in a drill press, it is too dangerous to use one in a hand-held electric drill. I like circle cutters because they cut a wider range of sizes than hole saws do, but the cutter must be reground so that it will cut a clean wheel instead of a clean hole. (The circle cutter at far right in the photo has a cutter that's been reground.)

Wheels on the lathe—With a lathe, you can turn wheels of almost any size and shape. Even a second-grader can turn a cylinder on our foot-powered lathe, smoothing off the spinning wood with a plane. You must decide whether a child is competent enough to use a power lathe safely; if not, you can turn a cylinder and the child can make wheels using the closet-rod method.

To make a lot of wheels quickly, bore a hole in the center of the stock on the lathe using a shell auger (p. 133). Shell augers come in sizes appropriate for axles (½ in., ⅜ in., ¼ in.) and they bore true down the center of the turning wood. Bore almost to the headstock end of the wood, then center the tailstock in the hole and turn the wood to a cylinder.

Use a parting tool to space out the wheels along the length of the cylinder. You can cut within about ¼ in. of the center hole without weakening the piece too much. Use a small gouge or beading tool to crown the edges of each wheel.

To turn details on the face of each wheel (a tire and hub, perhaps), work on the wheel nearest the tailstock. Carefully saw off each wheel by hand as it's finished. Move the tailstock over to engage the center hole of the next wheel and repeat the procedure. To shape both faces, space the wheels far enough apart to get a tool between them.

Rolling—Kids are thrilled when the car or truck they've just made rolls clear across the room with one push. It's not that hard to get a toy to do this, even if it's small.

The little train on p. 22 has wheels that are retained on separate, fixed stub axles, and they can barely turn. They would turn more easily if the holes in the wheels were larger, but then they would wobble too much. Wobbly wheels cause the toy to wander around rather than to roll in a definite direction because the wheels rub against the body of the toy and dig into the axle.

You can buy ready-made toy wheels on stub axles, but these don't roll any better than the homemade kind. It's much better when the wheels and axle turn as a unit, as shown below, because the wheels won't wobble out of control. Locking two wheels on one axle ensures that both wheels point in the same direction, and the vehicle won't be trying to roll in two directions at once. The bearing holes in the body of the toy can be very large if you use a wheel/axle unit, too. Large holes forgive axles that aren't quite straight or round, and if the holes aren't bored exactly parallel to each other or to the floor, no matter.

Another guideline: A short axle isn't as good as a long one. The wheels may wobble (unless the bearing hole is made smaller, which isn't a good idea).

Using big wheels and adding wooden washers between them and the body of the toy will also make the toy roll better. Big wheels gain more momentum and are less affected by rough surfaces; washers keep the wheels from rubbing against the toy. The washers should be smaller than the wheel (friction at a large diameter has more braking effect) and should run freely on the axle.

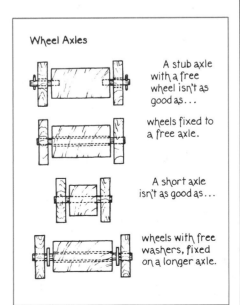

Wheel Axles

A stub axle with a free wheel isn't as good as...

wheels fixed to a free axle.

A short axle isn't as good as...

wheels with free washers, fixed on a longer axle.

Spokeshaves

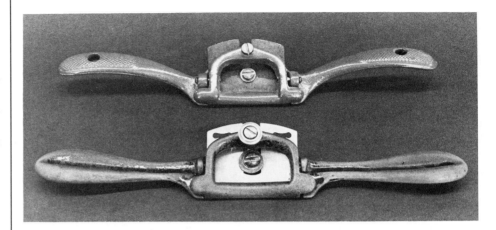

Spokeshaves are to drawknives as planes are to chisels. The spokeshave, like a drawknife, is a two-handled tool that works most comfortably when pulled toward you. The part of the tool that rests on the wood is called the sole; the space between the front of the blade and the sole is called the throat. A spokeshave's blade, like a plane's, is enclosed to control depth of cut.

Spokeshaves probably developed as wheelwrights' tools; they come in handy for work on spokelike objects, like stool parts. They're also good for chamfering boards and carving round shapes in spoons, toys and other projects.

A wide variety of spokeshaves can be classified by handle and sole shape. Handles can be raised or straight. Raised handles look pretty and keep your fingers clear of the work, but they tend to make the tool turn over in your hands, and are hard for kids to control. Straight-handled shaves, which place the force of the pull at the level of the blade, are harder to find these days, but worth looking for.

Spokeshave soles can be flat or curved, photo right. Flat-soled shaves are versatile: they work on convex, straight and concave surfaces. Those with soles that curve from front to back work well only on inside curves, but it's worth having one around.

Flat-soled spokeshaves with adjustable throats are the basic spokeshaves used in my shop. By turning a single knob, a child can get a very fine or very coarse shaving without an adult's help in adjusting the tool. These shaves can take extremely fine cuts in tricky grain or end grain; to take enormous bites, simply twist the knob. The raised-handled Stanley No. 53 and the straight-handled Stanley No. 54, at bottom in the photo above, have adjustable throats. Several spokeshaves produced by Kunz, a German firm, also have adjustable throats.

After sharpening the blade (p. 181), set the adjustable throat very fine and slide the blade into place. Be sure only a very small amount of the blade protrudes beyond the sole and the cutting edge is parallel to the sole. Tighten the hold-down screw and turn the throat-setting knob for the shaving you need.

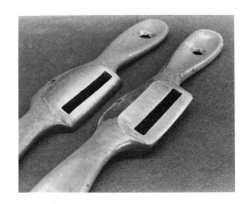

The only problem with adjustable-throat spokeshaves is that the shavings can get caught under the adjusting frame on either side of the blade; use a screwdriver to clear the shavings before they get too tightly packed.

To vary the thickness of the shaving using a spokeshave with a fixed throat, you must move the blade up or down in the frame.

A shave with half-round blades, at top in the photo below, is useful for smoothing stool parts; it won't leave facets as will a straight-bladed tool. Kids often try to round the edges of boards with these shaves, but they don't work nearly as well as straight-bladed tools for that job. Half-round and straight spokeshaves are combined in the double-cutter model, at bottom in the photo, which has two blades side by side in one spokeshave. The single, half-round blade is wider than the double cutter's half-round, but the radii are about the same. The narrower blade works as well and is easier to sharpen, so I prefer the double-cutter tool.

The curve of the half-round blade must match that of the sole—it's a tricky business, and that's why the narrower blade is easier to sharpen. To grind the curve of the blade, you'll need to round off the corners of an old grinding wheel with a wheel-dressing tool. Place the blade in the spokeshave regularly to test its shape, then finish sharpening the edge with a slip stone or a gouge stone.

The cooper's spokeshave that Brant Nicks is using in the photo above is 18 in. long and has a blade 2½ in. wide. It's a great substitute for a drawknife for little kids, or older kids who are shy of sharp edges. For an extra-thick shaving, file the throat wider. Originally produced as Stanley No. 56, these are now made by Kunz. Kunz spokeshave blades might not hold an edge well; you can harden them by following the directions on p. 134. Temper to a straw color.

Sharpening

Without a sharp edge, your planes, chisels, drawknives, spokeshaves and gouges would be worse than useless: dull tools are frustrating and dangerous. Working with kids, you'll want to be able to sharpen quickly; children will lose interest if they have to wait ten minutes while you put on that perfect edge.

In my shop, I'd rather keep kids working on their projects than have them puzzling over this precise and delicate skill, so I'm responsible for sharpening tools. You may want to start your child sharpening, but it takes a patient and mature kid to master the skill before he or she is fifteen or sixteen years old.

A cutting edge is formed by the intersection of two surfaces—on most tools, a bevel and the flat back of the blade. In theory, a sharp edge has no thickness, only length; it tapers to nothing, or at least appears to do so. A dull edge is rounded so you can actually see a bead of brightness where a sharp edge would be invisible. A sharp tool will shave hair: some woodworkers test their blades on the hair on their forearms.

When sharpening a cutting edge, metal is removed from the bevel until the newly exposed surface meets the flat side of the blade (or meets another bevel, as in double-beveled tools such as knives, some carving tools and skew chisels used for turning).

As the edge becomes thin, the metal near the tip becomes flexible and bends away from the grinding tool instead of being cut. This flap of metal is called a burr or wire edge; its appearance signals that grinding is done. All that's left to do is to use a finer abrasive on the tool's flat side to remove the burr and to smooth the rough texture on the bevel's surface left by grinding.

That's the theory—but every woodworker has his or her own way of getting it done. Here are the tools that you'll need.

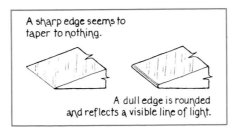

A sharp edge seems to taper to nothing.

A dull edge is rounded and reflects a visible line of light.

Grinders—Bench grinders use a circular grindstone. Some have built-in motors (as shown at left below), others are belt-driven from a separate motor. They can cost from twenty-five to several hundred dollars, depending on size and quality. Hand-powered grinders are slow but safer for kids to use; some are easily adapted for foot power, which leaves both hands free to hold the tool. Check out junk stores for old grinders.

Belt grinders use an abrasive cloth belt that runs over two or more wheels. I like those with a belt 2½ in. wide (wider than anything you're likely to grind except drawknives). My grinder (shown at right below) is a Mark II, made by Woodcraft Supply, Woburn, Mass.

Less expensive machines use a 1-in.-wide belt, and are made by Rockwell,

Sears, Belsaw and others. Some woodworkers grind tools on a portable belt sander, clamped upside down in a bench vise.

Grindstone surfaces that become misshapen or dull are resurfaced with a tool called a wheel dresser. Belt grinders never need reshaping because the wheels or platen (the flat back-up plate on some grinders) won't wear, and dull belts are replaced with new ones.

Belt grinders are somewhat less likely than a grindstone to overheat a tool, though the risk is increased by using a dull belt. Coarser belts cut quicker and cooler and last longer than finer ones. I use 60 grit in preference to 100 grit or 200 grit. All things considered, belt grinding probably costs a little more, but this is offset by the time it saves.

Sharpening stones—After grinding the tool, sharpening stones are used to remove the burr and smooth the bevel's surface. You can touch up an edge with stones several times before you will need to regrind.

Sharpening stones come in a variety of shapes, materials and degrees of coarseness. The basic kit in my shop consists of four stones, photo right. The silicon-carbide bench stone, at center, is called an India stone and is long and wide, with one side coarse, the other fine. It's good for sharpening chisels, plane blades and other straight-edged tools. The conical gouge stone, at left in the photo, can be used on the inside and outside surfaces of gouges and the edge of a half-round spokeshave.

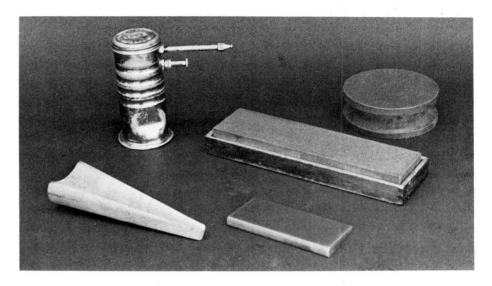

The small slip stone in the foreground is made of natural stone, which is called Arkansas; its fine texture makes it good for putting on a finished edge. This Arkansas slip stone has a wide edge and a narrow edge, both rounded for slipping into the channels of gouges to remove the burr. The faces of the slip stone are flat and can be used to finish straight-edged tools like plane blades. Arkansas stones come in two grades, hard and soft. Get hard if you can afford it. The round stone is used to sharpen drawknives (p. 189).

The squirt can contains light mineral oil, which is spread on the stones while sharpening to float away the metal particles that would otherwise clog the surface and keep it from cutting. After use, always rinse the stone in fresh oil and wipe it off.

Cloth buffing wheel—An alternative to hand stones is a cloth buffing wheel charged with polishing compound. The wheel is made of many layers of muslin sewn together and mounted on the shaft of a grinder or motor that rotates at about 1600 rpm. It stiffens up at speed, but remains flexible enough to conform to the shape of a gouge that is pressed

into it. The cloth wheel is used to polish off the burr on the back of the tool and to smooth the surface of the bevel.

Cloth wheels and bars of polishing compound are cheap and last a long time. Some woodworkers feel that the soft wheel rounds the edge too much, and for some tools I agree. But for most of our tools, the results with a cloth wheel are actually quite good and, most importantly, it's very fast. In my shop, it's the cloth wheel that lets me keep kids working with sharp tools.

Sharpening plane blades, spokeshave blades and chisels—The edges of these tools are straight, or almost straight, and they are sharpened in much the same way. Your grinder should have a tool rest that can be set to hold the blade against the wheel or belt and grind a bevel of between 25° and 30°. A bevel of this angle will be about twice as long as the blade is thick.

Rest the tool gently against the abrasive, moving it from side to side if the edge is wider than the wheel or belt. Hold short blades, like spokeshave blades, in a Vise-Grip pliers to keep your fingers away from the wheel or belt. On chisels or plow-plane blades, it's important that the cutting edge be

exactly at right angles to the sides, so check your work with a trysquare as you grind. The cutting edge of a plane blade may be perfectly straight or just slightly crowned, but never hollow. The cutting edges of spokeshave blades should be quite straight.

Dull stones or worn belts overheat tools quickly; dress the stone and replace your belts often. Overheating a blade draws the temper, softening the edge so it won't stay sharp in use. You can tell that you have overheated the metal if the edge turns blue—this is called burning the edge. If this happens, it's best to carefully grind past the burned section. To avoid overheating, keep a container of water near the grinder and dip the blade frequently. Watch the droplets of water on the blade as you grind; when they start to sizzle, it's time to cool the blade again.

Check your progress by running your finger down the back of the blade and across the edge. When you feel the burr all the way along the cutting edge, you've ground far enough. If grinding nicks out of the blade, keep grinding until the last nick is gone. Dub off the corners of the cutting edge on plane and spokeshave blades to keep them from marking the wood.

Now to the cloth wheel. If the wheel runs toward you, aim the blade downward; if away from you, point it upward. Point the bar of polishing compound in the same direction when you recharge the wheel every two or three sharpenings.

To avoid rounding the cutting edge as you polish, place it across the wheel at a large angle, as shown in the drawing at right. First polish off the burr on the back of the blade; work very lightly and touch the wheel only briefly. Use slightly heavier pressure and take a little longer on the bevel side to polish out the marks left by the grinder. You know the edge is sharp when it feels smooth and greasy when you drag your thumbnail over it.

For jointer-plane blades, I use hard stones rather than the cloth wheel after grinding, to get a straight edge. These blades need dead-straight edges and the flat India stone helps do a more accurate job. The method I'll describe is the one you would use for any edge tool if you don't have a cloth wheel.

Hold the blade at a large angle as you polish the edge on a cloth wheel.

Get the edge as straight as possible on the grinder: sight down the edge, or lay a straightedge along the tool's edge, and watch for light passing in between. If the edge is pretty straight, use the fine side of the India stone next; if the edge is not yet straight, use the coarse side. To sharpen a plane blade to a true edge, your stone should be flat; don't use a worn one. It's not hard to keep a stone flat—just use most of its surface as you work, rather than just the middle.

The stone must be held steady while in use. You can buy or make a box for the stone so it can be held in a vise without damage. Squirt some light mineral oil on the stone (put more on when the stone seems dry or when the oil already on it becomes black). Hold the blade in the palm of your hand and rest the bevel against the stone surface.

A blade ground on a wheel will have a hollow-ground bevel. The edge and the end of the bevel should touch the stone as you grind, as shown in the drawing below. Rock the blade up and down so you can feel a click, indicating that the edge and end of the bevel are in full contact with the stone.

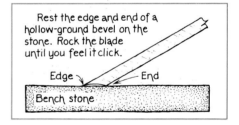

Rest the edge and end of a hollow-ground bevel on the stone. Rock the blade until you feel it click.
Edge
End
Bench stone

Sharpening a hollow-ground edge by hand is easy. You need remove only a little metal, and the back end of the bevel helps keep the blade in the correct position on the stone. A hollow-ground bevel can be resharpened many times, but as the flat portions of the bevel get wider, more metal must be removed with the hand stones. Restoring the edge will take longer each time; regrind it when sharpening becomes a chore.

Some belt grinders produce flat bevels. On the stone, lift the tail of a flat-beveled blade just a bit beyond the click so only the cutting edge is touching the stone. This will give you a small, second bevel, so you won't take metal off the whole bevel.

To help maintain the blade at the correct angle, let the tips of your fingers rest on the stone, as shown in the photo at left. Move the blade in a circular or figure-eight pattern.

Rocking the blade from side to side could crown the cutting edge, which is undesirable in a jointer plane. To grind back the center of a crowned blade, try pushing the blade across a corner of the stone so the stone cuts only in the middle of the edge.

When you have a straight cutting edge, and there's a burr along the entire edge, use the fine side of the stone to take off the burr. Hold the back of the blade flat on the stone; you don't want a counterbevel on the flat side of the blade. Rub the back of the blade until you feel the burr on the bevel side. Now flip the tool over and work on the bevel side. When you feel a burr on the flat side, turn the blade on its back and work it until the burr comes off.

The final touches, called honing, are done on a flat side of the Arkansas slip stone. On flat bevels, increase the second bevel just slightly; hone hollow-ground bevels in the position where you feel a click, or lift the tail of the blade to make a slight second bevel. Move the tool as you did on the other stones; you may need to go from bevel to back a few times, working more lightly each time.

Gouges—Veiner gouges, used for carving signs (Chapter 10), are a bit tricky to sharpen because they're thicker at the bottom of the U than at the sides. For a given bevel angle, the length of the bevel depends on the thickness of the blade. If the veiner's cutting edge has a uniformly angled bevel, the bevel will be longer at the bottom of the gouge than at the sides. New veiners don't come sharpened this way because it takes extra time, but the tool will cut much better when properly ground.

> The bevel on a veiner must be longer at the bottom than the sides.

Some grinders are equipped with special tool holders for gouges that allow you to roll the tool against the belt or wheel to create an even bevel, but you can do just as well with a normal rest or, with practice, freehand with no rest at all.

The bevel should be long and straight with no bulge behind the edge. Experimenting will tell you what the best bevel angle is, but I find it to be much lower than the usual 30° used for planes and chisels. As I sharpen, I look at the length of the bevel rather than its angle. Long, thin bevels, especially those on small gouges, accumulate heat quickly, so grind very lightly to avoid overheating the tool.

The cloth wheel is a great help in sharpening any gouge because it will conform to the inside shape (channel) of even the finest veiner. Slight rounding of this inside surface of the edge is permissible, so have no fear of pushing the gouge too hard into the wheel. Polish the bevel of the gouge with the tool held at a large angle to the wheel, rolling it to cover the whole surface of the bevel; work lightly to avoid rounding the bevel side of the edge.

If you don't have a cloth wheel, use a fine slip stone to clean the burr off the channel side of the edge. Roll the bevel back and forth on a flat side of the stone to help dislodge the burr. This is quicker and easier to do using the hollow side of the conical gouge stone.

Firmer gouges, used to make spoons (Chapter 11), have a uniformly thick cross section, so the bevel will be the same length at the bottom of the gouge as at its corners. Roll the gouge evenly as you grind; try to make the cutting edge straight and square to the length of the blade.

Spoon gouges should have a bevel that sweeps smoothly from the cutting edge to the curved bottom of the gouge; on a well-sharpened spoon gouge, you can't tell where the bevel ends and the

gouge bottom begins. The belt grinder is a great help here; use a section of the belt that isn't supported by a wheel or platen so it can flex slightly and conform to the curved surface. Move the handle up and down slightly as you roll the gouge from side to side.

Turning tools—Like veiners, deep-fluted long-and-strong gouges are extra thick at the bottom of the U, and the bevel should be longer there so the angle of the bevel is uniform. Experiment to see what bevel angle works best: many turners suggest 30°. A steeper angle will last longer on hardwoods, though kids might find a shallower angle easier to control. If you don't have a cloth wheel, try using the roughing-out gouge directly from the grinder without honing it on a slip stone. Some turners actually prefer a rough edge.

The ¼-in. turning gouge and larger, shallow turning gouges are usually ground to a nose or fingernail shape so they can reach deeper into a narrow cove. To grind them, swing the handle of the gouge so the portion of the edge you are grinding is perpendicular to the grindstone or belt; to do this, swing the handle as you roll the tool, as shown in the drawing below. This is tricky, but gets easier with practice.

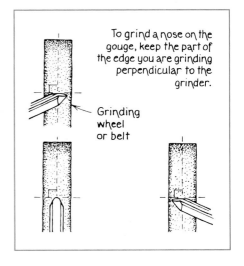

To grind a nose on the gouge, keep the part of the edge you are grinding perpendicular to the grinder.

Grinding wheel or belt

The ¼-in. skew can be ground quickly on the grindstone or belt and polished very lightly on the cloth wheel. Each bevel must be uniform along its length, and the length of the bevels on both sides must be equal, so that the cutting edge is parallel to the faces of the tool. If this is not the case, the tool will be difficult to control.

Larger skews require very careful sharpening. The bevel must be dead flat for about $\frac{1}{64}$ in. back from the cutting edge or the tool will tend to dig in suddenly. For this reason, never use the cloth wheel on a large turning skew. It's not hard to sharpen a large skew if the bevels are hollow-ground. You'll need a grindstone or a belt grinder on which the tool bears against a wheel rather than a platen. Grind the bevels to the same length and uniform width across the tool. Because of the skewed cutting edge, you may have to improvise a tool rest or hold the tool against the wheel without a rest. Grind each bevel until you can feel a burr.

Now hold the skew in a vise and sharpen it with a flat stone, held in your hand. Find the click position with the stone and take a few strokes to form a burr along the whole length of the edge, then turn the tool over and sharpen the other bevel the same way. Finally, hone both bevels with a flat Arkansas stone, also in the click position, and the tool is ready to go.

The parting tool is easy to sharpen. Grind one bevel slightly past the center, then grind the second bevel until the edge is centered. Take care to make the cutting edge parallel with the top and bottom edges of the tool; a crooked edge will cut poorly. Parting tools are tapered in thickness from front to back, so the sides of the tool won't bind in the cut. If yours seems to drag, grind a bit more taper.

If your parting tool doesn't cut well or leaves a lumpy bottom in the cut, try grinding it as a scraping tool, with a blunter edge, as shown in the drawing.

Grind the parting tool's bevels at about 50° to each other.

25°
25°

The cutting edge must be parallel to the tool's edges.

Grind a steep bevel if you want to use the parting tool to scrape.

Whittling knife—Kids have trouble finding the strength and coordination to use a knife well, so it helps if the blade is sharpened close to perfection. Grind knives with a long, flat bevel on each side of the blade, and sharpen them with the bevel held flat on an India stone, then on an Arkansas. As with most carving tools, avoid rounding the bevel near the edge. If you are in a hurry, you can hone the blade on the cloth wheel, but you will round the bevel a bit.

The all-purpose knife shown in the photo below is good for kids to use because the length of the blade can be varied for safety and convenience. The blade fits all the way through the handle and is locked in place by a set screw. It's convenient to remove the blade completely for sharpening.

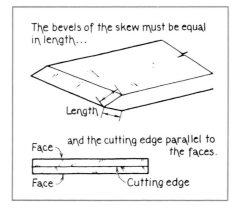

The bevels of the skew must be equal in length...

Length

Face
and the cutting edge parallel to the faces.
Face
Cutting edge

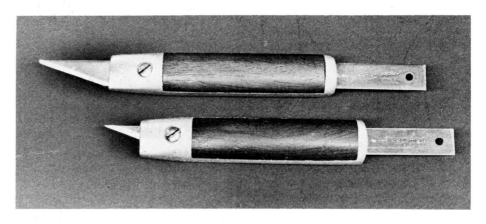

Scrapers

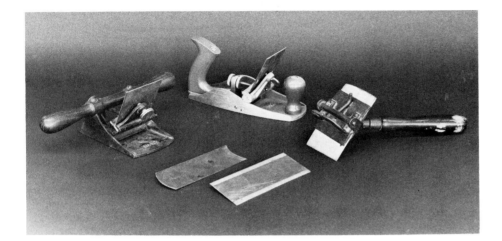

Scrapers remove a thin, lacy shaving with no danger of tearing the wood's surface or of taking off more than you want. Though not very effective on softwoods, they can clean up curly or fussy-grained hardwoods that a plane would tear badly.

A scraper blade is just a thin, flat piece of steel with a burr turned on its edge. When introducing a kid to the scraper, I have him or her feel the burr by moving a finger down the face and across the edge of the blade. "You feel the little bump? That's what does the cutting."

We use several styles of scrapers in my shop at school. The square-edged scraper, or cabinet scraper, is hand-held (two are shown in the foreground of the photo above) and is good for smoothing stool legs or spoons and for cleaning up tears in the face of a board. Scrapers come in other shapes, too, for working contours. For heavier work, a cabinet scraper can be set in a handle or in a planelike body for smoothing the surface of a whole board.

Scrapers are sharpened differently from other woodworking edge tools; it's not difficult to do if you know how a scraper cuts. The burr is a little hook-shaped ridge along the arris of the scraper's edge. The leading edge of the burr is very sharp, but the burr itself is so short that it can't take a deep bite into the wood. The shaving is thin and curled almost the instant the cut is made, so there's no possibility of the wood splitting ahead of the cut and tearing. Working with a scraper, you can almost disregard the grain direction.

To create a proper burr, you must first make the arris of the scraper's edge perfectly square. With the blade positioned upright in the vise, smooth the edge with a fine file held at right angles to the face, as shown in the photo at right. File until you can feel a burr on both face sides of the edge. The edge can be either straight along its length or have a slight bulge (called crown), but it should never be hollow. Dub off the corners.

Next, remove the burrs with a fine India stone. Make sure that you keep the stone flat on the faces, as shown in the photo at right, so you'll avoid rounding the edge. Now dress the edge of the scraper, using the stone as you did the file; hold it level and you won't round off the edges. Stone off the burrs on the face again. Now run your thumbnail down the arris of the edge of the scraper. A little roughness is okay for most work, but to get a glassy surface on the wood, the arris should feel really smooth. If it does not, try dressing the edge and faces again, but this time use a finer stone.

To create the cutting burr, you need a burnishing tool, a polished metal rod that is harder than the scraper steel. Some woodworkers use the back of a small gouge as a burnisher, but I prefer one that is triangular in section, as it requires less pressure to use. You can buy one, or make one by grinding smooth the edges of an old triangular file and polishing them on a cloth wheel charged with abrasive compound.

First, raise a fine burr on the arris, parallel to the face of the scraper, as shown in the drawing at near right and the photo above. Hold the scraper flat on a table's edge and place the burnisher on the far end of the arris. The burnisher should be almost parallel to the scraper face and held at a slight skew, so the handle is near the scraper.

As you pull the burnisher toward you, move the handle away from the edge of the scraper and pull it off so that you use a couple of inches of the burnisher's blade. Take a slow, definite stroke, touching every bit of the arris and pressing down firmly but not hard. One good stroke is enough; don't rub the burnisher back and forth. Raise a burr on each arris that you've prepared; some people sharpen all eight of them on a single steel scraper.

Now turn the burr. Set the scraper, edge up, in the vise, tip the burnisher about 5° below horizontal and draw it once across each arris, as in the photo below and the drawing at far right. This rolls the burr over into the cutting position. Here again, one firm stroke with the burnisher is enough.

Some woodworkers raise a large burr by rubbing the burnisher back and forth under great pressure. But I find a large burr doesn't cut as well as a fine one, is more easily damaged, and must be renewed more often.

You can usually raise and turn two or three burrs before the edge must be refiled, though second and third burrs are seldom as sharp as the first.

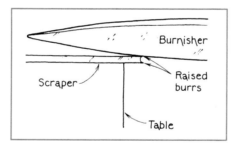

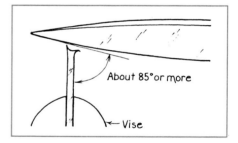

Using a cabinet scraper—Lean the scraper in the direction you're pushing it. The angle depends on the hook of the burr; try different angles to find where it cuts best.

To scrape a board, hold the scraper in two hands with your thumbs behind the edge. Push forward with your thumbs and pull back with your fingers to bend it slightly, so that the middle of the edge does most of the cutting.

Kids find bending the scraper hard on their thumbs. You can reduce or eliminate the need for this by filing the scraper's edge to a slight crown along its length.

If the scraper jumps or chatters across the wood, it probably needs to be leaned further forward. Chatter marks in the wood can be avoided by going over each section in a slightly different direction each time.

Using a scraper plane—Scraper planes combine the advantages of a plane with those of a scraper. They are easy to hold and will produce a smooth, flat surface, regardless of grain. You would use one after rough-planing and smooth-planing a board with fussy grain.

Scraper planes come with handles like those of a bench plane or with a cross-bar handle. The blade angle is adjusted by turning the two nuts on the horizontal threaded rod behind the blade. It's locked by tightening both nuts against the vertical post between them. Adjusting the angle causes the blade to move in or out slightly. Adjust the blade holder to an angle that looks right, insert the blade and set it where it projects the desired amount from the sole; lock it in place with the hold-down screw. Then try the tool; if it needs more angle you may need to retract the blade a little.

Sharpen the blade as you'd sharpen a cabinet scraper (p. 185): crown the edge slightly and dub off the corners. Some blades come beveled, so you can sharpen only one arris. If you file off the

bevel, you can sharpen two arrises on each end and have four burrs to use before you must rework the blade.

If your scraper plane has a cross-bar handle, place your palms on the handle, your thumbs on the back of the plane and your forefingers on the front of it. Plane in a slightly different direction on each stroke.

Scratch stocks—The scratch stock (also called a beading scraper) is used for cutting ornamental molding on the

edge of a board. Shown in the photo below is a Stanley No. 66 beading scraper, with extra blades and a sample of its work. The Stanley 66 is no longer made, but it can sometimes be found at flea markets or antique-tool stores.

It's not hard to make your own scratch stock; the drawing below shows how. You can file the blade to any shape you desire. This tool lets you cut moldings along curved or straight edges. An old marking gauge can be converted to a scratch stock, too.

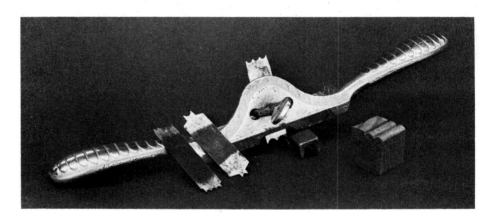

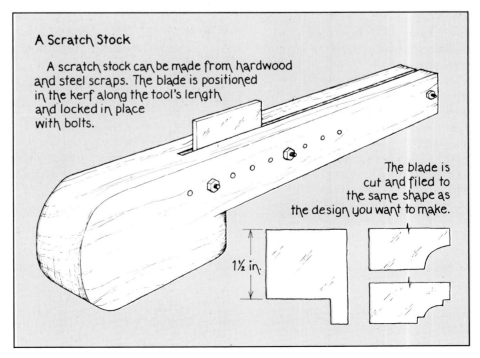

A Scratch Stock

A scratch stock can be made from hardwood and steel scraps. The blade is positioned in the kerf along the tool's length and locked in place with bolts.

The blade is cut and filed to the same shape as the design you want to make.

1½ in.

Drawknives

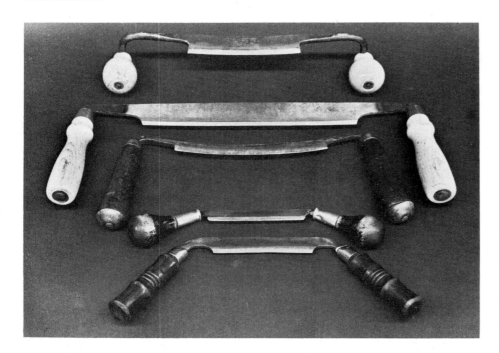

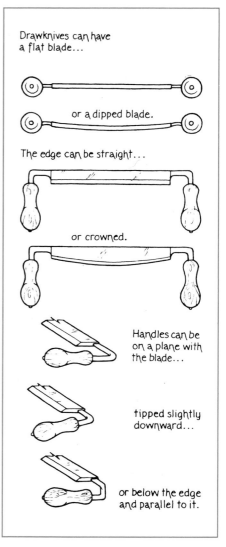

Drawknives can have a flat blade...

or a dipped blade.

The edge can be straight...

or crowned.

Handles can be on a plane with the blade...

tipped slightly downward...

or below the edge and parallel to it.

Drawknives come in many sizes and shapes. The cooper, log-cabin builder, carver and chair maker each used a different kind. Drawknives may be from 2 in. to 24 in. long. Their edges can be flat or curved, the handles in the same plane as the blade, tipped slightly downward or offset below the edge.

My own favorite drawknives are old ones resurrected from junk stores. They seem to stay sharp longer than new ones and they feel right in my hand. Look for drawknives with good, securely attached handles. Avoid drawknives with blades less than 1½ in. wide at the center, and knives made from old files.

For shaving stool parts, I prefer a knife with a straight edge, flat blade and handles on a plane with the blade. This style is made in England by both Marples and Sorby. Stay away from the French and German styles, which are carvers' tools; their ball-shaped handles are positioned well below the blade, and are hard to pull powerfully. We use small drawknives for carving spoons; my favorite has a straight, flat, 4-in. blade. Its egg-shaped handles allow you to swivel the tool in your hand for quick, accurate work. A full-sized pattern is given below, if you want to have a machinist make one. (Glue the handles on the tangs.) Or look for old ones made by Crescent or Cummings. Other small drawknives are available from companies specializing in carving tools.

A Drawknife Pattern

Made from ⅛-in. steel

Glue the tang with epoxy into a handle.

Drawknife blades are manufactured with one side flat and the other beveled. For shaving legs from green wood, I've found the tool's action is improved by grinding a small bevel, called a counterbevel, on the back of the blade.

Grind a small, slightly rounded counterbevel on the back of the drawknife's cutting edge. — 30°

Grind the large, top bevel of the drawknife to about 30°. Though the center of the blade wears most quickly because it's used more, you must grind the entire edge to maintain its shape. Don't grind more metal from the center than from the ends; it's okay to grind a bit more off the ends, but don't crown it too much.

If you grind a drawknife on most bench grinders, the motor housing usually gets in the way. Bevel the edge of the grindstone with a wheel-dressing tool, so that when the blade is held flat against the surface, its handles will clear the motor. You can also use a stationary belt sander (or a portable belt sander attached to a bench mount) to grind drawknives. My belt grinder has a wheel large enough to clear the motor housing and a wide belt to do a quick and even job. On belt grinders and sanders, grind with the edge facing the same way as the travel of the belt or you'll cut the belt in two.

In a shop full of kids, the edge of a drawknife gets nicked before it gets dull; run-ins with vises and other tools take their toll. (The drawknife rack, right, helps keep the knives from jostling against other tools.)

Grinding out nicks during every sharpening is tedious and wasteful work. A nicked blade will cut fine if it's sharp, and the trails the nicks leave are easily removed during scraping and sanding. If a drawknife is intended for fine work,

grind past the nicks, then treat the tool with extra care.

Old drawknives are usually pitted with rust. Pits on the top don't affect cutting action, but surface pits in the back become nicks when they intersect the top bevel. The edge of a pitted blade will be serrated with these nicks, but if you sharpen the knife with a counterbevel, the nicks in the back are ground away and won't become part of the edge. If you want to restore a really flat back to an old drawknife, ask a machinist to surface-grind it for you.

To sharpen drawknives quickly, I grind them lightly when they dull and finish them on a cloth wheel charged with abrasive compound. If you're not in a hurry, sharpen them by hand and grind only to restore the bevel or to take out nicks. I use a round oilstone that is coarse on one side, fine on the other, with a groove around the middle to keep fingers clear of the edge. Hold the drawknife, edge up, between your hand and shoulder, like a fiddle, as seventh-grader Michael Schruben does, and work the stone over the blade with a circular motion. Finish the edge with a soft Arkansas stone.

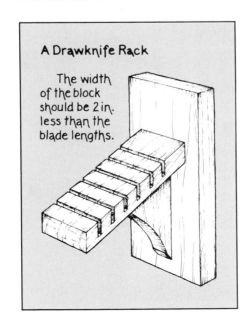

A Drawknife Rack

The width of the block should be 2 in. less than the blade lengths.

Surface Planing

The faces, edges and ends of boards you buy at the lumberyard, whether they are rough-sawn or planed, sometimes need further planing. For example, boards frequently have faces that are cupped and need to be planed flat. If you have glued several boards together edge to edge (p. 192), there will be some unevenness between them, and it will be necessary to plane the faces flat. Likewise, the edges and ends may not be straight enough or square enough for your purposes, and the edges of boards may need to be planed to make the board the correct width.

Face planing—It's easier to plane the hollow face of a cupped board first. (The face of a glued-up board may be rippled, and it probably won't matter which face you start on.) Clamp the board lengthwise between a vise dog and a bench stop, as shown above. Don't let the board overhang the bench more than an inch or two. Slip little wedges of scrap under the raised edges of a cupped board to keep it from rocking.

Use a jack plane (14 in.) or fore plane (18 in.), set to take a coarse shaving, to rough the board down quickly. Plane diagonally across the board in every

direction, pushing sideways to get a skew cut, as seventh-grader Rhonda Pillsbury does at left. To explain a skew cut to kids, I tell them to aim the tool at a corner of the room but push toward a wall. Plane off the edge of the board at an angle; if the blade is parallel to the edge, the board will chip.

Kids trying to flatten a board are mystified when the plane won't cut in certain areas. Show them the low points in the board by using the edge of the plane's sole as a straightedge. Tip the plane sideways to create a shadow on

the wood: light will show through where the board is low, as shown below. Be sure the child starts the cut at the near edge of the board and pushes it past the far edge. Pushing down on the front of the plane at the start of the cut, and on the end of the plane at the far edge, prevents rounding the ends of the cut.

Keep working all over the board until the plane takes off shavings everywhere. If the child planes too much in one section of the board, it will become much thinner; occasionally turn the board end for end to avoid this.

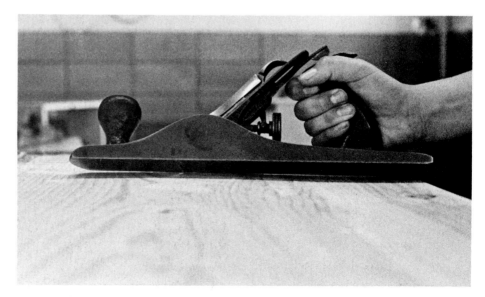

When the board is reasonably flat, set a long plane to take a fine shaving (we use a fore plane). Now plane along the grain from end to end, as shown in the photo below, in the direction that seems to leave the best surface. If there are knots in the board, if it has fussy grain, or if the board has edge-glued strips with grain running in different directions, plane each part in the most favorable direction. Should this be too confusing, set the plane very fine and plane across the grain. (Use a scraper plane on hardwoods.) As you smooth the board with the longer, finer-set plane, it will skip spots as it trims the high sections. Check progress with the edge of the sole, and plane down the high spots.

A dead-flat board will show no light under a straightedge in any position on its surface. Check across the board's ends, midsection and diagonals to see where the board needs further planing, as shown in the drawing below.

Thickness planing—Once you've flattened one face of a board, it's simple to plane it uniformly thick. Gauge the thickness with a wooden or metal marking gauge; the metal one shown in the photo seems to stand up best in a kid's shop.

Check the edges and ends of the board to find the thinnest part; set the distance between the marking-gauge fence and its pin to slightly less than that thickness. Hold the fence firmly against the flat face of the board and scribe a line around both edges and both ends, as eighth-grader Heidi Jernstadt is doing at left. Now plane down to the lines using the same techniques as for flattening the first face. (You can also use this method to plane a board to a desired thickness: just set the gauge to the thickness you want.)

Squaring up—If you need a board whose edges are parallel to each other and square to the faces (as when making the thin-walled box in Chapter 7), here's how to do it. After thickness planing, set the board on edge in the vise and plane the first edge straight and square to the face, as described on pp. 192-193. Check the squareness with a trysquare. Now set the marking gauge to the desired width and scribe the position of the second edge; be sure to push the fence firmly against the planed edge. If the board is too wide for the marking gauge, measure the distance across each of its ends and scribe along a straightedge between the marks. Plane to the line, checking the edge with a square to make sure it is at right angles to the face.

We usually use a miter box to square up the ends of small boards and a radial arm saw for larger ones. To do it by hand, use a trysquare and scribe a line across the end, then saw just outside the line. Plane to the line with a block plane, checking for squareness to the face with a trysquare.

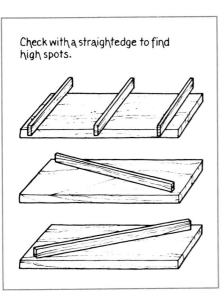

Check with a straightedge to find high spots.

Edge-Jointing

If you need a tabletop or box side that's wider than any board in your shop, you can glue several narrow boards together edge to edge. This method has several advantages: a wide board, made up of many small strips glued together, will stay flatter through seasonal changes in humidity than will a single board. A glued-up board is usually stronger than a solid piece because the weaknesses are redistributed throughout the board; glue joints are usually stronger than the wood itself. You can also flatten a cupped board by ripping it into strips and gluing them back together. Kids often like to glue woods of different colors together for a striped effect.

Edges to be glued together must be jointed, that is, planed flat, so there is perfect contact between them. Jointing takes care and practice; some kids pick it up right away but many find it frustrating. Sometimes I'll joint boards for my students so they can get on to the next step.

Boards to be edge-jointed should have knot-free edges and be cut several inches longer than the finished length. Badly cupped pieces should be ripped lengthwise into two or more pieces. Organize the boards on a table so the best-looking faces are up, and the grain patterns in adjacent pieces complement each other. Then draw a large triangle across the set to identify the position of each board, as in the drawing below.

Draw a large triangle to mark the position of the boards.

For boards 1 in. thick or less, it's best to plane mating edges of two boards at the same time. The wider surface makes it easier to hold the plane level, and planing two edges at once takes half the time. If the planed edges aren't perfectly square to the faces, the angles will be complementary, and the glued-up board will be flat. (When jointing thicker boards one at a time, the edge must be exactly square to the face. Use a trysquare to check as you plane.)

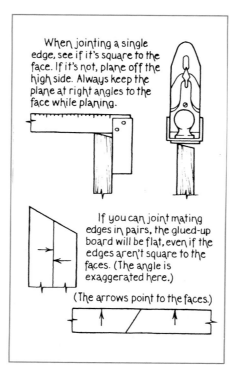

When jointing a single edge, see if it's square to the face. If it's not, plane off the high side. Always keep the plane at right angles to the face while planing.

If you can joint mating edges in pairs, the glued-up board will be flat, even if the edges aren't square to the faces. (The angle is exaggerated here.)

(The arrows point to the faces.)

Fold the faces of two adjacent boards together and set them in a vise with their mating edges up and flush with each other. A space between the edges means that the boards are slightly cupped and the hollow faces are facing away from each other. Put the hollow faces together without turning the boards end for end. Now the edges will press together when the vise tightens.

A jointer plane 22 in. or 24 in. long will bridge the low spots while trimming the high spots on the edge of a board. A shorter plane would follow the hills and valleys and emphasize them. If you don't have a jointer, use the longest plane you have and a good straightedge (a steel ruler is best) to locate the high points.

Though a jointer plane will flatten a lumpy or hollow edge, it won't automatically flatten a convex edge; it will just follow the curve. The trick in jointing is to plane the edge slightly concave before trying to flatten it: that way, you can be sure the plane is not following a bulge.

Be sure the jointer plane is well tuned with a sharp, straight-edged cutter, set to take a fine shaving. Hold the back handle in your right hand (if you're right-handed) and wrap the thumb of your left hand around the front knob. The fingers of the left hand should reach down under the plane, as Amy Lord's do in the photo below, to help guide the plane along the edge and to keep it level. On long boards, take a step with the plane rather than extend your arms too far, else you might tip the plane off level.

Start the cutting edge an inch or two in from the near end and plane along the edge, stopping an inch or two from the other end. At the end of each cut, lift the moving plane from the wood to avoid leaving an unfinished shaving on the wood. Press down firmly at the front of the plane as you begin the cut and at the back as you end it, in order to keep the plane bearing on the board.

The shavings indicate your progress: those spots along the length where no shaving comes off are low; shavings narrower than the edge of the board indicate a low point across the width. After several passes, the shavings should get longer and wider as the high spots on the edge get lower.

As the middle of the edge becomes lower than the ends, the plane will take thinner shavings, and eventually none at all. When the edge is very slightly hollow, plane it straight by working from the middle toward each end; two or three shots in each direction should do it. When the plane again begins to take shavings in the middle of the edge, try a few passes along the entire length of the edge: you should get a complete shaving, in width and length, along the whole edge. If there are sections where a piece of the shaving is missing, continue planing until the shaving is complete. If you've been planing a single edge, now work up its mate so you can check the fit.

Check the joint between two edges by holding one board in each hand and pressing the edges together, as Amy does at right. (For long or heavy boards, put one in the vise, edge up.) Try to rotate the boards against each other; if their edges are convex along their length, they will touch only in the center and pivot easily on one another. You will also be able to see light coming through at the ends of the joint. Place them back in the vise and plane them without cutting the ends of the edges, as previously described.

If the boards don't rotate against one another, but you can see light through the middle of the joint, the edges are still hollow. If they are very hollow, plane from the center outward to straighten them. Some woodworkers prefer to leave the edges slightly hollow so that when the joint is clamped, the ends will be pressed together extra tightly. This is useful if you're not sure your boards are completely seasoned or if you are gluing during very humid weather; because of the extra tension, the joint is unlikely to open as the boards lose moisture. The gap should be no more than $\frac{1}{32}$ in. in boards of $1\frac{1}{2}$ ft. to 2 ft. long, a bit more in longer stock (shorter pieces should be dead flat). If your edges are completely flat, you can make them slightly hollow with a few jointer strokes that do not touch the ends: each stroke should start and end a little closer to the middle of the edge.

For the second test, rock the boards across the width of the edges. The edges of a good joint will click, but a rounded edge will roll with no clear, correct position. Back in the vise, plane the boards without allowing the plane to tip sideways.

Look for spaces along the joint even if no light shows through: these may be low spots that don't go all the way across the edge or chips in the arris of an edge. Keep planing until there are no spaces in the edges of the shavings.

When all the joints in a set of boards are done, you are ready to glue up. In my shop, we usually do this right in the vise because it is quick, neat and easy to apply glue. Put the first board in the vise and spread glue thinly and evenly on its edge. Set its mating board in place (the triangle mark will tell you which board this is) and rub the two edges back and forth a few times to help them stick in position. Then spread glue on the next edge and fit its mate in place, and so on. Now align the ends of the boards. You don't have to be too fussy about this, because they are overlong and will be trimmed later.

Use bar or pipe clamps to hold the assembly together. Amy put one on each end and on the same side. Next, she'll move the boards sideways in the vise so she can put a clamp in the middle of the boards on the opposite face. Pinch the two ends of each joint between your thumb and fingers to align the faces. Snug the center clamp first, and then the outer ones. Check that everything is aligned properly, tighten the center clamp, then the others. On longer boards, you may want to use five clamps. Glue should squeeze out along every joint if the fit is good, the clamps tight, and enough glue is on the edge. If you don't get glue beads somewhere along a joint, pull off the clamps and open up the joint to find out why.

When you're gluing up many strips, or thin boards that won't stand upright, you're better off working horizontally. Cover the table with newspaper and make a rack to hold your clamps in place. Put the two end clamps in the rack and put the pieces in place, as sixth-grader Mark Joseph does at right. When all the glued edges are mated, place a third clamp in the center of the boards; snug that one up first, then the outer ones, and then tighten them all.

The faces of two jointed boards whose edges aren't square to their faces usually slide out of alignment. Pinch the ends of the joint with handscrew clamps or *C*-clamps to hold them in place.

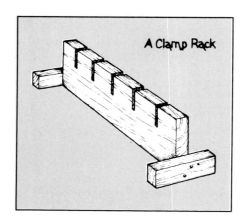

A Clamp Rack

The Workbench

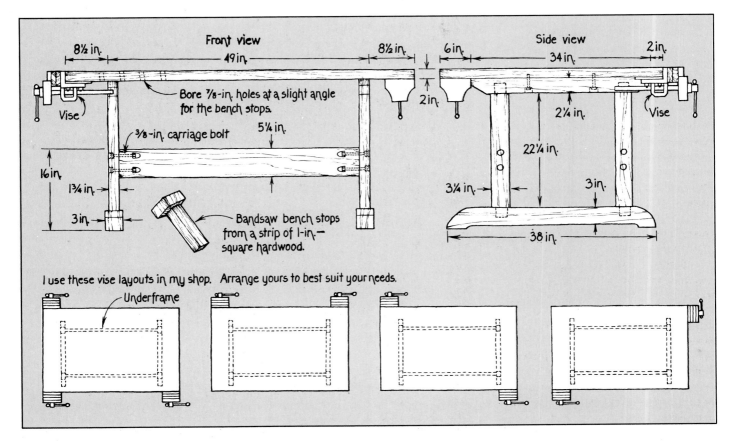

Front view

8½ in. | 49 in. | 8½ in. | 2 in.

Bore ⅞-in. holes at a slight angle for the bench stops.

Vise

⅜-in. carriage bolt

5¼ in.

16 in.

1¾ in.

3 in.

Bandsaw bench stops from a strip of 1-in.-square hardwood.

Side view

6 in. | 34 in. | 2 in.

2 in.

Vise

2¼ in.

22¼ in.

3¼ in. | 3 in.

38 in.

I use these vise layouts in my shop. Arrange yours to best suit your needs.

Underframe

My workbench design has proven to be flexible and comfortable for kids even after ten years of heavy use. Though you may not need a bench that can handle three or four kids at a time, you should consider the following features as you design or modify your own bench.

A height of 30 in. seems about right. That's about 4 in. lower than most adult benches. Small kids might prefer a lower bench, but they can get along on a 30-in. bench by standing on a block of wood or climbing on the benchtop to bore holes or carve.

Heavy benches stay put. My benches have heavy tops made of 2-in. by 2-in. strips of maple glued up butcher-block style. I can jump on the benchtop's overhang without upending the table (I weigh about 200 lb.). If your bench is small or lightweight, consider weighting its base with concrete blocks.

It's useful to have two different-sized vises. Small vises are easy to operate, and best for small work; the larger ones can hold wide, deep or thick work. Vises should be mounted flush with the corners of the benchtop to allow kids to saw close to the vise jaws and to facilitate the assembly of projects. Make sure that the benchtop overhangs enough so that the vise mechanisms will clear the underframe.

Vises mounted on both right and left-hand corners of the benchtop will accommodate kids of both handedness, and projects that may fit better in one vise than the other. It's also handy to have a benchtop with two vises mounted on the same side to hold long projects. In my shop, no two benches have the same vise layout.

The tops of the vise jaws should be flush with the surface of the benchtop or

slightly below it, but never above it. Shim between the vise and the bottom of the bench with washers or a plywood spacer to position the jaws properly. Countersink the heads of the mounting bolts below the benchtop surface.

Using the bench-stop dog on a vise and a bench stop on the bench, you can hold a piece of wood in position for planing or carving. I make bench stops quickly on the bandsaw from strips of 1-in.-square hardwood. First cut the shoulders, then rip along the length of the stop on all four sides to clear the waste. These wooden bench stops are superior in every way to the metal stops that are commercially made. They won't chip a plane blade; the heads can be sawn off short if you need to plane thin wood; they are quickly and easily replaced if lost or broken; and best of all, they don't cost anything.

Bore the holes for the bench stops at an angle of about 5° to the benchtop, inclined toward the vise so pressure will push the stop into the hole rather than lift it out. The space between the holes should be at least an inch or two less than the maximum opening of the vise jaws. This spacing will accommodate every length of board.

Clamp-on vises can be attached to a bench anywhere. The Versa-Vise, with a clamp-on base, is especially useful for working on pieces too small or delicate for bench vises. The vise can be rotated and set on its side to hold odd pieces in convenient positions, as shown in the photo below.

A benchtop corner without a vise is very useful; you can clamp work to it, as when rabbeting a cupped board (p. 166), or you can hang a project over the corner for support (p. 45). Benchtop corners should overhang the bench understructure enough to avoid interfering with such work.

A nicely finished workbench top encourages good work, so try to keep it in good shape. But no matter how careful you are, a benchtop will always take abuse. In my shop, kids know they must not nail into the top, plane it or try gouges on it. I remind them to use scrap as a backing and a depth gauge when boring holes. Clean up minor dings and glue spots with a scraper. Apply paste wax once or twice a year to keep glue from sticking, and have a separate table on which to oil, stain or paint.

Shaving Horse

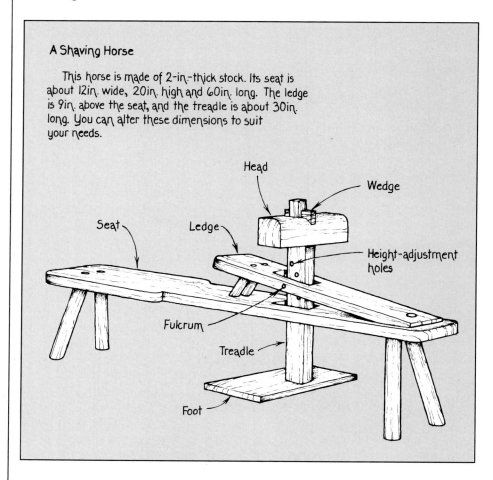

A Shaving Horse

This horse is made of 2-in.-thick stock. Its seat is about 12in. wide, 20in. high and 60in. long. The ledge is 9in. above the seat, and the treadle is about 30in. long. You can alter these dimensions to suit your needs.

Head

Wedge

Seat

Ledge

Height-adjustment holes

Fulcrum

Treadle

Foot

A shaving horse is a great help in making legs and stretchers for green-wood stools, benches and tables. The horse is easy and fun for kids to use; pushing down on the treadle wedges the wood firmly between the horse's head and the slanted ledge.

You can make the seat as you would a four-legged bench (p. 113), using a good hardwood, if possible. The seat narrows to allow space for the child's knees. The slanted ledge is also made like a bench, and its legs are tenoned and through-wedged into the seat.

The slots in the seat and the ledge should be long enough to allow for the treadle to swing and wide enough so it doesn't bind. Bore a hole through the slot in the ledge to take a fulcrum made of ½-in. steel rod (a long, ½-in. bolt will

also work). The hole should be slightly oversized so you can remove the pin easily to adjust the height of the head.

The horse's head can be a solid block of wood, mortised to take the treadle, or you can bolt thick pieces on either side of the treadle to form the head. A series of pivot holes in the treadle will allow you to adjust the horse to hold various thicknesses of wood.

Make sure that the treadle and its foot are long enough for the child to reach, but not so long that they hit the floor when working with thin pieces. The foot in the drawing is a board, mortised or nailed to the end of the treadle. You could also use a piece of round closet rod: bore a hole through the bottom end of the treadle and then glue or nail the rod in place.

Lathe

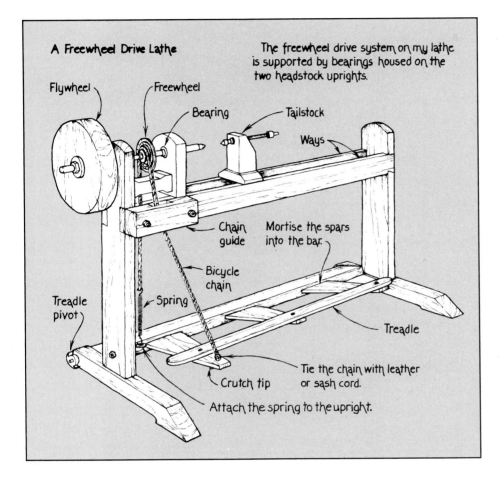

A Freewheel Drive Lathe

The freewheel drive system on my lathe is supported by bearings housed on the two headstock uprights.

Flywheel · Freewheel · Bearing · Tailstock · Ways · Chain guide · Mortise the spars into the bar. · Treadle pivot · Spring · Bicycle chain · Treadle · Tie the chain with leather or sash cord. · Crutch tip · Attach the spring to the upright.

Children like woodturning it because they see results quickly, and it's almost effortless once they have acquired skill. The shapes they can create, imaginative sweeping curves and crinkly details in three dimensions, would be difficult to produce any other way. Kids like the way shavings fly off the tool. In woodturning, the process may be even more fun than the product.

In my school shop, I've reduced the risks of woodturning by building a foot-powered lathe. It is slow and low-powered, but capable of fine work. Mishaps like catching a tool or throwing stock out of the machine have a lot less energy behind them than they would on a motor-driven lathe, so serious injury is far less likely. Kids still need to wear face protection, to dress properly and to

take care where they put their hands. They learn the same skills and safety habits as they would on a power machine, but I'm a lot more secure knowing that accidents are less likely to be serious.

This design for a foot-powered lathe has proven itself through many years of heavy work and abuse in my school shop. Building one is fun, but it is not a simple project. Homemade machinery requires seat-of-the-pants engineering and a period of development during which nothing seems to work right. At first you'll spend more time tuning your lathe than turning.

If you really enjoy this sort of work, as I do, then building a foot-powered lathe will be fun for you and it will broaden the woodworking opportunities available

to your child. If your child becomes involved in the project, it will be even more meaningful.

If you start from scratch, use my drawings as a guide. Visit a museum to get a close look at an authentic old-style wooden lathe and see if there are any good ideas. Then build away.

If you'd prefer not to build a whole lathe, adapt a commercial lathe to foot power. Buy a lightweight, inexpensive machine, mount it on a stand and find a way to adapt my drive system to the headstock. It may be easiest to replace the original metal headstock with a wooden one similar to mine.

The drive system on my lathe wastes very little energy. The system converts the up-and-down motion of your foot to continuous rotation by draping a bicycle chain over the sprocket from a ten-speed bike. When you push the treadle down, it pulls the chain and turns the sprocket, which is mounted on the machine's input shaft. As you release the treadle, a spring mounted at the far end of the chain pulls the system back to the starting position. The ratchet mechanism in the bicycle freewheel allows the sprocket to click backward while the shaft continues to coast forward, its momentum maintained by a flywheel.

The drive is made from inexpensive parts easily obtained at bike shops and hardware stores. Unlike the crank-and-flywheel system found on sewing machines, this treadle drive starts instantly and always in the right direction. You don't have to pump a rigid rhythm and the treadle doesn't kick back with the lathe's accumulated momentum when pumping stops. All these features make it safer and easier for kids to do woodturning.

The flywheel keeps the lathe turning between treadle strokes; without a flywheel, the thing would stop instantly. A relatively light flywheel allows the lathe to stop quickly if something gets caught in it, like a sleeve, hair or a finger. My flywheel is made of two cherry discs, each 1½ in. thick and 11 in. in diameter.

The lathe's speed depends on the number of teeth on the freewheel sprocket. Get a cluster with the smallest high gear available, usually 12 or 13 teeth. The larger sprockets are best for lower speeds where higher power is required, like when climbing a hill on a bike. Lathe speed can be increased by attaching the chain farther from the pivot of the treadle to pull more chain over the sprocket on each stroke.

Screen-door springs are too stiff for foot power. Find a selection of springs at a hardware store, and choose one that is about 1 in. in diameter and 14 in. long. If your treadle doesn't return quickly, attach a second spring at its right end.

The chain will usually slap and jump around between the treadle and the freewheel, which could cause it to jump the sprocket. A chain guide fitted near the freewheel, as shown in the drawing on p. 197, will solve the problem.

The bottom drawing at right shows you how to make a Morse-taper socket for the lathe. If you don't want to go to the trouble of making a Morse-taper socket, you can purchase a spur center that fastens to the shaft by a setscrew. These are available for ShopSmith and Williams and Hussey lathes, but make sure the spur center will fit your shaft before purchasing one. Chucks that mount the same way are also available.

Turning wood—Woodturning is one of those skills you should know well before trying to teach it to a child, for safety's sake and to avoid unnecessary frustration. There are many books written on woodturning, so I won't try to condense the skills into a few pages. (See the bibliography on p. 203 for some books on woodturning.) I learned from a book and so can you, but the

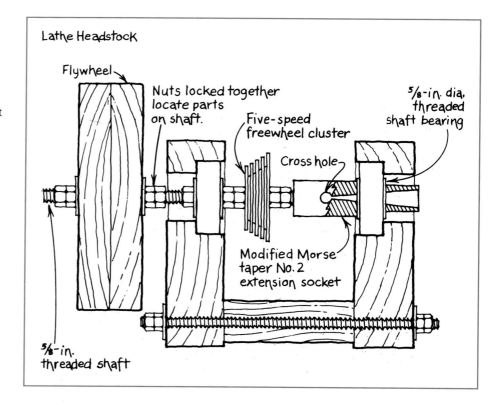

Lathe Headstock

Flywheel

Nuts locked together locate parts on shaft.

Five-speed freewheel cluster

Cross hole

⅝-in. dia. threaded shaft bearing

Modified Morse taper No. 2 extension socket

⅝-in. threaded shaft

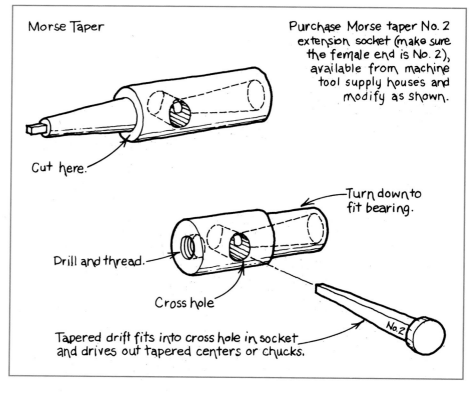

Morse Taper

Purchase Morse taper No. 2 extension socket (make sure the female end is No. 2), available from machine tool supply houses and modify as shown.

Cut here.

Turn down to fit bearing.

Drill and thread.

Cross hole

No. 2

Tapered drift fits into cross hole in socket and drives out tapered centers or chucks.

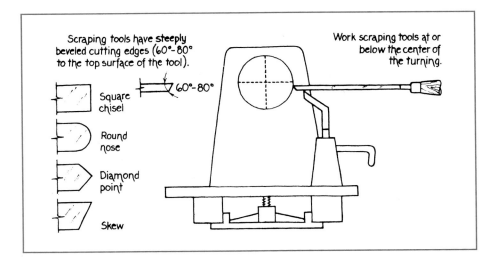

Scraping tools have steeply beveled cutting edges (60°-80° to the top surface of the tool).

60°-80°

Square chisel

Round nose

Diamond point

Skew

Work scraping tools at or below the center of the turning.

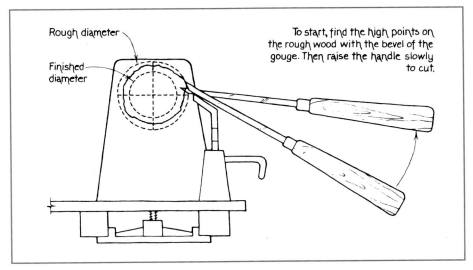

Rough diameter

Finished diameter

To start, find the high points on the rough wood with the bevel of the gouge. Then raise the handle slowly to cut.

just stand back and make sure they're safe. Some children find it frustrating to learn but eventually pick it up, and a few never get shearing cuts at all.

Scraping, shown in the drawing at left, is a much easier method to teach—all you have to do is apply the tool gently at somewhere near the correct angle. Scrapers come in a variety of shapes and sizes that can define the form you are trying to cut. There are scrapers that will cut beads in one motion, for example, and you can cut a cove simply by pushing a cove-sized tool right into the wood. Both of these operations require multiple strokes and lots of skill if you are shearing with a gouge or skew chisel.

Scraping is best at higher lathe speeds, though with a properly sharpened tool you can get a good surface on a slow lathe when working hard woods. Thin, flexible work will climb the scraping tool, causing chatter and possible breakage, but in skilled hands, the shearing tool can actually support flexible stock as it cuts.

For scraping cuts, be sure the tool rest is very close to the wood's surface, both for steadiness and safety. Help your child experiment with the tool's angle of attack by raising or lowering the handle to get the smoothest cut.

For rounding off lumpy stock, the shearing cut is safer. When shearing rough stock, you approach the wood from above, gingerly, with the bevel of the tool. You make contact with the bumpy surface before starting a cut. With a scraper, you push the tool straight in—do this too fast and you could catch the edge and flip the tool or throw the stock out of the lathe.

So which cut to teach first? It all depends on which one you are most comfortable with, how adept your child is and what your first turning projects will be. As with any other project or skill in this book, your judgment is the last word.

quickest and safest way is to study with an expert. Look for workshops at a local craft center, or ask a friend whose skills you trust. Another way to develop some skill is to find a good videotape on turning. Watching the moves of woodturning repeatedly on the screen makes things clearer.

Expert woodturners switch from shearing cuts to scraping cuts, depending on the job at hand. Which to teach kids? There are a couple of things to consider.

The shearing cut, shown in the drawing above, is harder to master. It requires moving the tool in three-dimensional space, even to cut a simple cove. Once mastered, the shearing cut is the key to fluid turning and quick results. Shearing puts less stress on the wood than scraping. That makes it good for turning slender work or soft materials. It works well at low lathe speeds, which is a safety plus for kids. On a slow-running foot-powered lathe, the shearing cut gives the best results.

Certain kids are intuitive woodturners, and learn the shearing cut instantly. They seem to take to woodturning so easily that you scarcely teach them; you

Here are two turning techniques that you probably won't find in a videotape, but they're safe and easy for kids to learn, and handy for adults, too. Turned parts for doll furniture, miniature baseball bats, small drawer pulls and drumsticks are easy to make from store-bought dowels with a file. Dowels up to ½ in. in diameter will fit a drill chuck mounted on the lathe's spindle. For work longer than 4 in., use the tailstock to support the right end of the dowel. Even short pieces of ¼-in. dowel can be turned with precision.

A round (rattail) file or sandpaper wrapped around a dowel works well for shaping and smoothing coves, and kids like to make drumsticks from ½-in. dowel, shaping them with a half-round file. The details, like the tip of the stick and decorative rings on the handle, can be cut with the edge of the file, while long tapers are easily formed with the flat side of the file.

Always remove the tool rest when filing, and make sure that the tangs of the files you use have handles. Also, be sure to clean the file frequently with a

possible to do without the tool rest entirely if you angle the plane almost parallel with the work so the plane's bottom is actually supported by the turning stock.

Here are some things kids should remember when they turn wood. These are part of my introduction to turning, and things I watch for when supervising a child on the lathe.

● Wear a full face mask for all activities on the lathe.

● Tie back long hair securely or tuck it down the back of the shirt.

● Remove rings and wrist jewelry, along with neckties and necklaces. Whirling spindles and gears love to eat dangling bits of anything.

● Tighten all adjustments, and position the tool rest appropriately for the cut.

● Keep your tool-rest hand away from the work to avoid getting pinched, especially when rounding off rough stock.

● Press the tool onto the tool rest, not into the work.

● Move the tool slowly. Fast moves leave rough work and can be dangerous. On my foot-powered lathe, where kids have direct control of speed, I say, "fast lathe, slow tool."

● Work downhill, from large diameters to small diameters. Working uphill leaves a rough surface and can cause a surprise catch and a thrown tool.

● Remove the tool rest when sanding to avoid pinched fingers. Wear a dust mask if you are doing a lot of sanding.

● Sand under the object.

file card, a short-bristle wire brush made for the job. Brush in the direction of the lines on the file until no wood is left in the crevices.

You can also plane on the lathe. A wood plane makes easy work of turning smooth cylinders and tapers. Planes on the lathe can shape stool legs, baseball bats and rolling pins, for example. Kids who have a rough time doing smooth work with a gouge get over their frustration fast when they see how easily they can clean up their work with a plane.

Turning stock should first be rounded off and rough-shaped with a gouge; you may wish to do this for young kids. Always travel downhill on a taper, and always aim the plane a few degrees toward the direction of travel rather than at right angles to the work. Angling the tool gives a skew cut, which encounters less resistance and leaves a smoother surface. The skew angle also keeps the corners of the plane's blade off the wood, so they leave no marks. Crowning the blade slightly and dubbing the corners (p. 159 and p. 182) will prevent marking in case you don't center the blade properly on the wood. A sharp plane, set fine, will leave a surface so smooth you may not need to sand it.

Select a standard bench plane, or for finer work, a low-angle block plane (p. 157 and p. 162). Set the lathe's tool rest away from the work so it supports the back end of the plane, and raise it until the plane is almost level. It is

The books listed here will help extend your woodworking knowledge and inspire your kids. Begin a shop library and encourage kids who are between projects to browse through.

Carving

Jarman, Christopher. **Teach Your Children Woodwork.** New York: Drake Publishers, 1974.
This is an elementary carving book, despite the title.

Johnstone, James B., et al., eds. **Woodcarving: Techniques and Projects.** Menlo Park, Calif.: Lane Publishing Co., 1971.
A clear and comprehensive book, beautifully illustrated.

Tangerman, E.J. **Whittling and Woodcarving.** New York: Dover Publications, 1962.
This is a classic. Though the photos are small and crowded together, you will find some inspiring things.

Green Woodworking

Alexander, John. **Make a Chair from a Tree.** Newtown, Conn.: The Taunton Press, 1978.
Interesting approach to non-Windsor stick furniture, though the chairs may be too difficult for some kids.

Dunbar, Michael. **Windsor Chairmaking.** New York: Hastings House, 1976.
Wordy and not very clear, but one of the few books on the subject.

Langsner, Drew. **Country Woodcraft.** Emmaus, Penn.: Rodale Press, 1978.
Lots of ideas for working green wood, including pitchforks, rakes and baskets.

Underhill, Roy. **The Woodwright's Shop: A Practical Guide to Traditional Woodcraft.** Chapel Hill, N.C.: University of North Carolina Press, 1981.
A survey of old woodworking techniques, including chair making.

Musical Instruments

Robinson, Trevor. **The Amateur Wind Instrument Maker.** Amherst, Mass.: University of Massachusetts Press, 1973.
A spare book, but you can glean shapes, proportions and crucial dimensions for flutes and recorders.

Sloane, Irving. **Classic Guitar Construction.** New York: E.P. Dutton Co., 1966.
Though Sloane's methods are too sophisticated to use with kids, it's nice to be able to explain how guitars are made.

Waring, Dennis. **Making Folk Instruments in Wood.** New York: Sterling Publishing Co., 1979.
A book about making instruments with kids—lots of ideas and specifications.

Project Ideas

Andrews, Edward Deming, and Faith Andrews. **Shaker Furniture.** New York: Dover Publications, 1937.
Shaker furniture is simple and elegant, perfect for kids in a hand-tool shop. This is a classic, with inspiring photographs.

Brann, Donald R. **How to Build Gun Cabinets and Racks.** Briarcliff Manor, N.Y.: Directions Simplified, Inc., 1967.
Rack proportions are critical—this book will help you get them right.

Clark, David E., et al., eds. **Sunset Woodworking Projects.** La Jolla, Calif.: Lane Publishing Co., 1975.
Lots of good ideas. Many rely on quick plywood assembly.

Meras, Phyllis. **A Yankee Way With Wood.** Boston, Mass.: Houghton-Mifflin Co., 1975.
Profiles of New England craftsmen with plans for a project by each of them.

Shea, John G. **The American Shakers and Their Furniture.** New York: Van Nostrand Reinhold Co., 1971.
Plans for Shaker furniture.

Sloan, Eric. **Diary of an Early American Boy.** New York: Funk and Wagnalls, 1962.
————. **A Museum of Early American Tools.** New York: Funk and Wagnalls, 1964.
————. **A Reverence For Wood.** New York: Funk and Wagnalls, 1965.
These books have been an inspiration for a whole generation of hand woodworkers. They will each be referred to again and again for their ideas.

Thomas, David. **Easy Woodstuff for Kids.** Mt. Rainier, Md.: Gryphon House, 1981.
Simple, delightful stuff made from twigs, spools, logs and boards.

Wigginton, Eliot, ed. **The Foxfire Books.** Garden City, N.Y.: Anchor Press/Doubleday, 1973.
A series of books collecting the best articles on folk craft from a high-school magazine. A superb resource.

Reference Books

Hayward, Charles H. **The Complete Book of Woodwork.** London: Evans Brothers, Ltd., 1959.
A good reference book, a little easier to understand than Joyce (below).

Hoadley, R. Bruce. **Understanding Wood.** Newtown, Conn.: The Taunton Press, 1980.
Easily the most thorough and readable technical book on wood—its structure, cutting, gluing and a lot more.

Joyce, Ernest. **The Encyclopedia of Furniture Making.** New York: Drake Publishers, 1976.
Everything you ever wanted to know. . . . A bit stuffy, but well illustrated and authoritative.

Safety

American Medical Association Staff. **The AMA Handbook of First Aid & Emergency Care.** New York: Random House, 1980.
A thorough, authoritative guide to first aid. A good reference book.

Spoons

Gould, Mary Earle. **Early American Wooden Ware.** Rutland, Vt.: Charles E. Tuttle Co., 1962.
Lots of ideas for the kitchen.

Nilsson, Ake R. **Woodware.** New York: Drake Publishers, 1973.
Stylish spoons, dishes and cutting boards. Well illustrated and inspiring.

Sundqvist, Wille. **Swedish Carving Techniques** (book), **Carving Swedish Woodenware with Jögge Sundqvist** (video). Newtown, Conn.: The Taunton Press, 1990.
A fine introduction to the carving of woodenware. The companion video is especially useful to beginners.

Tools

Adkins, Jan. **Toolchest.** New York: Walker and Co., 1973.
Wonderful illustrations of hand tools at work. Not much of a technical guide, but some of the drawings may help clarify difficult points for kids.

Christoforo, R.J. **Handtool Handbook.** Tucson, Ariz.: H.P. Books, 1977.
Useful information, though not always in-depth, on hand tools and joints. Clear illustrations.

Clifford, E., and Hampton, C.W. **Planecraft.** Sheffield, England: C&J Hampton, 1959. Reprinted by Woodcraft Supply, Woburn, Mass.
Based on the Record planes, which are virtually identical to Stanley tools, this is the best book I know of on the subject of planes and planing.

Dunbar, Michael. **Restoring, Tuning and Using Classic Woodworking Tools.** New York: Sterling Publishing Co., 1989.
If you are a yard-sale buff, this book tells how to get your finds in shape. Unique information on tuning molding planes and other specialized planes.

Gentry, George. **Hardening and Tempering Engineering Tools.** Hertfordshire, England: Argus Books, 1978.
Contains in-depth information about hardening tools.

Larkman, Brian. **How to Do It—Woodwork.** Loughborough, England: Ladybird Books Ltd., 1973.
A sweet introduction to the craft for children, focusing on tools. Fine color illustrations.

McDonnell, Leo P. **Hand Woodworking Tools.** Albany, N.Y.: Delmar Publishers, 1962.
A complete survey of modern hand tools, written as a textbook. A good reference.

Sellens, Alvin. **The Stanley Plane: A Historic and Descriptive Inventory.** Early American Industries Association, 1975.
A reference book for tool collectors, but helpful if you want to date that rusted hulk you just bought.

Weygers, Alexander G. **The Making of Tools.** New York: Van Nostrand Reinhold Co., 1973.
Basics of tool making, focusing on gouges and knives. Clear drawings.

Toys

Accorsi, William. **Accorsi Puzzles.** New York: Simon and Schuster, 1978.
Good variations of the jigsaw puzzle that kids love to make.

Hayward, Charles. **Making Toys in Wood.** New York: Sterling Publishing Co., 1980.
Directed to adults, but may give ideas to some kids. Includes large toys, like slides and playhouses.

Johnson, Gene. **Ship Model Building.** Centreville, Md.: Cornell Maritime Press, 1961.
For sophisticated builders, but useful for details on kids' boats, too.

Peppe, Rodney. **Rodney Peppe's Moving Toys.** New York: Sterling Publishing Co., 1980.
Provides some clever and colorful ideas, and plans are included.

Studley, Vance. **The Woodworker's Book of Wooden Toys.** New York: Van Nostrand Reinhold Co., 1980.
Some interesting ideas, but they're given as plans with little leeway for flexibility. A good chapter on the history of toys.

Turning

Klenke, William. **The Art of Woodturning.** Peoria, Ill.: Chas. A. Bennett Co., 1954.
An American text, this book is not so rigorous as the English one by Frederick Pain (below), but it is also a little less colorful. Some neat projects.

Nish, Dale. **Creative Woodturning.** Provo, Utah: Brigham Young University Press, 1975.
A good source of ideas for advanced turners, though not a suitable introduction for beginners.

Pain, Frederick. **The Practical Wood Turner.** London: Evans Brothers, Ltd., 1958.
I learned turning from this book. It wanders a bit, but the more I know about the subject, the more I learn from Pain.

Raffan, Richard. **Turning Wood with Richard Raffan** (book and video), 1985; **Turned-Bowl Design** (book), 1987; **Turning Projects** (book and video), available March 1991. Newtown, Conn.: The Taunton Press.
An excellent comprehensive guide to the art of turning wood. Beginners will appreciate the guidance provided in the videos.

Editor: Andrew Schultz

Designer: Roger Barnes

Layout and Illustration: Lee Hochgraf Hov, Henry Roth

Illustrators: Vince Babak, Christopher Clapp, E. Marino III, Karen Pease

Woodcuts: E. Marino III

Copy/Production Editor: Ruth Dobsevage

Typesetter: Lisa Carlson

Print Production Manager: Tom Greco

Typeface: Univers 9 point

Paper: Warren Patina, 70 lb., neutral pH

Printer: The Maple-Vail Book Manufacturing Group, Binghamton, N.Y.

Choose your specialty.